Beethoven's Letters
1790-1826
Volume I & II

Ludwig van Beethoven
Translated by Lady Grace Wallace
Compiled by Ludwig Nohl & Ludwig Köchel

Copyright © Ludwig van Beethoven, Lady Grace Wallace, Ludwig Nohl, & Ludwig Köchel
All rights reserved.
ISBN-13:9798455487675

**Published in New York
1867**

Table of Contents

Volume I   4

Volume II   93

VOL. I

TRANSLATOR'S PREFACE.

Since undertaking the translation of Dr. Ludwig Nohl's valuable edition of "Beethoven's Letters," an additional collection has been published by Dr. Ludwig Ritter von Köchel, consisting of many interesting letters addressed by Beethoven to his illustrious pupil, H.R.H. the Archduke Rudolph, Cardinal-Archbishop of Olmütz. These I have inserted in chronological order, and marked with the letter K., in order to distinguish them from the correspondence edited by Dr. Nohl. I have only omitted a few brief notes, consisting merely of apologies for non-attendance on the Archduke.

The artistic value of these newly discovered treasures will no doubt be as highly appreciated in this country as in the great *maestro's* Father-land.

I must also express my gratitude to Dr. Th.G. v. Karajan, for permitting an engraving to be made expressly for this work, from an original Beethoven portrait in his possession, now for the first time given to the public. The grand and thoughtful countenance forms a fitting introduction to letters so truly depicting the brilliant, fitful genius of the sublime master, as well as the touching sadness and gloom pervading his life, which his devotion to Art alone brightened, through many bitter trials and harassing cares.

The love of Beethoven's music is now become so universal in England, that I make no doubt his Letters will receive a hearty welcome from all those whose spirits have been elevated and soothed by the genius of this illustrious man.

GRACE WALLACE.

AINDERBY HALL, March 28, 1866.

PREFACE
BY DR. LUDWIG NOHL
TO THE
LETTERS OF LUDWIG VAN BEETHOVEN.

In accompanying the present edition of the Letters of Ludwig van Beethoven with a few introductory remarks, I at once acknowledge that the compilation of these letters has cost me no slight sacrifices. I must also, however, mention that an unexpected Christmas donation, generously bestowed on me with a view to further my efforts to promote the science of music, enabled me to undertake one of the journeys necessary for my purpose, and also to complete the revision of the Letters and of the press, in the milder air and repose of a country residence, long since recommended to me for the restoration of my health, undermined by overwork.

That, in spite of every effort, I have not succeeded in seeing the original of each letter, or even discovering the place where it exists, may well be excused, taking into consideration the slender capabilities of an individual, and the astonishing manner in which Beethoven's Letters are dispersed all over the world. At the same time, I must state that not only have the hitherto inaccessible treasures of Anton Schindler's "Beethoven's Nachlass" been placed at my disposal, but also other letters from private sources, owing to various happy chances, and the kindness and complaisance of collectors of autographs. I know better, however, than most people--being in a position to do so--that in the present work there can be no pretension to any thing approaching to a complete collection of Beethoven's Letters. The master, so fond of writing, though he often rather amusingly accuses himself of being a lazy correspondent, may very probably have sent forth at least double the amount of the letters here given, and there is no doubt whatever that a much larger number are still extant in the originals. The only thing that can be done at this moment, however, is to make the attempt to bring to light, at all events, the letters that could be discovered in Germany. The mass of those which I gradually accumulated, and now offer to the public (with the exception of some insignificant notes), appeared to me sufficiently numerous and important to interest the world, and also to form a substantial nucleus for any letters that may hereafter be discovered. On the other hand, as many of Beethoven's Letters slumber in foreign lands, especially in the unapproachable cabinets of curiosities belonging to various close-fisted English collectors, an entire edition of the correspondence could only be effected by a most disproportionate outlay of time and expense.

When revising the text of the Letters, it seemed to me needless perpetually to impair the pleasure of the reader by retaining the mistakes in orthography; but enough of the style of writing of that day is adhered to, to prevent its peculiar charm being entirely destroyed. Distorted and incorrect as Beethoven's mode of expression sometimes is, I have not presumed to alter his grammar, or rather syntax, in the smallest degree: who would presume to do so with an individuality which, even amid startling clumsiness of style, displays those inherent intellectual powers that often did violence to language as well as to his fellow-men? Cyclopean masses of rock are here hurled with Cyclopean force; but hard and massive as they are, the man is not to be envied whose heart is not touched by these glowing fragments, flung apparently at random right and left, like meteors, by a mighty intellectual being, however perverse the treatment language may have received from him.

The great peculiarity, however, in this strange mode of expression is, that even such incongruous language faithfully reflects the mind of the man whose nature was of prophetic depth and heroic force; and who that knows anything of the creative genius of a Beethoven can deny him these attributes?

The antique dignity pervading the whole man, the ethical contemplation of life forming the basis of his nature, prevented even a momentary wish on my part to efface a single word of the oft-recurring expressions so painfully harsh, bordering on the unaesthetic, and even on the repulsive, provoked by his wrath against the meanness of men. In the last part of these genuine documents, we learn with a feeling of sadness, and with almost a tragic sensation, how low was the standard of moral worth, or rather how great was the positive unworthiness, of the intimate society surrounding the master, and with what difficulty he could maintain the purity of the nobler part of his being in such an atmosphere. The manner, indeed, in which he strives to do so, fluctuating between explosions of harshness and almost weak yieldingness, while striving to master the base thoughts and conduct of these men, though never entirely succeeding in doing so, is often more a diverting than an offensive spectacle. In my opinion, nevertheless, even this less pleasing aspect of the Letters ought not to be in the slightest degree softened (which it has hitherto been, owing to false views of propriety and morality), for it is no moral deformity here displayed. Indeed, even when the irritable master has recourse to expressions repugnant to our sense of conventionality, and which may well be called harsh and rough, still the wrath that seizes on our hero is a just and righteous wrath, and we disregard it, just as in Nature, whose grandeur constantly elevates us above the inevitable stains of an earthly soil. The coarseness and ill-breeding, which would claim toleration because this great man now and then showed such feelings, must beware of doing so, being certain to make shipwreck when coming in contact with the massive rock of true morality on which, with all his faults and deficiencies, Beethoven's being was surely grounded. Often, indeed, when absorbed in the unsophisticated and genuine utterances of this great man, it seems as if these peculiarities and strange asperities were the results of some mysterious law of Nature, so that we are inclined to adopt the paradox by which a wit once described the singular groundwork of our nature,--"The faults of man are the night in which he rests from his virtues."

Indeed, I think that the lofty morality of such natures is not fully evident until we are obliged to confess with regret, that even the great ones of the earth must pay their tribute to humanity, and really do pay it (which is the distinction between them and base and petty characters), without being ever entirely hurled from their pedestal of dignity and virtue. The soul of that man cannot fail to be elevated, who can seize the real spirit of the scattered pages that a happy chance has preserved for us. If not fettered by petty feelings, he will quickly surmount the casual obstacles and stumbling-blocks which the first perusal of these Letters may seem to present, and quickly feel himself transported at a single stride into a stream, where a strange roaring and rushing is heard, but above which loftier tones resound with magic and exciting power. For a peculiar life breathes in these lines; an under-current runs through their apparently unconnected import, uniting them as with an electric chain, and with firmer links than any mere coherence of subjects could have effected. I experienced this myself, to the most remarkable degree, when I first made the attempt to arrange, in accordance with their period and substance, the hundreds of individual pages bearing neither date nor address, and I was soon convinced that a connecting text (such as Mozart's Letters have, and ought to have) would be here entirely superfluous, as even the best biographical commentary would be very dry work, interrupting the electric current of the whole, and thus destroying its peculiar effect.

And now, what is this spirit which, for an intelligent mind, binds together these scattered fragments into a whole, and what is its actual power? I cannot tell; but I feel to this day just as I felt to the innermost depths of my heart in the days of my youth when I first heard a symphony of Beethoven's,--that a spirit breathes from it bearing us aloft with giant power out of the oppressive atmosphere of sense, stirring to its inmost recesses the heart of man, bringing him to the full consciousness of his loftier being, and of the undying within him. And even more distinctly than when a new world was thus disclosed to his youthful feelings is the *man* fully conscious that not only was this a new world to him, but a new world of feeling in itself, revealing to the spirit phases of its own, which, till Beethoven appeared, had never before been fathomed. Call it by what name you will, when one of the great works of the sublime master is heard, whether indicative of proud self-consciousness, freedom, spring, love, storm, or battle, it grasps the soul with singular force, and enlarges the laboring breast. Whether a man understands music or not, every one who has a heart beating within his breast will feel with enchantment that here is concentrated the utmost promised to us by the most imaginative of our poets, in bright visions of happiness and freedom. Even the only great hero of action, who in those memorable days is worthy to stand beside the great master of harmony, having diffused among mankind new and priceless earthly treasures, sinks in the scale when we compare these with the celestial treasures of a purified and deeper feeling, and a more free, enlarged, and sublime view of the world, struggling gradually and distinctly upwards out of the mere frivolity of an art devoid of words to express itself, and impressing its stamp on the spirit of the age. They convey, too, the knowledge of this brightest victory of genuine German intellect to those for whom the sweet Muse of Music is as a book with seven seals, and reveal, likewise, a more profound sense of Beethoven's being to many who already, through the sweet tones they have imbibed, enjoy some dawning conviction of the master's grandeur, and who now more and more eagerly lend a listening ear to the intellectual clearly worded strains so skilfully interwoven, thus soon to arrive at the full and blissful comprehension of those grand outpourings of the spirit, and finally to add another bright delight to the enjoyment of those who already know and love Beethoven. All these may be regarded as the objects I had in view when I undertook to edit his Letters, which have also bestowed on myself the best recompense of my labors, in the humble conviction that by this means I may have vividly reawakened in the remembrance of many the mighty mission which our age is called on to perform for the development of our race, even in the realm of harmony,--more especially in our Father-land.

LUDWIG NOHL.

LA TOUR DE PERLZ--LAKE OF GENEVA, March, 1865.

FIRST PART.

LIFE'S JOYS AND SORROWS.
1783 TO 1815.

1.
TO THE ELECTOR OF COLOGNE, FREDERICK MAXIMILIAN.[1]

ILLUSTRIOUS PRINCE,--

Music from my fourth year has ever been my favorite pursuit. Thus early introduced to the sweet Muse, who attuned my soul to pure harmony, I loved her, and sometimes ventured to think that I was beloved by her in return. I have now attained my eleventh year, and my Muse often whispered to me in hours of inspiration,--Try to write down the harmonies in your soul. Only eleven years old! thought I; does the character of an author befit me? and what would more mature artists say? I felt some trepidation; but my Muse willed it--so I obeyed, and wrote.

May I now, therefore, Illustrious Prince, presume to lay the first-fruits of my juvenile labors at the foot of your throne? and may I hope that you will condescend to cast an encouraging and kindly glance on them? You will; for Art and Science have ever found in you a judicious protector and a generous patron, and rising talent has always prospered under your fostering and fatherly care. Encouraged by this cheering conviction, I venture to approach you with these my youthful efforts. Accept them as the pure offering of childlike reverence, and graciously vouchsafe to regard with indulgence them and their youthful composer,

LUDWIG VAN BEETHOVEN.

[Footnote 1: The dedication affixed to this work, "Three Sonatas for the Piano, dedicated to my illustrious master, Maximilian Friedrich, Archbishop and Elector of Cologne, by Ludwig van Beethoven in his eleventh year," is probably not written by the boy himself, but is given here as an amusing contrast to his subsequent ideas with regard to the homage due to rank.]

2.
TO DR. SCHADE,--AUGSBURG.

Bonn, 1787. Autumn.

MY MOST ESTEEMED FRIEND,--

I can easily imagine what you must think of me, and I cannot deny that you have too good grounds for an unfavorable opinion. I shall not, however, attempt to justify myself, until I have explained to you the reasons why my apologies should be accepted. I must tell you that from the time I left Augsburg[1] my cheerfulness, as well as my health, began to decline; the nearer I came to my native city, the more frequent were the letters from my father, urging me to travel with all possible speed, as my mother's health was in a most precarious condition. I therefore hurried forwards as fast as I could, although myself far from well. My longing once more to see my dying mother overcame every obstacle, and assisted me in surmounting the greatest difficulties. I found my mother indeed still alive, but in the most deplorable state; her disease was consumption, and about seven weeks ago, after much pain and suffering, she died [July 17]. She was indeed a kind, loving mother to me, and my best friend. Ah! who was happier than I, when I could still utter the sweet name of mother, and it was heard? But to whom can I now say it? Only to the silent form resembling her, evoked by the power of imagination. I have passed very few pleasant hours since my arrival here, having during the whole time been suffering from asthma, which may, I fear, eventually turn to consumption; to this is added melancholy,--almost as great an evil as my malady itself. Imagine yourself in my place, and then I shall hope to receive your forgiveness for my long silence. You showed me extreme kindness and friendship by lending me three Carolins in Augsburg, but I must entreat your indulgence for a time. My journey cost me a great deal, and I have not the smallest hopes of earning anything here. Fate is not propitious to me in Bonn. Pardon my intruding on you so long with my affairs, but all that I have said was necessary for my own justification.

I do entreat you not to deprive me of your valuable friendship; nothing do I wish so much as in any degree to become worthy of your regard. I am, with all esteem, your obedient servant and friend,

L. V. BEETHOVEN,
Cologne Court Organist.

[Footnote 1: On his return from Vienna, whither Max Franz had sent him for the further cultivation of his talents.]

3.
TO THE ELECTOR MAXIMILIAN FRANCIS.[1]

1793.

MOST ILLUSTRIOUS AND GRACIOUS PRINCE,--

Some years ago your Highness was pleased to grant a pension to my father, the Court tenor Van Beethoven, and further graciously to decree that 100 R. Thalers of his salary should be allotted to me, for the purpose of maintaining, clothing, and educating my two younger brothers, and also defraying the debts incurred by our father. It was my intention to present this decree to your Highness's treasurer, but my father earnestly implored me to desist from doing so, that he might not be thus publicly proclaimed incapable himself of supporting his family, adding that he would engage to pay me the 25 R.T. quarterly, which he punctually did. After his death, however (in December last), wishing to reap the benefit of your Highness's gracious boon, by presenting the decree, I was startled to find that my father had destroyed it.

I therefore, with all dutiful respect, entreat your Highness to renew this decree, and to order the paymaster of your Highness's treasury to grant me the last quarter of this benevolent addition to my salary (due the beginning of February). I have the honor to remain,

Your Highness's most obedient and faithful servant,

LUD. V. BEETHOVEN,
Court Organist.

[Footnote 1: An electoral decree was issued in compliance with this request on May 3, 1793.]

4.
TO ELEONORE VON BREUNING,--BONN.

Vienna, Nov. 2, 1793.

MY HIGHLY ESTEEMED ELEONORE, MY DEAREST FRIEND,--

A year of my stay in this capital has nearly elapsed before you receive a letter from me, and yet the most vivid remembrance of you is ever present with me. I have often conversed in thought with you and your dear family, though not always in the happy mood I could have wished, for that fatal misunderstanding still hovered before me, and my conduct at that time is now hateful in my sight. But so it was, and how much would I give to have the power wholly to obliterate from my life a mode of acting so degrading to myself, and so contrary to the usual tenor of my character!

Many circumstances, indeed, contributed to estrange us, and I suspect that those tale-bearers who repeated alternately to you and to me our mutual expressions were the chief obstacles to any good understanding between us. Each believed that what was said proceeded from deliberate conviction, whereas it arose only from anger, fanned by others; so we were both mistaken. Your good and noble disposition, my dear friend, is sufficient security that you have long since forgiven me. We are told that the best proof of sincere contrition is to acknowledge our faults; and this is what I wish to do. Let us now draw a veil over the whole affair, learning one lesson from it,--that when friends are at variance, it is always better to employ no mediator, but to communicate directly with each other.

With this you will receive a dedication from me [the variations on "Se vuol ballare"]. My sole wish is that the work were greater and more worthy of you. I was applied to here to publish this little work, and I take advantage of the opportunity, my beloved Eleonore, to give you a proof of my regard and friendship for yourself, and also a token of my enduring remembrance of your family. Pray then accept this trifle, and do not forget that it is offered by a devoted friend. Oh! if it only gives you pleasure, my wishes will be fulfilled. May it in some degree recall the time when I passed so many happy hours in your house! Perhaps it may serve to remind you of me till I return, though this is indeed a distant prospect. Oh! how we shall then rejoice together, my dear Eleonore! You will, I trust, find your friend a happier man, all former forbidding, careworn furrows smoothed away by time and better fortune.

When you see B. Koch [subsequently Countess Belderbusch], pray say that it is unkind in her never once to have written to me. I wrote to her twice, and three times to Malchus (afterwards Westphalian Minister of Finance), but no answer. Tell her that if she does not choose to write herself, I beg that she will at least urge Malchus to do so. At the close of my letter I venture to make one more request--I am anxious to be so fortunate as again to possess an Angola waistcoat knitted by your own hand, my dear friend. Forgive my indiscreet request; it proceeds from my great love for all that comes from you; and I may privately admit that a little vanity is connected with it, namely, that I may say I possess something from the best and most admired young lady in Bonn. I still have the one you were so good as to give me in Bonn; but change of fashion has made it look so antiquated, that I can only treasure it in my wardrobe as your gift, and thus still very dear to me. You would make me very happy by soon writing me a kind letter. If mine cause you any pleasure, I promise you to do as you wish, and write as often as it lies in my power; indeed everything is acceptable to me that can serve to show you how truly I am your admiring and sincere friend,

L. V. BEETHOVEN.

P.S. The variations are rather difficult to play, especially the shake in the *Coda*; but do not be alarmed at this, being so contrived that you only require to play the shake, and leave out the other notes, which also occur in the violin part. I never would have written it in this way, had I not occasionally observed that there was a certain individual in Vienna who, when I extemporized the previous evening, not unfrequently wrote down next day many of the peculiarities of my music, adopting them as his own [for instance, the Abbé Gelinek]. Concluding, therefore, that some of these things would soon appear, I resolved to anticipate this. Another reason also was to puzzle some of the pianoforte teachers here, many of whom are my mortal foes; so I wished to revenge myself on them in this way, knowing that they would occasionally be asked to play the variations, when these gentlemen would not appear to much advantage.

BEETHOVEN.

5.
TO ELEONORE VON BREUNING,--BONN.

The beautiful neckcloth, embroidered by your own hand, was the greatest possible surprise to me; yet, welcome as the gift was, it awakened within me feelings of sadness. Its effect was to recall former days, and to put me to shame by your noble conduct to me. I, indeed, little thought that you still considered me worthy of your remembrance.

Oh! if you could have witnessed my emotions yesterday when this incident occurred, you would not think that I exaggerate in saying that such a token of your recollection brought tears to my eyes, and made me feel very sad. Little as I may deserve favor in your eyes, believe me, my dear *friend*, (let me still call you so,) I have suffered, and still suffer severely from the privation of your friendship. Never can I forget you and your dear mother. You were so kind to me that your loss neither can nor will be easily replaced. I know what I have forfeited, and what you were to me, but in order to fill up this blank I must recur to scenes equally painful for you to hear and for me to detail.

As a slight requital of your kind *souvenir*, I take the liberty to send you some variations, and a Rondo with violin accompaniment. I have a great deal to do, or I would long since have transcribed the Sonata I promised you. It is as yet a mere sketch in manuscript, and to copy it would be a difficult task even for the clever and practised Paraquin [counter-bass in the Electoral orchestra]. You can have the Rondo copied, and return the score. What I now send is the only one of my works at all suitable for you; besides, as you are going to Kerpen [where an uncle of the family lived], I thought these trifles might cause you pleasure.

Farewell, my friend; for it is impossible for me to give you any other name. However indifferent I may be to you, believe me, I shall ever continue to revere you and your mother as I have always done. If I can in any way contribute to the fulfilment of a wish of yours, do not fail to let me know, for I have no other means of testifying my gratitude for past friendship.

I wish you an agreeable journey, and that your dear mother may return entirely restored to health! Think sometimes of your affectionate friend,

BEETHOVEN.

6.
TO HERR SCHENK.

June, 1794.

DEAR SCHENK,[1]--

I did not know that I was to set off to-day to Eisenstadt. I should like to have talked to you again. In the mean time rest assured of my gratitude for your obliging services. I shall endeavor, so far as it lies in my power, to requite them. I hope soon to see you, and once more to enjoy the pleasure of your society. Farewell, and do not entirely forget your

BEETHOVEN.

[Footnote 1: Schenk, afterwards celebrated as the composer of the "Dorf Barbier," was for some time Beethoven's teacher in composition. This note appears to have been written in June, 1794, and first printed in the "Freischütz," No. 183, about 1836, at the time of Schenk's death, when his connection with Beethoven was mentioned.]

7.
TO DR. WEGELER,--VIENNA.[1]

... In what an odious light have you exhibited me to myself! Oh! I acknowledge it, I do not deserve your friendship. It was no intentional or deliberate malice that induced me to act towards you as I did, but inexcusable thoughtlessness alone.

I say no more. I am coming to throw myself into your arms, and to entreat you to restore me my lost friend; and you will give him back to me, to your penitent, loving, and ever-grateful

BEETHOVEN.

[Footnote 1: Dr. Wegeler, in answer to my request that he would send me the entire letter, replied that "the passages omitted in the letter consisted chiefly in eulogiums of his father, and enthusiastic expressions of friendship, which did not seem to him to be of any value; but besides this, the same reasons that induced his father to give only a portion of the letter were imperative with him also." I do not wish to contest the point with the possessor of the letter; still I may remark that all the utterances and letters of a great man belong to the world at large, and that in a case like the present, the conscientious biographer, who strives faithfully to portray such a man, is alone entitled to decide what portion of these communications is fitted for publication, and what is not. Any considerations of a personal character seem to me very trivial.]

8.
TO DR. WEGELER,--VIENNA.

Vienna, May 1797.

God speed you, my dear friend! I owe you a letter which you shall shortly have, and my newest music besides, *I am going on well; indeed, I may say every day better.* Greet those to whom it will give pleasure from me. Farewell, and do not forget your

BEETHOVEN.

9.
WRITTEN IN THE ALBUM OF LENZ VON BREUNING.

Vienna, Oct. 1, 1797.

Truth for the wise,
Beauty for a feeling heart,
And both for each other.

MY DEAR, GOOD BREUNING,--

Never can I forget the time I passed with you, not only in Bonn, but here. Continue your friendship towards me, for you shall always find me the same true friend,

L. V. BEETHOVEN.

10.
TO BARON ZMESKALL VON DOMANOWECZ.

1800.[1]

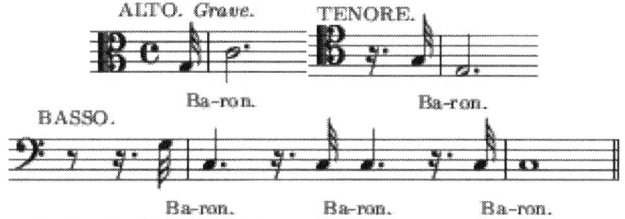

MY CHEAPEST (NOT DEAREST) BARON,--

Desire the guitar-player to come to me to-day. Amenda (instead of an *amende* [fine], which he sometimes deserves for not observing his rests properly) must persuade this popular guitarist to visit me, and if possible to come at five o'clock this evening; if not then, at five or six o'clock to-morrow morning; but he must not waken me if I chance to be still asleep. *Adieu, mon ami à bon marché.* Perhaps we may meet at the "Swan"?

[Footnote 1: As it appears from the following letters that Amenda was again at home in 1800, the date of this note is thus ascertained. It is undoubtedly addressed to Baron Zmeskall von Domanowecz, Royal Court Secretary, a good violoncello-player, and one of Beethoven's earliest friends in Vienna. The "guitarist" was probably the celebrated Giuliani, who lived in Vienna.]

11.

The musical Count is from this day forth *cashiered* with infamy. The first violin [Schuppanzigh] ruthlessly transported to *Siberia*. The Baron [see No. 10] for a whole month *strictly interdicted from asking questions*; no longer to be so hasty, and to devote himself exclusively to his *ipse miserum*.[1]

B.

[Footnote 1: Written in gigantic characters in pencil on a large sheet of paper. The "musical Count" is probably Count Moritz Lichnowsky, brother of Prince Carl Lichnowsky, in whose house were held those musical performances in which Beethoven's works were first produced. Even at that time he behaved in a very dictatorial manner to those gentlemen when his compositions were badly executed. Thence the name given him by Haydn of "The Great Mogul."]

12.
TO PASTOR AMENDA,--COURLAND.

Does Amenda think that I can ever forget him, because I do not write? in fact, never have written to him?--as if the memory of our friends could only thus be preserved! The *best man I ever knew* has a thousand times recurred to my thoughts! Two persons alone once possessed my whole love, one of whom still lives, and you are now the third. How can my remembrance of you ever fade? You will shortly receive a long letter about my present circumstances and all that can interest you. Farewell, beloved, good, and noble friend! Ever continue your love and friendship towards me, just as I shall ever be your faithful

BEETHOVEN.

13.
TO PASTOR AMENDA.

1800.

MY DEAR, MY GOOD AMENDA, MY WARM-HEARTED FRIEND,--

I received and read your last letter with deep emotion, and with mingled pain and pleasure. To what can I compare your fidelity and devotion to me? Ah! it is indeed delightful that you still continue to love me so well. I know how to prize you, and to distinguish you from all others; you are not like my Vienna friends. No! you are one of those whom the soil of my fatherland is wont to bring forth; how often I wish that you were with me, for your Beethoven is very unhappy. You must know that one of my most precious faculties, that of hearing, is become very defective; even while you were still with me I felt indications of this, though I said nothing; but it is now much worse. Whether I shall ever be cured remains yet to be seen; it is supposed to proceed from the state of my digestive organs, but I am almost entirely recovered in that respect. I hope indeed that my hearing may improve, but I scarcely think so, for attacks of this kind are the most incurable of all. How sad my life must now be!--forced to shun all that is most dear and precious to me, and to live with such miserable egotists as ----, &c. I can with truth say that of all my friends Lichnowsky [Prince Carl] is the most genuine. He last year settled 600 florins on me, which, together with the good sale of my works, enables me to live free from care as to my maintenance. All that I now write I can dispose of five times over, and be well paid into the bargain. I have been writing a good deal latterly, and as I hear that you have ordered some pianos from ----, I will send you some of my compositions in the packing-case of one of these instruments, by which means they will not cost you so much.

To my great comfort, a person has returned here with whom I can enjoy the pleasures of society and disinterested friendship,--one of the friends of my youth [Stephan von Breuning]. I have often spoken to him of you, and told him that since I left my fatherland, you are one of those to whom my heart specially clings. Z. [Zmeskall?] does not seem quite to please him; he is, and always will be, too weak for true friendship, and I look on him and ---- as mere instruments on which I play as I please, but never can they bear noble testimony to my inner and outward energies, or feel true sympathy with me; I value them only in so far as their services deserve. Oh! how happy should I now be, had I my full sense of hearing; I would then hasten to you; whereas, as it is, I must withdraw from everything. My best years will thus pass away, without effecting what my talents and powers might have enabled me to perform. How melancholy is the resignation in which I must take refuge! I had determined to rise superior to all this, but how is it possible? If in the course of six months my malady be pronounced incurable then, Amenda! I shall appeal to you to leave all else and come to me, when I intend to travel (my affliction is less distressing when playing and composing, and most so in intercourse with others), and you must be my companion. I have a conviction that good fortune will not forsake me, for to what may I not at present aspire? Since you were here I have written everything except operas and church music. You will not, I know, refuse my petition; you will help your friend to bear his burden and his calamity. I have also very much perfected my pianoforte playing, and I hope that a journey of this kind may possibly contribute to your own success in life, and you would thenceforth always remain with me. I duly received all your letters, and though I did not reply to them, you were constantly present with me, and my heart beats as tenderly as ever for you. I beg you will keep the fact of my deafness a profound secret, and not confide it to any human being. Write to me frequently; your letters, however short, console and cheer me; so I shall soon hope to hear from you.

Do not give your quartet to any one [in F, Op. 18, No. 1], as I have altered it very much, having only now succeeded in writing quartets properly; this you will at once perceive when you receive it. Now, farewell, my dear kind friend! If by any chance I can serve you here, I need not say that you have only to command me.

Your faithful and truly attached
L. V. BEETHOVEN.

14.
TO WEGELER.

Vienna, June 29, 1800.

MY DEAR AND VALUED WEGELER,--

How much I thank you for your remembrance of me, little as I deserve it, or have sought to deserve it; and yet you are so kind that you allow nothing, not even my unpardonable neglect, to discourage you, always remaining the same true, good, and faithful friend. That I can ever forget you or yours, once so dear and precious to me, do not for a moment believe. There are times when I find myself longing to see you again, and wishing that I could go to stay with you. My father-land, that lovely region where I first saw the light, is still as distinct and beauteous in my eyes as when I quitted you; in short, I shall esteem the time when I once more see you, and again greet Father Rhine, as one of the happiest periods of my life. When this may be I cannot yet tell; but at all events I may say that you shall not see me again till I have become eminent, not only as an artist, but better and more perfect as a man; and if the condition of our father-land be then more prosperous, my art shall be entirely devoted to the benefit of the poor. Oh, blissful moment!--how happy do I esteem myself that I can expedite it and bring it to pass!

You desire to know something of my position; well! it is by no means bad. However incredible it may appear, I must tell you that Lichnowsky has been, and still is, my warmest friend (slight dissensions occurred occasionally between us, and yet they only served to strengthen our friendship). He settled on me last year the sum of 600 florins, for which I am to draw on him till I can procure some suitable situation. My compositions are very profitable, and I may really say that I have almost more commissions than it is possible for me to execute. I can have six or seven publishers or more for every piece, if I choose; they no longer bargain with me--I demand, and they pay--so you see this is a very good thing. For instance, I have a friend in distress, and my purse does not admit of my assisting him at once; but I have only to sit down and write, and in a short time he is relieved. I am also become more economical than formerly. If I finally settle here, I don't doubt I shall be able to secure a particular day every year for a concert, of which I have already given several. That malicious demon, however, bad health, has been a stumbling-block in my path; my hearing during the last three years has become gradually worse. The chief cause of this infirmity proceeds from the state of my digestive organs, which, as you know, were formerly bad enough, but have latterly become much worse, and being constantly afflicted with diarrhoea, has brought on extreme weakness. Frank [Director of the General Hospital] strove to restore the tone of my digestion by tonics, and my hearing by oil of almonds; but alas! these did me no good whatever; my hearing became worse, and my digestion continued in its former plight. This went on till the autumn of last year, when I was often reduced to utter despair. Then some medical *asinus* recommended me cold baths, but a more judicious doctor the tepid ones of the Danube, which did wonders for me; my digestion improved, but my hearing remained the same, or in fact rather got worse. I did indeed pass a miserable winter; I suffered from most dreadful spasms, and sank back into my former condition. Thus it went on till about a month ago, when I consulted Vering [an army surgeon], under the belief that my maladies required surgical advice; besides, I had every confidence in him. He succeeded in almost entirely checking the violent diarrhoea, and ordered me the tepid baths of the Danube, into which I pour some strengthening mixture. He gave me no medicine, except some digestive pills four days ago, and a lotion for my ears. I certainly do feel better and stronger, but my ears are buzzing and ringing perpetually, day and night. I can with truth say that my life is very wretched; for nearly two years past I have avoided all society, because I find it impossible to say to people, *I am deaf!* In any other profession this might be more tolerable, but in mine such a condition is truly frightful. Besides, what would my enemies say to this?--and they are not few in number.

To give you some idea of my extraordinary deafness, I must tell you that in the theatre I am obliged to lean close up against the orchestra in order to understand the actors, and when a little way off I hear none of the high notes of instruments or singers. It is most astonishing that in conversation some people never seem to observe this; being subject to fits of absence, they attribute it to that cause. I often can scarcely hear a person if speaking low; I can distinguish the tones, but not the words, and yet I feel it intolerable if any one shouts to me. Heaven alone knows how it is to end! Vering declares that I shall certainly improve, even if I be not entirely restored. How often have I cursed my existence! Plutarch led me to resignation. I shall strive if possible to set Fate at defiance, although there must be moments in my life when I cannot fail to be the most unhappy of God's creatures. I entreat you to say nothing of my affliction to any one, not even to Lorchen [see Nos. 4 and 5]. I confide the secret to you alone, and entreat you some day to correspond with Vering on the subject. If I continue in the same state, I shall come to you in the ensuing spring, when you must engage a house for me somewhere in the country, amid beautiful scenery, and I shall then become a rustic for a year, which may perhaps effect a change. Resignation!--what a miserable refuge! and yet it is my sole remaining one. You will forgive my thus appealing to your kindly sympathies at a time when your own position is sad enough. Stephan Breuning is here, and we are together almost every day; it does me so much good to revive old feelings! He has really become a capital good fellow, not devoid of talent, and his heart, like that of us all, pretty much in the right place. [See No. 13.]

I have very charming rooms at present, adjoining the Bastei [the ramparts], and peculiarly valuable to me on account of my health [at Baron Pasqualati's]. I do really think I shall be able to arrange that Breuning shall come to me. You shall have your Antiochus [a picture], and plenty of my music besides--if, indeed, it will not cost you too much. Your love of art does honestly rejoice me. Only say how it is to be done, and I will send you all my works, which now amount to a considerable number, and are daily increasing. I beg you will let me have my grandfather's portrait as soon as possible by the post, in return for which I send you that of his grandson, your loving and attached Beethoven. It has been brought out here by Artaria, who, as well as many other publishers, has often urged this on me. I intend soon to write to Stoffeln [Christoph von Breuning], and plainly admonish him about his surly humor. I mean to sound in his ears our old friendship, and to insist on his promising me not to annoy you further in your sad circumstances. I will also write to the amiable Lorchen. Never have I forgotten one of you, my kind friends, though you did not hear from me; but you know well that writing never was my *forte*, even my best friends having received no letters from me for years. I live wholly in my music, and scarcely is one work finished when another is begun; indeed, I am now often at work on three or four things at the same time. Do write to me frequently, and I will strive to find time to write to you also. Give my remembrances to all, especially to the kind Frau Hofräthin [von Breuning], and say to her that I am still subject to an occasional *raptus*. As for K----, I am not at all surprised at the change in her: Fortune rolls like a ball, and does not always stop before the best and noblest. As to Ries [Court musician in Bonn], to whom pray cordially remember me, I must say one word. I will write to you more particularly about his son [Ferdinand], although I believe that he would be more likely to succeed in Paris than in Vienna, which is already overstocked, and where even those of the highest merit find it a hard matter to maintain themselves. By next autumn or winter, I shall be able to see what can be done for him, because then all the world returns to town. Farewell, my kind, faithful Wegeler! Rest assured of the love and friendship of your

BEETHOVEN.

15.
TO COUNTESS GIULIETTA GUICCIARDI.[1]

Morning, July 6, 1800.

MY ANGEL! MY ALL! MY SECOND SELF!

Only a few words to-day, written with a pencil (your own). My residence cannot be settled till to-morrow. What a tiresome loss of time! Why this deep grief when necessity compels?--can our love exist without sacrifices, and by refraining from desiring all things? Can you alter the fact that you are not wholly mine, nor I wholly yours? Ah! contemplate the beauties of Nature, and reconcile your spirit to the inevitable. Love demands all, and has a right to do so, and thus it is *I feel towards you* and *you towards me*; but you do not sufficiently remember that I must live both *for you* and *for myself*. Were we wholly united, you would feel this sorrow as little as I should. My journey was terrible. I did not arrive here till four o'clock yesterday morning, as no horses were to be had. The drivers chose another route; but what a dreadful one it was! At the last stage I was warned not to travel through the night, and to beware of a certain wood, but this only incited me to go forward, and I was wrong. The carriage broke down, owing to the execrable roads, mere deep rough country lanes, and had it not been for the postilions I must have been left by the wayside. Esterhazy, travelling the usual road, had the same fate with eight horses, whereas I had only four. Still I felt a certain degree of pleasure, which I invariably do when I have happily surmounted any difficulty. But I must now pass from the outer to the inner man. We shall, I trust, soon meet again; to-day I cannot impart to you all the reflections I have made, during the last few days, on my life; were our hearts closely united forever, none of these would occur to me. My heart is overflowing with all I have to say to you. Ah! there are moments when I find that speech is actually nothing. Take courage! Continue to be ever my true and only love, my all! as I am yours. The gods must ordain what is further to be and shall be!

Your faithful
LUDWIG.

Monday Evening, July 6.

You grieve! dearest of all beings! I have just heard that the letters must be sent off very early. Mondays and Thursdays are the only days when the post goes to K. from here. You grieve! Ah! where I am, there you are ever with me; how earnestly shall I strive to pass my life with you, and what a life will it be!!! Whereas now!! without you!! and persecuted by the kindness of others, which I neither deserve nor try to deserve! The servility of man towards his fellow-man pains me, and when I regard myself as a component part of the universe, what am I, what is he who is called the greatest?--and yet herein are displayed the godlike feelings of humanity!--I weep in thinking that you will receive no intelligence from me till probably Saturday. However dearly you may love me, I love you more fondly still. Never conceal your feelings from me. Good-night! As a patient at these baths, I must now go to rest [a few words are here effaced by Beethoven himself]. Oh, heavens! so near, and yet so far! Is not our love a truly celestial mansion, but firm as the vault of heaven itself?

July 7.

GOOD-MORNING!

Even before I rise, my thoughts throng to you, my immortal beloved!--sometimes full of joy, and yet again sad, waiting to see whether Fate will hear us. I must live either wholly with you, or not at all. Indeed I have resolved to wander far from you [see No. 13] till the moment arrives when I can fly into your arms, and feel that they are my home, and send forth my soul in unison with yours into the realm of spirits. Alas! it must be so! You will take courage, for you know my fidelity. Never can another possess my heart--never, never! Oh, heavens! Why must I fly from her I so fondly love? and yet my existence in W. was as miserable as here. Your love made me the most happy and yet the most unhappy of men. At my age, life requires a uniform equality; can this be found in our mutual relations? My angel! I have this moment heard that the post goes every day, so I must conclude, that you may get this letter the sooner. Be calm! for we can only attain our object of living together by the calm contemplation of our existence. Continue to love me. Yesterday, to-day, what longings for you, what tears for you! for you! for you! my life! my all! Farewell! Oh! love me forever, and never doubt the faithful heart of your lover, L.

Ever thine.
Ever mine.
Ever each other's.

[Footnote 1: These letters to his "immortal beloved," to whom the C sharp minor Sonata is dedicated, appear here for the first time in their integrity, in accordance with the originals written in pencil on fine notepaper, and given in Schindler's *Beethoven's Nachlass*. There has been much discussion about the date. It is certified, in the first place, in the church register which Alex. Thayer saw in Vienna, that Giulietta was married to Count Gallenberg in 1801; and in the next place, the 6th of July falls on a Monday in 1800. The other reasons which induce me decidedly to fix this latter year as the date of the letter, I mean to give at full length in the second volume of *Beethoven's Biography*. I may also state that Beethoven was at baths in Hungary at that time. Whether the K---- in the second letter means Komorn, I cannot tell.]

16.
TO MATTHISSON.

Vienna, August 4, 1800.

MOST ESTEEMED FRIEND,--

You will receive with this one of my compositions published some years since, and yet, to my shame, you probably have never heard of it. I cannot attempt to excuse myself, or to explain why I dedicated a work to you which came direct from my heart, but never acquainted you with its existence, unless indeed in this way, that at first I did not know where you lived, and partly also from diffidence, which led me to think I might have been premature in dedicating a work to you before ascertaining that you approved of it. Indeed, even now I send you "Adelaide" with a feeling of timidity. You know yourself what changes the lapse of some years brings forth in an artist who continues to make progress; the greater the advances we make in art, the less are we satisfied with our works of an earlier date. My most ardent wish will be fulfilled if you are not dissatisfied with the manner in which I have set your heavenly "Adelaide" to music, and are incited by it soon to compose a similar poem; and if you do not consider my request too indiscreet, I would ask you to send it to me forthwith, that I may exert all my energies to approach your lovely poetry in merit. Pray regard the dedication as a token of the pleasure which your "Adelaide" conferred on me, as well as of the appreciation and intense delight your poetry always has inspired, and *always will inspire in me*.

When playing "Adelaide," sometimes recall

Your sincere admirer,
BEETHOVEN.

17.
TO FRAU FRANK,--VIENNA

October, 1800.

DEAR LADY,--

At the second announcement of our concert, you must remind your husband that the public should be made acquainted with the names of those whose talents are to contribute to this concert. Such is the custom here; and indeed, were it not so, what is there to attract a larger audience? which is after all our chief object. Punto [the celebrated horn-player, for whom Beethoven wrote Sonata 17] is not a little indignant about the omission, and I must say he has reason to be so; but even before seeing him it was my intention to have reminded you of this, for I can only explain the mistake by great haste or great forgetfulness. Be so good, then, dear lady, as to attend to my hint otherwise you will certainly expose yourself to *many annoyances*. Being at last convinced in my own mind, and by others, that I shall not be quite superfluous in this concert, I know that not only I, but also Punto, Simoni [a tenorist], and Galvani will demand that the public should be apprised of our zeal for this charitable object; otherwise we must all conclude that we are not wanted.

Yours,
BEETHOVEN.

18.
TO HERR VON WEGELER.

Vienna, Nov. 16, 1800.

MY DEAR WEGELER,--

I thank you for this fresh proof of your interest in me, especially as I so little deserve it. You wish to know how I am, and what remedies I use. Unwilling as I always feel to discuss this subject, still I feel less reluctant to do so with you than with any other person. For some months past Vering has ordered me to apply blisters on both arms, of a particular kind of bark, with which you are probably acquainted,--a disagreeable remedy, independent of the pain, as it deprives me of the free use of my arms for a couple of days at a time, till the blisters have drawn sufficiently. The ringing and buzzing in my ears have certainly rather decreased, particularly in the left ear, in which the malady first commenced, but my hearing is not at all improved; in fact I fear that it is become rather worse. My health is better, and after using the tepid baths for a time, I feel pretty well for eight or ten days. I seldom take tonics, but I have begun applications of herbs, according to your advice. Vering will not hear of plunge baths, but I am much dissatisfied with him; he is neither so attentive nor so indulgent as he ought to be to such a malady; if I did not go to him, which is no easy matter, I should never see him at all. What is your opinion of Schmidt [an army surgeon]? I am unwilling to make any change, but it seems to me that Vering is too much of a practitioner to acquire new ideas by reading. On this point Schmidt appears to be a very different man, and would probably be less negligent with regard to my case. I hear wonders of galvanism; what do you say to it? A physician told me that he knew a deaf and dumb child whose hearing was restored by it (in Berlin), and likewise a man who had been deaf for seven years, and recovered his hearing. I am told that your friend Schmidt is at this moment making experiments on the subject.

I am now leading a somewhat more agreeable life, as of late I have been associating more with other people. You could scarcely believe what a sad and dreary life mine has been for the last two years; my defective hearing everywhere pursuing me like a spectre, making me fly from every one, and appear a misanthrope; and yet no one is in reality less so! This change has been wrought by a lovely fascinating girl [undoubtedly Giulietta], who loves me and whom I love. I have once more had some blissful moments during the last two years, and it is the first time I ever felt that marriage could make me happy. Unluckily, she is not in my rank of life, and indeed at this moment I can marry no one; I must first bestir myself actively in the world. Had it not been for my deafness, I would have travelled half round the globe ere now, and this I must still do. For me there is no pleasure so great as to promote and to pursue my art.

Do not suppose that I could be happy with you. What indeed could make me happier? Your very solicitude would distress me; I should read your compassion every moment in your countenance, which would make me only still more unhappy. What were my thoughts amid the glorious scenery of my father-land? The hope alone of a happier future, which would have been mine but for this affliction! Oh! I could span the world were I only free from this! I feel that my youth is only now commencing. Have I not always been an infirm creature? For some time past my bodily strength has been increasing, and it is the same with my mental powers. I feel, though I cannot describe it, that I daily approach the object I have in view, in which alone can your Beethoven live. No rest for him!--I know of none but in sleep, and I do grudge being obliged to sacrifice more time to it than formerly.[1] Were I only half cured of my malady, then I would come to you, and, as a more perfect and mature man, renew our old friendship.

You should then see me as happy as I am ever destined to be here below--not unhappy. No! that I could not endure; I will boldly meet my fate, never shall it succeed in crushing me. Oh! it is so glorious to live one's life a thousand times over! I feel that I am no longer made for a quiet existence. You will write to me as soon as possible? Pray try to prevail on Steffen [von Breuning] to seek an appointment from the Teutonic Order somewhere. Life here is too harassing for his health; besides, he is so isolated that I do not see how he is ever to get on. You know the kind of existence here. I do not take it upon myself to say that society would dispel his lassitude, but he cannot be persuaded to go anywhere. A short time since, I had some music in my house, but our friend Steffen stayed away. Do recommend him to be more calm and self-possessed, which I have in vain tried to effect; otherwise he can neither enjoy health nor happiness. Tell me in your next letter whether you care about my sending you a large selection of music; you can indeed dispose of what you do not want, and thus repay the expense of the carriage, and have my portrait into the bargain. Say all that is kind and amiable from me to Lorchen, and also to mamma and Christoph. You still have some regard for me? Always rely on the love as well as the friendship of your

BEETHOVEN.

[Footnote 1: "Too much sleep is hurtful" is marked by a thick score in the Odyssey (45, 393) by Beethoven's hand. See Schindler's *Beethoven's Nachlass*.]

19.
TO KAPELLMEISTER HOFMEISTER,--LEIPZIG.[1]

Vienna, Dec. 15, 1800.

MY DEAR BROTHER IN ART,--

I have often intended to answer your proposals, but am frightfully lazy about all correspondence; so it is usually a good while before I can make up my mind to write dry letters instead of music. I have, however, at last forced myself to answer your application. *Pro primo*, I must tell you how much I regret that you, my much-loved brother in the science of music, did not give me some hint, so that I might have offered you my quartets, as well as many other things that I have now disposed of. But if you are as conscientious, my dear brother, as many other publishers, who grind to death us poor composers, you will know pretty well how to derive ample profit when the works appear. I now briefly state what you can have from me. 1st. A Septet, *per il violino, viola, violoncello, contra-basso, clarinetto, corno, fagotto;--tutti obbligati* (I can write nothing that is not *obbligato*, having come into the world with an *obbligato* accompaniment!) This Septet pleases very much. For more general use it might be arranged for one more *violino, viola*, and *violoncello*, instead of the three wind-instruments, *fagotto, clarinetto*, and *corno*.[2] 2d. A Grand Symphony with full orchestra [the 1st]. 3rd. a pianoforte Concerto [Op. 19], which I by no means assert to be one of my best, any more than the one Mollo is to publish here [Op. 15], (this is for the benefit of the Leipzig critics!) because *I reserve the best for myself* till I set off on my travels; still the work will not disgrace you to publish. 4th. A Grand Solo Sonata [Op. 22]. These are all I can part with at this moment; a little later you can have a quintet for stringed instruments, and probably some quartets also, and other pieces that I have not at present beside me. In your answer you can yourself fix the prices; and as you are neither an *Italian* nor a *Jew*, nor am I either, we shall no doubt quickly agree. Farewell, and rest assured,

My dear brother in art, of the esteem of your

BEETHOVEN.

[Footnote 1: The letters to Hofmeister, formerly of Vienna, who conducted the correspondence with Beethoven in the name of the firm of "Hofmeister & Kühnel, Bureau de Musique," are given here as they first appeared in 1837 in the *Neue Zeitschrift für Musik*. On applying to the present representative of that firm, I was told that those who now possess these letters decline giving them out of their own hands, and that no copyist can be found able to decipher or transcribe them correctly.]

[Footnote 2: This last phrase is not in the copy before me, but in Marx's *Biography*, who appears to have seen the original.]

20.
TO KAPELLMEISTER HOFMEISTER.

Vienna, Jan. 15 (or thereabouts), 1801.

I read your letter, dear brother and friend, with much pleasure, and I thank you for your good opinion of me and of my works, and hope I may continue to deserve it. I also beg you to present all due thanks to Herr K. [Kühnel] for his politeness and friendship towards me. I, on my part, rejoice in your undertakings, and am glad that when works of art do turn out profitable, they fall to the share of true artists, rather than to that of mere tradesmen.

Your intention to publish Sebastian Bach's works really gladdens my heart, which beats with devotion for the lofty and grand productions of this our father of the science of harmony, and I trust I shall soon see them appear. I hope when golden peace is proclaimed, and your subscription list opened, to procure you many subscribers here.[1]

With regard to our own transactions, as you wish to know my proposals, they are as follows. I offer you at present the following works:--The Septet (which I already wrote to you about), 20 ducats; Symphony, 20 ducats; Concerto, 10 ducats; Grand Solo Sonata, *allegro, adagio, minuetto, rondo*, 20 ducats. This Sonata [Op. 22] is well up to the mark, my dear brother!

Now for explanations. You may perhaps be surprised that I make no difference of price between the sonata, septet, and symphony. I do so because I find that a septet or a symphony has not so great a sale as a sonata, though a symphony ought unquestionably to be of the most value. (N.B. The septet consists of a short introductory *adagio*, an *allegro, adagio, minuetto, andante*, with variations, *minuetto*, and another short *adagio* preceding a *presto*.) I only ask ten ducats for the concerto, for, as I already wrote to you, I do not consider it one of my best. I cannot think that, taken as a whole, you will consider these prices exorbitant; at least, I have endeavored to make them as moderate as possible for you.

With regard to the banker's draft, as you give me my choice, I beg you will make it payable by Germüller or Schüller. The entire sum for the four works will amount to 70 ducats; I understand no currency but Vienna ducats, so how many dollars in gold they make in your money is no affair of mine, for really I am a very bad man of business and accountant. Now this *troublesome* business is concluded;--I call it so, heartily wishing that it could be otherwise here below! There ought to be only one grand *dépôt* of art in the world, to which the artist might repair with his works, and on presenting them receive what he required; but as it now is, one must be half a tradesman besides-- and how is this to be endured? Good heavens! I may well call it *troublesome*!

As for the Leipzig oxen,[2] let them talk!--they certainly will make no man immortal by their prating, and as little can they deprive of immortality those whom Apollo destines to attain it.

Now may Heaven preserve you and your colleagues! I have been unwell for some time; so it is rather difficult for me at present to write even music, much more letters. I trust we shall have frequent opportunities to assure each other how truly you are my friend, and I yours.

I hope for a speedy answer. Adieu!

L. V. BEETHOVEN.

[Footnote 1: I have at this moment in my hands this edition of Bach, bound in one thick volume, together with the first part of Nägeli's edition of the *Wohltemperirtes Clavier*, also three books of exercises (D, G, and C minor), the *Toccata in D Minor*, and *Twice Fifteen Inventions*.]

[Footnote 2: It is thus that Schindler supplies the gap. It is probably an allusion to the *Allgemeine Musikalische Zeitung*, founded about three years previously.]

21.
TO HERR HOFMEISTER.

Vienna, April 22, 1801.

You have indeed too good cause to complain not a little of me. My excuse is that I have been ill, and in addition had so much to do, that I could scarcely even think of what I was to send you. Moreover, the only thing in me that resembles a genius is, that my papers are never in very good order, and yet no one but myself can succeed in arranging them. For instance, in the score of the concerto, the piano part, according to my usual custom, was not yet written down; so, owing to my hurry, you will receive it in my own very illegible writing. In order that the works may follow as nearly as possible in their proper order, I have marked the numbers to be placed on each, as follows:--

Solo Sonata, Op. 22.
Symphony,   Op. 21.
Septet,   Op. 20.
Concerto,   Op. 19.

I will send you their various titles shortly.

Put me down as a subscriber to Sebastian Bach's works [see Letter 20], and also Prince Lichnowsky. The arrangement of Mozart's Sonatas as quartets will do you much credit, and no doubt be profitable also. I wish I could contribute more to the promotion of such an undertaking, but I am an irregular man, and too apt, even with the best intentions, to forget everything; I have, however, mentioned the matter to various people, and I everywhere find them well disposed towards it. It would be a good thing if you would arrange the septet you are about to publish as a quintet, with a flute part, for instance; this would be an advantage to amateurs of the flute, who have already importuned me on the subject, and who would swarm round it like insects and banquet on it.

Now to tell you something of myself. I have written a ballet ["Prometheus"], in which the ballet-master has not done his part so well as might be. The F---- von L---- has also bestowed on us a production which by no means corresponds with the ideas of his genius conveyed by the newspaper reports. F---- seems to have taken Herr M---- (Wenzel Müller?) as his ideal at the Kusperle, yet without even rising to his level. Such are the fine prospects before us poor people who strive to struggle upwards! My dear friend, pray lose no time in bringing the work before the notice of the public, and write to me soon, that I may know whether by my delay I have entirely forfeited your confidence for the future. Say all that is civil and kind to your partner, Kühnel. Everything shall henceforth be sent finished, and in quick succession. So now farewell, and continue your regards for

Your friend and brother,
BEETHOVEN.

22.
TO HERR HOFMEISTER.

Vienna, June, 1801.

I am rather surprised at the communication you have desired your business agent here to make to me; I may well feel offended at your believing me capable of so mean a trick. It would have been a very different thing had I sold my works to rapacious shopkeepers, and then secretly made another good speculation; but, from *one artist to another*, it is rather a strong measure to suspect me of such a proceeding! The whole thing seems to be either a device to put me to the test, or a mere suspicion. In any event I may tell you that before you received the septet from me I had sent it to Mr. Salomon in London (to be played at his own concert, which I did solely from friendship), with the express injunction to beware of its getting into other hands, as it was my intention to have it engraved in Germany, and, if you choose, you can apply to him for the confirmation of this. But to give you a further proof of my integrity, "I herewith give you the faithful assurance that I have neither sold the septet, the symphony, the concerto, nor the sonata to any one but to Messrs. Hofmeister and Kühnel, and that they may consider them to be their own exclusive property. And to this I pledge my honor." You may make what use you please of this guarantee.

Moreover, I believe Salomon to be as incapable of the baseness of engraving the septet as I am of selling it to him. I was so scrupulous in the matter, that when applied to by various publishers to sanction a pianoforte arrangement of the septet, I at once declined, though I do not even know whether you proposed making use of it in this way. Here follow the long-promised titles of the works. There will no doubt be a good deal to alter and to amend in them; but this I leave to you. I shall soon expect a letter from you, and, I hope, the works likewise, which I wish to see engraved, as others have appeared, and are about to appear, in connection with these numbers. I look on your statement as founded on mere rumors, which you have believed with too much facility, or based entirely on supposition, induced by having perchance heard that I had sent the work to Salomon; I cannot, therefore, but feel some coolness towards such a credulous friend, though I still subscribe myself

Your friend,
BEETHOVEN.

23.
DEDICATION TO DR. SCHMIDT.[1]

1801.

MONSIEUR,--

Je sens parfaitement bien, que la Celebrité de Votre nom ainsi que l'amitié dont Vous m'honorez, exigeroient de moi la dédicace d'un bien plus important ouvrage. La seule chose qui a pu me déterminer à Vous offrir celui-ci de préférence, c'est qu'il me paroît d'une exécution plus facile et par la même plus propre à contribuer à la Satisfaction dont Vous jouissez dans l'aimable Cercle de Votre Famille.--C'est surtout, lorsque les heureux talents d'une fille chérie se seront developpés davantage, que je me flatte de voir ce but atteint. Heureux si j'y ai réussi et si dans cette faible marque de ma haute estime et de ma gratitude Vous reconnoissez toute la vivacité et la cordialité de mes sentiments.

LOUIS VAN BEETHOVEN.

[Footnote 1: Grand Trio, Op. 38.]

24.
TO HIS SCHOLAR, FERDINAND RIES.[1]

1801.

DEAR RIES,--

I send you herewith the four parts corrected by me; please compare the others already written out with these. I also enclose a letter to Count Browne. I have told him that he must make an advance to you of fifty ducats, to enable you to get your outfit. This is absolutely necessary, so it cannot offend him; for after being equipped, you are to go with him to Baden on the Monday of the ensuing week. I must, however, reproach you for not having had recourse to me long ago. Am I not your true friend? Why did you conceal your necessities from me? No friend of mine shall ever be in need, so long as I have anything myself. I would already have sent you a small sum, did I not rely on Browne; if he fails us, then apply at once to your

BEETHOVEN.

[Footnote 1: Ries names 1801 as the date of this letter, and it was no doubt during that summer that Count Browne was in Baden. Ries's father had assisted the Beethoven family in every way in his power at the time of the mother's death.]

25.
TO HERR HOFMEISTER,--LEIPZIG.

Vienna, April 8, 1802.

Do you mean to go post-haste to the devil, gentlemen, by proposing that I should write *such* a *sonata*? During the revolutionary fever, a thing of the kind might have been appropriate, but now, when everything is falling again into the beaten track, and Bonaparte has concluded a *Concordat* with the Pope--such a sonata as this? If it were a *missa pro Sancta Maria à tre voci*, or a *vesper*, &c., then I would at once take up my pen and write a *Credo in unum*, in gigantic semibreves. But, good heavens! such a sonata, in this fresh dawning Christian epoch. No, no!--it won't do, and I will have none of it.

Now for my answer in quickest *tempo*. The lady can have a sonata from me, and I am willing to adopt the general outlines of her plan in an *aesthetical* point of view, without adhering to the keys named. The price to be five ducats; for this sum she can keep the work a year for her own amusement, without either of us being entitled to publish it. After the lapse of a year, the sonata to revert to me--that is, I can and will then publish it, when, if she considers it any distinction, she may request me to dedicate it to her.

I now, gentlemen, commend you to the grace of God. My Sonata [Op. 22] is well engraved, but you have been a fine time about it! I hope you will usher my Septet into the world a little quicker, as the P---- is waiting for it, and you know the Empress has it; and when there are in this imperial city people like ----, I cannot be answerable for the result; so lose no time!

Herr ---- [Mollo?] has lately published my Quartets [Op. 18] full of faults and *errata*, both large and small, which swarm in them like fish in the sea; that is, they are innumerable. *Questo è un piacere per un autore*--this is what I call engraving [*stechen*, stinging] with a vengeance.[1] In truth, my skin is a mass of punctures and scratches from this fine edition of my Quartets! Now farewell, and think of me as I do of you. Till death, your faithful

L. V. BEETHOVEN.

[Footnote 1: In reference to the musical piracy at that time very prevalent in Austria.]

26.[1]
TO MY BROTHERS CARL AND JOHANN BEETHOVEN.

Heiligenstadt, Oct. 6, 1802.

Oh! ye who think or declare me to be hostile, morose, and misanthropical, how unjust you are, and how little you know the secret cause of what appears thus to you! My heart and mind were ever from childhood prone to the most tender feelings of affection, and I was always disposed to accomplish something great. But you must remember that six years ago I was attacked by an incurable malady, aggravated by unskilful physicians, deluded from year to year, too, by the hope of relief, and at length forced to the conviction of a *lasting affliction* (the cure of which may go on for years, and perhaps after all prove impracticable).

Born with a passionate and excitable temperament, keenly susceptible to the pleasures of society, I was yet obliged early in life to isolate myself, and to pass my existence in solitude. If I at any time resolved to surmount all this, oh! how cruelly was I again repelled by the experience, sadder than ever, of my defective hearing!--and yet I found it impossible to say to others: Speak louder; shout! for I am deaf! Alas! how could I proclaim the deficiency of a sense which ought to have been more perfect with me than with other men,--a sense which I once possessed in the highest perfection, to an extent, indeed, that few of my profession ever enjoyed! Alas, I cannot do this! Forgive me therefore when you see me withdraw from you with whom I would so gladly mingle. My misfortune is doubly severe from causing me to be misunderstood. No longer can I enjoy recreation in social intercourse, refined conversation, or mutual outpourings of thought. Completely isolated, I only enter society when compelled to do so. I must live like an exile. In company I am assailed by the most painful apprehensions, from the dread of being exposed to the risk of my condition being observed. It was the same during the last six months I spent in the country. My intelligent physician recommended me to spare my hearing as much as possible, which was quite in accordance with my present disposition, though sometimes, tempted by my natural inclination for society, I allowed myself to be beguiled into it. But what humiliation when any one beside me heard a flute in the far distance, while I heard *nothing*, or when others heard *a shepherd singing*, and I still heard *nothing*! Such things brought me to the verge of desperation, and wellnigh caused me to put an end to my life. *Art! art* alone, deterred me. Ah! how could I possibly quit the world before bringing forth all that I felt it was my vocation to produce?[2] And thus I spared this miserable life--so utterly miserable that any sudden change may reduce me at any moment from my best condition into the worst. It is decreed that I must now choose *Patience* for my guide! This I have done. I hope the resolve will not fail me, steadfastly to persevere till it may please the inexorable Fates to cut the thread of my life. Perhaps I may get better, perhaps not. I am prepared for either. Constrained to become a philosopher in my twenty-eighth year![3] This is no slight trial, and more severe on an artist than on any one else. God looks into my heart, He searches it, and knows that love for man and feelings of benevolence have their abode there! Oh! ye who may one day read this, think that you have done me injustice, and let any one similarly afflicted be consoled, by finding one like himself, who, in defiance of all the obstacles of Nature, has done all in his power to be included in the ranks of estimable artists and men. My brothers Carl and Johann, as soon as I am no more, if Professor Schmidt [see Nos. 18 and 23] be still alive, beg him in my name to describe my malady, and to add these pages to the analysis of my disease, that at least, so far as possible, the world may be reconciled to me after my death. I also hereby declare you both heirs of my small fortune (if so it may be called). Share it fairly, agree together and assist each other. You know that anything you did to give me pain has been long forgiven. I thank you, my brother Carl in particular, for the attachment you have shown me of late. My wish is that you may enjoy a happier life, and one more free from care, than mine has been. Recommend *Virtue* to your children; that alone, and not wealth, can ensure happiness. I speak from experience. It was *Virtue* alone which sustained me in my misery; I have to thank her and Art for not having ended my life by suicide. Farewell! Love each other. I gratefully thank all my friends, especially Prince Lichnowsky and Professor Schmidt. I wish one of you to keep Prince L----'s instruments; but I trust this will give rise to no dissension between you. If you think it more beneficial, however, you have only to dispose of them. How much I shall rejoice if I can serve you even in the grave! So be it then! I joyfully hasten to meet Death. If he comes before I have had the opportunity of developing all my artistic powers, then, notwithstanding my cruel fate, he will come too early for me, and I should wish for him at a more distant period; but even then I shall be content, for his advent will release me from a state of endless suffering. Come when he may, I shall meet him with courage. Farewell! Do not quite forget me, even in death; I deserve this from you, because during my life I so often thought of you, and wished to make you happy. Amen!

LUDWIG VAN BEETHOVEN.

(*Written on the Outside.*)

Thus, then, I take leave of you, and with sadness too. The fond hope I brought with me here, of being to a certain degree cured, now utterly forsakes me. As autumn leaves fall and wither, so are my hopes blighted. Almost as I came, I depart. Even the lofty courage that so often animated me in the lovely days of summer is gone forever. O Providence! vouchsafe me one day of pure felicity! How long have I been estranged from the glad echo of true joy! When! O my God! when shall I again feel it in the temple of Nature and of man?--never? Ah! that would be too hard!

(*Outside*.)

To be read and fulfilled after my death by my brothers Carl and Johann.

[Footnote 1: This beautiful letter I regret not to have seen in the original, it being in the possession of the violin *virtuoso* Ernst, in London. I have adhered to the version given in the Leipzig *Allgemeine Musikalische Zeitung*, Oct. 1827.]

[Footnote 2: A large portion of the *Eroica* was written in the course of this summer, but not completed till August, 1804.]

[Footnote 3: Beethoven did not at that time know in what year he was born. See the subsequent letter of May 2, 1810. He was then far advanced in his thirty-third year.]

27.
NOTICE.

November, 1802.

I owe it to the public and to myself to state that the two quintets in C and E flat major--one of these (arranged from a symphony of mine) published by Herr Mollo in Vienna, and the other (taken from my Septet, Op. 20) by Herr Hofmeister in Leipzig--are not original quintets, but only versions of the aforesaid works given by the publishers. Arrangements in these days (so fruitful in-- arrangements) an author will find it vain to contend against; but we may at least justly demand that the fact should be mentioned in the title-page, neither to injure the reputation of the author nor to deceive the public. This notice is given to prevent anything of the kind in future. I also beg to announce that shortly a new original quintet of my composition, in C major, Op. 29, will appear at Breitkopf & Härtel's in Leipzig.

LUDWIG VAN BEETHOVEN.

28.
TO FERDINAND RIES.

Summer of 1803.

You no doubt are aware that I am here. Go to Stein, and ask if he can send me an instrument, on hire. I am afraid of bringing mine here. Come to me this evening about seven o'clock. I lodge in Oberdöbling, on the left side of the street, No. 4, going down the hill towards Heiligenstadt.

29.
TO HERR HOFMEISTER,--LEIPZIG.

Vienna, Sept. 22, 1803.

I hereby declare all the works you have ordered to be your property. The list of these shall be made out and sent to you with my signature, as the proof of their being your own. I also agree to accept the sum of fifty ducats for them. Are you satisfied?

Perhaps, instead of the variations with violoncello and violin,[1] I may send you variations for the piano, arranged as a duet on a song of mine; but Goethe's poetry must also be engraved, as I wrote these variations in an album, and consider them better than the others. Are you satisfied?

The arrangements are not by me, though I have revised and much improved various passages; but I do not wish you to say that I have arranged them, for it would be false, and I have neither time nor patience to do so. Are you satisfied?

Now farewell! I sincerely wish that all may go well with you. I would gladly make you a present of all my works, if I could do so and still get on in the world; but--remember most people are provided for, and know what they have to live on, while, good heavens! where can an appointment be found at the Imperial Court for such a *parvum talentum com ego*?

Your friend,
L. V. BEETHOVEN.

[Footnote 1: These are the six variations in D, on the air *Ich denke Dein* written in 1800 in the album of the Countesses Josephine Deym and Thérèse of Brunswick.]

30.
CAUTION.

November, 1803.

Herr Carl Zulehner, a piratical engraver in Mayence, has announced an edition of my collected works for the pianoforte and also stringed instruments. I consider it my duty publicly to inform all friends of music that I have no share whatever in this edition.

I would never have in any way authorized any collection of my works (which, moreover, I consider premature) without previously consulting the publishers of single pieces, and ensuring that correctness in which editions of my individual works are so deficient. I must also observe that this illegal edition cannot be complete, as several new works of mine are shortly to appear in Paris, and these Herr Zulehner, being a French subject, dare not pirate. I intend to take another opportunity of enumerating the details of the collection of my works to be brought out under my own auspices and careful revision.

LUDWIG VAN BEETHOVEN.

31.
TO HERR RIES.[1]

1804.

Be so good as to make out a list of the mistakes and send it at once to Simrock, and say that the work must appear as soon as possible. I will send him the Sonata [Op. 47] and the Concerto the day after to-morrow.

BEETHOVEN.

[Footnote 1: Ries relates that the three following notes refer to the pianoforte Sonata, Op. 31, No. 1, carefully engraved by Nägeli in Zurich, which Beethoven consequently sent forthwith to Simrock in Bonn, desiring him to bring out "*une édition très-correcte*" of the work. He also states that Beethoven was residing in Heiligenstadt at the time the work was first sent [see No. 26]. In

Nottebohm's *Skizzenbuch von Beethoven*, he says (p. 43) that the first notice of the appearance of this sonata was on May 21st, 1803; but Simrock writes to me that the date of the document making over the sonata to him is 1804.]

32.
TO HERR RIES.

I must again ask you to undertake the disagreeable task of making a fair copy of the errors in the Zurich Sonata. I have got your list of *errata* "*auf der Wieden*."

33.
TO HERR RIES.

DEAR RIES,--
The signs are wrongly marked, and many of the notes misplaced; so be careful! or your labor will be vain. *Ch' a detto l' amato bene?*

34.
TO HERR RIES.

DEAR RIES,--
May I beg you to be so obliging as to copy this *andante* [in the Kreuzer Sonata] for me, however indifferently? I must send it off to-morrow, and as Heaven alone knows what its fate may then be, I wish to get it transcribed. But I must have it back to-morrow about one o'clock. The cause of my troubling you is that one of my copyists is already very much occupied with various things of importance, and the other is ill.

35.
TO THE COMPOSER LEIDESDORF,--VIENNA.[1]

DORF DES LEIDES [VILLAGE OF SORROW--LEIDESDORF],--
Let the bearer of this, Herr Ries, have some easy duets, and, better still, let him have them for nothing. Conduct yourself in accordance with the reformed doctrines. Farewell!

BEETHOVEN
Minimus.

[Footnote 1: Date unknown. Leidesdorf was also a music-seller.]

36.
TO HERR RIES.

Baden, July 14, 1804.

DEAR RIES,--
If you can find me better lodgings, I shall be very glad. Tell my brothers not to engage these at once; I have a great desire to get one in a spacious, quiet square or on the Bastei. It it really inexcusable in my brother not to have provided wine, as it is so beneficial and necessary to me. I shall take care to be present at the rehearsal on Wednesday. I am not pleased to hear that it is to be at Schuppanzigh's. He may well be grateful to me if my impertinences make him thinner! Farewell, dear Ries! We have bad weather here, and I am not safe from visitors; so I must take flight in order to be alone.

Your true friend,
L. V. BEETHOVEN.

37.
TO HERR RIES.

Baden, July, 1804.

DEAR RIES,--
As Breuning [see Nos. 13, 14, and 18] by his conduct has not scrupled to display my character to you and the house-steward as that of a mean, petty, base man, I beg you will convey my reply at once in person to Breuning. I answer only one point, the first in his letter, and I do so solely because it is

the only mode of justifying myself in your eyes. Say also to him that I had no intention of reproaching him on account of the delay of the notice to quit, and even if Breuning were really to blame for this, our harmonious relations are so dear and precious in my sight, that, for the sake of a few hundreds more or less, I would never subject any friend of mine to vexation. You are aware, indeed, that I jestingly accused you as the cause of the notice arriving too late. I am quite sure that you must remember this. I had entirely forgotten the whole matter, but at dinner my brother began to say that he thought Breuning was to blame in the affair, which I at once denied, saying that you were in fault. I think this shows plainly enough that I attributed no blame to Breuning; but on this he sprang up like a madman, and insisted on sending for the house-steward. Such behavior, in the presence of all those with whom I usually associate, and to which I am wholly unaccustomed, caused me to lose all self-control; so I also started up, upset my chair, left the room, and did not return. This conduct induced Breuning to place me in a pretty light to you and the house-steward, and also to send me a letter which I only answered by silence. I have not another word to say to Breuning. His mode of thinking and of acting, with regard to me, proves that there never ought to have been such friendly intimacy between us, and assuredly it can never more be restored. I wished to make you acquainted with this, as your version of the occurrence degraded both my words and actions. I know that, had you been aware of the real state of the affair, you would not have said what you did, and with this I am satisfied.

I now beg of you, dear Ries, to go to my brother, the apothecary, as soon as you receive this letter, and say to him that I mean to leave Baden in the course of a few days, and that he is to engage the lodging in Döbling as soon as you have given him this message. I had nearly left this to-day; I detest being here--I am sick of it. For Heaven's sake urge him to close the bargain at once, for I want to take possession immediately. Neither show nor speak to any one of what is written in the previous page of this letter. I wish to prove to him in every respect that I am not so meanly disposed as he is. Indeed I have written to him, although my resolve as to the dissolution of our friendship remains firm and unchangeable.

Your friend,
BEETHOVEN.

38.
TO HERR RIES.

Berlin, July 24, 1804.

... You were no doubt not a little surprised about the affair with Breuning; believe me, my dear friend, that the ebullition on my part was only an outbreak caused by many previous scenes of a disagreeable nature. I have the gift of being able to conceal and to repress my susceptibility on many occasions; but if attacked at a time when I chance to be peculiarly irritable, I burst forth more violently than any one. Breuning certainly possesses many admirable qualities, but he thinks himself quite faultless; whereas the very defects that he discovers in others are those which he possesses himself to the highest degree. From my childhood I have always despised his petty mind. My powers of discrimination enabled me to foresee the result with Breuning, for our modes of thinking, acting, and feeling are entirely opposite; and yet I believed that these difficulties might be overcome, but experience has disproved this. So now I want no more of his friendship! I have only found two friends in the world with whom I never had a misunderstanding; but what men these were! One is dead, the other still lives. Although for nearly six years past we have seen nothing of each other, yet I know that I still hold the first place in his heart, as he does in mine [see No. 12]. The true basis of friendship is to be found in sympathy of heart and soul. I only wish you could have read the letter I wrote to Breuning, and his to me. No! never can he be restored to his former place in my heart. The man who could attribute to his friend so base a mode of thinking, and could himself have recourse to so base a mode of acting towards him, is no longer worthy of my friendship.

Do not forget the affair of my apartments. Farewell! Do not be too much addicted to tailoring,[1] remember me to the fairest of the fair, and send me half a dozen needles.

I never could have believed that I could be so idle as I am here. If this be followed by a fit of industry, something worth while may be produced.

Vale! Your
BEETHOVEN.

[Footnote 1: Ries says, in Wegeler's *Biographical Notices*:--"Beethoven never visited me more frequently than when I lived in the house of a tailor, with three very handsome but thoroughly respectable daughters."]

39.
TO MESSRS. ARTARIA & CO.[1]

Vienna, June 1, 1805.

I must inform you that the affair about the new quintet is settled between Count Fries and myself.

The Count has just assured me that he intends to make you a present of it; it is too late to-day for a written agreement on the subject, but one shall be sent early in the ensuing week. This intelligence must suffice for the present, and I think I at all events deserve your thanks for it.

Your obedient servant,
LUDWIG VAN BEETHOVEN.

[Footnote 1: The quintet is probably not that in C, Op. 29, dedicated to Count v. Fries, previously published in 1803 by Breitkopf & Härtel [see No. 27]. It is more likely that he alludes to a new quintet which the Count had no doubt ordered.]

40.
TO MADAME LA PRINCESSE LIECHTENSTEIN, &C.[1]

November, 1805.

Pray pardon me, illustrious Princess, if the bearer of this should cause you an unpleasant surprise. Poor Ries, my scholar, is forced by this unhappy war to shoulder a musket, and must moreover leave this in a few days, being a foreigner. He has nothing, literally nothing, and is obliged to take a long journey. All chance of a concert on his behalf is thus entirely at an end, and he must have recourse to the benevolence of others. I recommend him to you. I know you will forgive the step I have taken. A noble-minded man would only have recourse to such measures in the most utter extremity. Confident of this, I send the poor youth to you, in the hope of somewhat improving his circumstances. He is forced to apply to all who know him.

I am, with the deepest respect, yours,
L. VAN BEETHOVEN.

[Footnote 1: Communicated by Ries himself, who, to Beethoven's extreme indignation, did not deliver the note. See Wegeler's work, p. 134. The following remark is added:--"Date unknown; written a few days before the entrance of the French in 1805" (which took place Nov. 13). Ries, a native of Bonn, was now a French subject, and recalled under the laws of conscription. The Sonata, Op. 27, No. 1, is dedicated to Princess Liechtenstein.]

41.
TO HERR MEYER.[1]

1805.

DEAR MEYER,--

Pray try to persuade Herr v. Seyfried to direct my Opera, as I wish on this occasion to see and hear it myself *from a distance*; in this way my patience will at all events not be so severely tried as when I am close enough to hear my music so bungled. I really do believe that it is done on purpose to annoy me! I will say nothing of the wind-instruments; but all *pp.*'s, *cresc.*, *discresc.*, and all *f.*'s and *ff.*'s may as well be struck out of my Opera, for no attention whatever is paid to them. I shall lose all pleasure in composing anything in future, if I am to hear it given thus. To-morrow or the day after I will come to fetch you to dinner. To-day I am again unwell.

Your friend,
BEETHOVEN.

If the Opera is to be performed the day after to-morrow, there must be another private rehearsal to-morrow, or *each time it will be given worse and worse*.

[Footnote 1: Meyer, the husband of Mozart's eldest sister-in-law, Josepha (Hofer's widow), sang the part of Pizarro at the first performance of *Fidelio*, Nov. 20, 1805, and also at a later period. Seyfried was at that time Kapellmeister at the Theatre "an der Wien."]

42.
TESTIMONIAL FOR C. CZERNY.

Vienna, Dec. 7, 1805.

I, the undersigned, am glad to bear testimony to young Carl Czerny having made the most extraordinary progress on the pianoforte, far beyond what might be expected at the age of fourteen. I consider him deserving of all possible assistance, not only from what I have already referred to, but from his astonishing memory, and more especially from his parents having spent all their means in cultivating the talent of their promising son.

LUDWIG VAN BEETHOVEN.

43.
TO HERR RÖCKEL.[1]

DEAR RÖCKEL,--

Be sure that you arrange matters properly with Mdlle. Milder, and say to her previously from me, that I hope she will not sing anywhere else. I intend to call on her to-morrow, to kiss the hem of her garment. Do not also forget Marconi, and forgive me for giving you so much trouble.

Yours wholly,
BEETHOVEN.

[Footnote 1: Röckel, in 1806 tenor at the Theatre "an der Wien," sang the part of Florestan in the spring of that year, when *Fidelio* was revived. Mdlle. Milder, afterwards Mdme. Hauptmann, played Leonore; Mdme. Marconi was also prima donna.]

44.
TO HERR COLLIN,[1] COURT SECRETARY AND POET.

MY ESTEEMED COLLIN,--

I hear that you are about to fulfil my greatest wish and your own purpose. Much as I desire to express my delight to you in person, I cannot find time to do so, having so much to occupy me. Pray do not then ascribe this to any want of proper attention towards you. I send you the "Armida"; as soon as you have entirely done with it, pray return it, as it does not belong to me. I am, with sincere esteem,

Yours,
BEETHOVEN.

[Footnote 1: Collin, Court Secretary, was the author of *Coriolanus*, a tragedy for which Beethoven in 1807 wrote the celebrated Overture dedicated to that poet. According to Reichardt, Collin offered the libretto of *Bradamante* to Beethoven in 1808, which Reichardt subsequently composed. This note evidently refers to a *libretto*.]

45.
TO HERR GLEICHENSTEIN.[1]

I should like very much, my good Gleichenstein, to speak to you this forenoon between one and two o'clock, or in the afternoon, and where you please. To-day I am too busy to call early enough to find you at home. Give me an answer, and don't forget to appoint the place for us to meet. Farewell, and continue your regard for your

BEETHOVEN.

[Footnote 1: Probably in reference to a conference with regard to a contract for the publication of his works, Op. 58, 59, 60, 61, and 62, that Beethoven had made on the 20th April, 1807, with Muzio Clementi, who had established a large music firm in London; it was also signed by Baron Gleichen.

Beethoven's first intention was to dedicate Op. 58 to him, which is evident from a large page in Schindler's work, on which is written in bold characters, by the master's own hand, "*Quatrième Concerto pour le Piano, avec accompagnement, etc., dédié à son ami Gleichenstein*," &c. The name of the Archduke Rudolph had been previously written, and was eventually adopted, and Gleichenstein afterwards received the dedication of the Grand Sonata with violoncello, Op. 69.]

46.
TO THE DIRECTORS OF THE COURT THEATRE.[1]

Vienna, December, 1807.

The undersigned has cause to flatter himself that during the period of his stay in Vienna he has gained some favor and approbation from the highest nobility, as well as from the public at large, his works having met with an honorable reception both in this and other countries. Nevertheless he has had difficulties of every kind to contend against, and has not hitherto been so fortunate as to acquire a position that would enable him *to live solely for art*, and to develop his talents to a still higher degree of perfection, which ought to be the aim of every artist, thus ensuring future independence instead of mere casual profits.

The mere wish *to gain a livelihood* has never been the leading clew that has hitherto guided the undersigned on his path. His great aim has been the *interest of art* and the ennobling of taste, while his genius, soaring to a higher ideal and greater perfection, frequently compelled him to sacrifice his talents and profits to the Muse. Still works of this kind won for him a reputation in distant lands, securing him the most favorable reception in various places of distinction, and a position befitting his talents and acquirements.

The undersigned does not, however, hesitate to say that this city is above all others the most precious and desirable in his eyes, owing to the number of years he has lived here, the favor and approval he has enjoyed from both high and low, and his wish fully to realize the expectations he has had the good fortune to excite, but most of all, he may truly say, from his *patriotism as a German*. Before, therefore, making up his mind to leave a place so dear to him, he begs to refer to a hint which the reigning Prince Lichnowsky was so kind as to give him, to the effect that the directors of the theatre were disposed to engage the undersigned on reasonable conditions in the service of their theatre, and to ensure his remaining in Vienna by securing to him a permanent position, more propitious to the further exercise of his talents. As this assurance is entirely in accordance with the wishes of the undersigned, he takes the liberty, with all due respect, to place before the directors his readiness to enter into such an engagement, and begs to state the following conditions for their gracious consideration.

1. The undersigned undertakes and pledges himself to compose each year at least *one grand opera*, to be selected by the directors and himself; in return for this he demands a *fixed salary* of 2400 florins a year, and also a free benefit at the third performance of each such opera.

2. He also agrees to supply the directors annually with a little *operetta* or a *divertissement*, with choruses or occasional music of the kind, as may be required, *gratis*; he feels confident that on the other hand the directors will not refuse, in return for these various labors, to grant him *a benefit concert* at all events once a year in one of the theatres. Surely the above conditions cannot be thought exorbitant or unreasonable, when the expenditure of time and energy entailed by the production of an *opera* is taken into account, as it entirely excludes the possibility of all other mental exertion; in other places, too, the author and his family have a share in the profits of every individual performance, so that even *one* successful work at once ensures the future fortunes of the composer. It must also be considered how prejudicial the present rate of exchange is to artists here, and likewise the high price of the necessaries of life, while a residence in foreign countries is open to them.

But in any event, whether the directors accede to or decline this present proposal, the undersigned ventures to request that he may be permitted to give a concert for his own benefit in one of the theatres. For if his conditions be accepted, the undersigned must devote all his time and talents to the composition of such an opera, and thus be prevented working in any other way for profit. In case of the non-acceptance of these proposals, as the concert he was authorized to give last year did not take place owing to various obstacles, he would entreat, as a parting token of the favor hitherto vouchsafed to him, that the promise of last year may now be fulfilled. In the former case, he would beg to suggest *Annunciation Day* [March 25.] for his concert, and in the latter a day during the ensuing Christmas vacation.

LUDWIG VAN BEETHOVEN, M.P.
[*Manu propria.*]

[Footnote 1: This application was fruitless. See Reichardt's *Vertraute Briefe*. "These two (Lobkowitz and Esterhazy) are the heads of the great theatrical direction, which consists entirely of princes and counts, who conduct all the large theatres on their own account and at their own risk." The close of this letter shows that it was written in December.]

47.
TO COUNT FRANZ VON OPPERSDORF.[1]

Vienna, Nov. 1, 1808 [*sic!*].

MY DEAR COUNT,--

I fear you will look on me with displeasure when I tell you that necessity compelled me not only to dispose of the symphony I wrote for you, but to transfer another also to some one else. Be assured, however, that you shall soon receive the one I intend for you. I hope that both you and the Countess, to whom I beg my kind regards, have been well since we met. I am at this moment staying with Countess Erdödy in the apartments below those of Prince Lichnowsky. I mention this in case you do me the honor to call on me when you are in Vienna. My circumstances are improving, without having recourse to the intervention of people *who treat their friends insultingly*. I have also the offer of being made *Kapellmeister* to the King of Westphalia, and it is possible that I may accept the proposal. Farewell, and sometimes think of your attached friend,

BEETHOVEN.

[Footnote 1: The fourth Symphony is dedicated to Count Oppersdorf.]

48.[1]

I fear I am too late for to-day, but I have only now been able to get back your memorial from C----, because H---- wished to add various items here and there. I do beg of you to dwell chiefly on the great importance to me of adequate opportunities to exercise my art; by so doing you will write what is most in accordance with my head and my heart. The preamble must set forth what I am to have in Westphalia--600 ducats in gold, 150 ducats for travelling expenses; all I have to do in return for this sum being to direct the King's [Jerome's] concerts, which are short and few in number. I am not even bound to direct any opera I may write. So, thus freed from all care, I shall be able to devote myself entirely to the most important object of my art--to write great works. An orchestra is also to be placed at my disposition.

N.B. As member of a theatrical association, the title need not be insisted on, as it can produce nothing but annoyance. With regard to the *Imperial service*, I think that point requires delicate handling, and not less so the solicitation for the title of *Imperial Kapellmeister*. It must, however, be made quite clear that I am to receive a sufficient salary from the Court to enable me to renounce the annuity which I at present receive from the gentlemen in question [the Archduke Rudolph, Prince Kinsky, and Prince Lobkowitz], which I think will be most suitably expressed by my stating that it is my hope, and has ever been my most ardent wish, to enter the Imperial service, when I shall be ready to give up as much of the above salary as the sum I am to receive from His Imperial Majesty amounts to. (N.B. We must have it to-morrow at twelve o'clock, as we go to Kinsky then. I hope to see you to-day.)

[Footnote 1: This note, now first published, refers to the call Beethoven had received, mentioned in the previous No. The sketch of the memorial that follows is not, however, in Beethoven's writing, and perhaps not even composed by him [see also No. 46]. It is well known that the Archduke Rudolph, Prince Kinsky, and Prince Lobkowitz had secured to the *maestro* a salary of 4000 gulden.]

49.

The aim and endeavor of every true artist must be to acquire a position in which he can occupy himself exclusively with the accomplishment of great works, undisturbed by other avocations or by considerations of economy. A composer, therefore, can have no more ardent wish than to devote himself wholly to the creation of works of importance, to be produced before the public. He must also keep in view the prospect of old age, in order to make a sufficient provision for that period.

The King of Westphalia has offered Beethoven a salary of 600 gold ducats for life, and 150 ducats for travelling expenses, in return for which his sole obligations are, occasionally to play before His Majesty, and to conduct his chamber concerts, which are both few and short. This proposal is of a most beneficial nature both to art and the artist.

Beethoven, however, much prefers a residence in this capital, feeling so much gratitude for the many proofs of kindness he has received in it, and so much patriotism for his adopted father-land, that he will never cease to consider himself an Austrian artist, nor take up his abode elsewhere, if anything approaching to the same advantages are conferred on him here.

As many persons of high, indeed of the very highest rank, have requested him to name the conditions on which he would be disposed to remain here, in compliance with their wish he states as follows:--

1. Beethoven must receive from some influential nobleman security for a permanent salary for life: various persons of consideration might contribute to make up the amount of this salary, which, at the present increased price of all commodities, must not consist of less than 4000 florins *per annum*. Beethoven's wish is that the donors of this sum should be considered as cooperating in the production of his future great works, by thus enabling him to devote himself entirely to these labors, and by relieving him from all other occupations.

2. Beethoven must always retain the privilege of travelling in the interests of art, for in this way alone can he make himself known, and acquire some fortune.

3. His most ardent desire and eager wish is to be received into the Imperial service, when such an appointment would enable him partly or wholly to renounce the proposed salary. In the mean time the title of *Imperial Kapellmeister* would be very gratifying to him; and if this wish could be realized, the value of his abode here would be much enhanced in his eyes.

If his desire be fulfilled, and a salary granted by His Majesty to Beethoven, he will renounce so much of the said 4000 florins as the Imperial salary shall amount to; or if this appointment be 4000 florins, he will give up the whole of the former sum.

4. As Beethoven wishes from time to time to produce before the public at large his new great works, he desires an assurance from the present directors of the theatre on their part, and that of their successors, that they will authorize him to give a concert for his own benefit every year on Palm Sunday, in the Theatre "an der Wien." In return for which Beethoven agrees to arrange and direct an annual concert for the benefit of the poor, or, if this cannot be managed, at all events to furnish a new work of his own for such a concert.

50.
TO ZMESKALL.

December, 1808.

MY EXCELLENT FRIEND,--

All would go well now if we had only a curtain, without it the *Aria* ["Ah! Perfido"] *will be a failure*.[1] I only heard this to-day from S. [Seyfried], and it vexes me much: a curtain of any kind will do, even a bed-curtain, or merely a *kind of gauze screen*, which could be instantly removed. There must be something; for the Aria is in the *dramatic style*, and better adapted for the stage than for effect in a concert-room. *Without a curtain, or something of the sort, the Aria will be devoid of all meaning, and ruined! ruined! ruined!! Devil take it all!* The Court will probably be present. Baron Schweitzer [Chamberlain of the Archduke Anton] requested me earnestly to make the application myself. Archduke Carl granted me an audience and promised to come. The Empress *neither promised nor refused*.

A hanging curtain!!!! or the Aria and I will both be hanged to-morrow. Farewell! I embrace you as cordially on this new year as in the old one. *With or without a curtain!* Your

BEETHOVEN.

[Footnote 1: Reichardt, in his *Vertraute Briefe* relates among other things about the concert given by Beethoven in the Royal Theatre "an der Wien," Oct. 22, 1808, as follows:--"Poor Beethoven, who derived from this concert the first and only net profits which accrued to him during the whole year, met with great opposition and very slender support in arranging and carrying it out. First came the *Pastoral Symphony; or, Reminiscences of Rural Life*; then followed, as the sixth piece, a long

Italian *scena*, sung by Demoiselle Killitzky, a lovely Bohemian with a lovely voice." The above note [to Zmeskall?] certainly refers to this concert.]

51.
TO FERDINAND RIES.[1]

1809.

MY DEAR FELLOW,--

Your friends have at any rate given you very bad advice; but I know all about them: they are the very same to whom you sent that fine news about me from Paris; the very same who inquired about my age--information that you contrived to supply so correctly!--the very same who have often before injured you in my opinion, but now permanently. Farewell!

BEETHOVEN.

[Footnote 1: Ries himself gives the date of this note as 1809, though he cannot recall what gave rise to it. It is probably connected with a fact mentioned by Wegeler, p. 95, that Reichardt, who was at that time in Vienna, had advised Beethoven's young pupil, Ries, to apply to the King of Westphalia for the appointment of Kapellmeister, which he had recently given up. This was reported to Beethoven, and roused his ire. Ries, too, had written from Paris that the taste in music there was very indifferent; that Beethoven's works were little known or played in that city. Beethoven was also very susceptible with regard to his age. At the request of some of Beethoven's friends, Ries, in 1806, obtained Beethoven's baptismal certificate, and sent it to Vienna. But the *maestro's* wrath on this occasion passed away as quickly as usual.]

52.
TO ZMESKALL.[1]

March 7, 1809.

It is just what I expected! As to the blows, that is rather far-fetched. The story is at least three months' old, and very different from what he now makes it out to be. The whole stupid affair was caused by a female huckster and a couple of low fellows. I lose very little. He no doubt was corrupted in the very house where I am now living.

[Footnote 1: [See No. 10.] The notes to Zmeskall generally have the dates written by himself. This one bears the date March 7, 1809. In all points connected with domestic life, and especially in household matters and discords, Zmeskall was always a kind and consolatory friend. Beethoven at that time lived in the same house with Countess Erdödy. [See No. 74.]]

53.
TO ZMESKALL.

My most excellent, high, and well-born Herr v. Zmeskall, Court Secretary and Member of the Society of the Single Blessed,--If I come to see you to-day, ascribe it to the fact that a person wishes to speak to me at your house whom I could not refuse to see. I come without any *card* from you, but I hope you will not on that account *discard* me.

Yours truly--most truly,
L. V. BEETHOVEN.

54.
TO ZMESKALL.

It seems to me, dear Zmeskall, if war really does break out, when it comes to an end you will be the very man for an appointment in the Peace Legation. What a glorious office!!! I leave it entirely to you to do the best you can about my servant, only henceforth Countess Erdödy must not attempt to exercise the smallest influence over him. She says she made him a present of twenty-five florins, and gave him five florins a month, solely to induce him to stay with me. I cannot refuse to believe this trait of generosity, but I do not choose that it should be repeated. Farewell! I thank you for your friendship, and hope soon to see you.

Yours ever,
BEETHOVEN.

55.
TO ZMESKALL.[1]

April 16, 1809.

If I cannot come to-day, dear Zmeskall which is very possible, ask Baroness von ---- [name illegible] to give you the pianoforte part of the Trios, and be so good as to send them and the other parts to me to-day.

In haste, your
BEETHOVEN.

[Footnote 1: April 16, 1809. By the Terzetts he no doubt means the Trios, Op. 70, dedicated to Countess Erdödy.]

56.
TO ZMESKALL.

April 17, 1809.

DEAR Z.,--

A suitable lodging has just been found out for me, but I need some one to help me in the affair. I cannot employ my brother, because he only recommends what costs least money. Let me know, therefore, if we can go together to look at the house. It is in the Klepperstall.[1]

[Footnote 1: An der Mölker Bastei.]

57.
TO ZMESKALL.

April 25, 1809.

I shall be glad, right glad, to play. I send you the violoncello part; if you find that you can manage it, play it yourself, or let old Kraft[1] do so. I will tell you about the lodging when we meet.

Your friend,
BEETHOVEN.

[Footnote 1: Anton Kraft (and likewise his son, Nicolaus Kraft) was a most admirable violoncello-player, with whom Beethoven from the earliest days of his residence in Vienna had played a great deal at Prince Lichnowsky's. Kraft was at that time in Prince Lobkowitz's band.]

58.
TO ZMESKALL.[1]

May 14, 1809.

MY DEAR LITTLE MUSICAL OLD COUNT!--

I think after all it would be advisable to let old Kraft play, as the trios are to be heard for the first time (in society), and you can play them afterwards; but I leave it all to your own option. If you meet with any difficulties, one of which may possibly be that Kraft and S. [Schuppanzigh] do not harmonize well together, then Herr v. Zmeskall must distinguish himself, not as a mere musical Count, but as an energetic musician.

Your friend,
BEETHOVEN.

[Footnote 1: Kraft and Schuppanzigh were then each giving quartet *soirées*.]

59.
TO FREIHERR V. HAMMER-PURGSTALL.[1]

1809.

I feel almost ashamed of your complaisance and kindness in permitting me to see the MS. of your as yet unknown literary treasures. Pray receive my sincere thanks. I also beg to return both your operettas. Wholly engrossed by my professional avocations, it is impossible for me to give an opinion, especially with regard to the Indian Operetta; as soon as time permits, I will call on you for the purpose of discussing this subject, and also the Oratorio of "The Deluge." Pray always include me among the warm admirers of your great talents.

> I am, sir, with sincere esteem, your obedient
> BEETHOVEN.

[Footnote 1: I see in Schindler's *Beethoven*, that he wished to have "an Indian Chorus of a religious character" from this renowned Orientalist, who, in sending his *Persian Operetta*, written "rather with an ideal than a musical object," and likewise an oratorio, *The Deluge*, remarks:--"Should you not find these works in all respects executed quite to your taste, still I feel convinced that through the genius of a Beethoven alone can music portray the rising of the great flood and the pacifying of the surging waters."]

60.
TO FREIHERR V. HAMMER-PURGSTALL.[1]

1809.

Forgive me, my dear H----, for not having brought you the letter for Paris. I have been, and still am, so much occupied, that day after day I am obliged to delay writing it, but you shall have it to-morrow, even if I am unable to come myself to see you, which I am most anxious to do.

There is another matter that I would most earnestly press on you; perhaps you might succeed in doing something for a *poor unfortunate man*. I allude to Herr Stoll, son of the celebrated physician. With many persons the question is whether a man has been ruined by his own fault or by that of others, but this is not so with either you or me; it is sufficient that Stoll is unfortunate, and looks on a journey to Paris as his sole resource, having last year made many influential acquaintances, who, when he goes there, are to endeavor to procure him a professorship in Westphalia. Stoll has therefore applied to Herr v. Neumann, in the State Chancery Office, to send him with a government courier to Paris, but the latter refuses to take him for less than twenty-five louis d'or. Now I request you, my dear friend, to speak to Herr v. Neumann to arrange, if possible, that the courier should either take Stoll *gratis*, or for a small sum. I am persuaded that if there is nothing particular against it, you will be glad to interest yourself in poor Stoll. I return to the country to-day, but hope soon to be so fortunate as to enjoy an hour of your society. In the mean time I send you my best wishes, and beg you will believe in the sincere esteem of

> Your obedient
> LUDWIG v. BEETHOVEN.

[Footnote 1: Reichardt states that Stoll was in Vienna in the spring of 1809, which fixes the date of this letter. Napoleon bestowed a pension on the young poet (who appears to have gone to Paris), mistaking him for his father, the celebrated physician.]

61.
TO BARONESS VON DROSSDICK.

MY ESTEEMED THÉRÈSE,--

You will receive with this what I promised. Had not many serious obstacles intervened, I would have sent you more, in order to show you that where my friends are concerned *I always perform more than I promise*. I hope, and do not doubt, that you are agreeably occupied and enjoying society, but not too much, I trust, to prevent your thinking of us. It would show too much confidence in you, or too high an estimation of my own merits, were I to attribute the sentiment to you, "That people are not together only when present, but that the absent and the dead also live with us." Who could ascribe such a thought to the volatile Thérèse, who takes the world so lightly? Among your various occupations, do not forget the piano, or rather, music in general, for which you have so fine a talent: why not then seriously cultivate it? You, who have so much feeling for the good and the beautiful, should strive to recognize the perfections of so charming an art, which in return always casts so bright a reflection on us.

I live in entire quiet and solitude, and even though occasional flashes of light arouse me, still since you all left this I feel a hopeless void which even my art, usually so faithful to me, has not yet triumphed over. Your pianoforte is ordered, and you shall soon have it. What a difference you must have discovered between the treatment of the theme I extemporized on the other evening and the mode in which I have recently written it out for you? You must explain this yourself, only do not find the solution in the punch! How happy you are to get away so soon to the country! I cannot enjoy this luxury till the 8th. I look forward to it with the delight of a child. What happiness I shall feel in wandering among groves and woods, and among trees, and plants, and rocks! No man on earth can love the country as I do! Thickets, trees, and rocks supply the echo man longs for!

You shall soon receive some more of my compositions, which will not cause you to complain so much of difficulties. Have you read Goethe's "Wilhelm Meister," and Schlegel's "Translations of Shakspeare"? People have so much leisure in the country, that perhaps you would like me to send you these works? It happens that I have an acquaintance in your neighborhood; so perhaps you may see me some morning early for half an hour, after which I must be off again. You will also observe that I intend to bore you for as short a time as possible.[1]

Commend me to the regard of your father and mother, though I have as yet no right to claim it. Remember me also to your cousin M. [Mathilde]. Farewell, my esteemed Thérèse; I wish you all the good and charm that life can offer. Think of me kindly, and forget my follies. Rest assured that no one would more rejoice to hear of your happiness, even were you to feel no interest in your devoted servant and friend,

BEETHOVEN.

N.B. It would be very amiable in you to write me a few lines, to say if I can be of any use to you here.

[Footnote: Herr v. Malfatti Rohrenbach, nephew of the renowned physician who was so prominent in Beethoven's last illness, lately related to me in Vienna as follows:--Beethoven went to pay a visit to young Frau Thérèse, Baroness Drossdick, at Mödling, but not finding her at home, he tore a sheet of music-paper out of a book, and wrote some music to a verse of Matthisson's, and on the other side, inscribed, in large letters, "To my dear Thérèse." The "Mathilde" mentioned farther on was, according to Bärmann, a Baroness Gleichenstein. [See No. 45.]]

62.
À MDLLE. MDLLE. DE GERARDI.[1]

DEAR MDLLE. G.,--

I cannot with truth deny that the verses you sent have considerably embarrassed me. It causes a strange sensation to see and hear yourself praised, and yet to be conscious of your own defects, as I am. I consider such occurrences as mere incitements to strive to draw nearer the unattainable goal set before us by Art and Nature, difficult as it may be. These verses are truly beautiful, with the exception of one fault that we often find in poets, which is, their being misled by Fancy to believe that they really do see and hear *what they wish to see and hear*, and yet even this is far below their ideal. You may well believe that I wish to become acquainted with the poet or poetess; pray receive also yourself my thanks for the kindly feeling you show towards your sincere friend,

L. V. BEETHOVEN.

[Footnote 1: Nothing has hitherto been ascertained respecting either the date of this note, or the lady to whom it is addressed.]

63.
TO ZMESKALL.[1]

January 23, 1810.

What are you about? My gayety yesterday, though only assumed, has not only vexed but offended you. The *uninvited guests* seemed so little to deserve your ill-humor, that I endeavored to use all my friendly influence to prevent your giving way to it, by my pretended flow of spirits. I am still suffering from indigestion. Say whether you can meet me at the "Swan" to-day.

Your true friend,
BEETHOVEN.

[Footnote 1: The cause that gave rise to this note is not known.]

64.
TO WEGELER.

Vienna, May 2, 1810.

MY DEAR OLD FRIEND,--

These lines may very possibly cause you some surprise, and yet, though you have no written proof of it, I always retain the most lively remembrance of you. Among my MSS. is one that has long been destined for you, and which you shall certainly receive this summer. For the last two years my secluded and quiet life has been at an end, and I have been forcibly drawn into the vortex of the world; though as yet I have attained no good result from this,--nay, perhaps rather the reverse, --but who has not been affected by the storms around us? Still I should not only be happy, but the happiest of men, if a demon had not taken up his settled abode in my ears. Had I not somewhere read that man must not voluntarily put an end to his life while he can still perform even one good deed, I should long since have been no more, and by my own hand too! Ah! how fair is life; but for me it is forever poisoned!

You will not refuse me one friendly service, which is to procure me my baptismal certificate. As Steffen Breuning has an account with you, he can pay any expenses you may incur, and I will repay him here. If you think it worth while to make the inquiry in person, and choose to make a journey from Coblenz to Bonn, you have only to charge it all to me. I must, however, warn you that I had an *elder brother* whose name was also Ludwig, with the second name of *Maria*, who died. In order to know my precise age, the date of my birth must be first ascertained, this circumstance having already led others into error, and caused me to be thought older than I really am. Unluckily, I lived for some time without myself knowing my age [see Nos. 26 and 51]. I had a book containing all family incidents, but it has been lost, Heaven knows how! So pardon my urgently requesting you to try to discover *Ludwig Maria's* birth, as well as that of the present Ludwig. The sooner you can send me the certificate of baptism the more obliged shall I be.[1] I am told that you sing one of my songs in your Freemason Lodge, probably the one in E major, which I have not myself got; send it to me, and I promise to compensate you threefold and fourfold.[2] Think of me with kindness, little as I apparently deserve it. Embrace your dear wife and children, and all whom you love, in the name of your friend,

BEETHOVEN.

[Footnote 1: Wegeler says:--"I discovered the solution of the enigma (why the baptismal certificate was so eagerly sought) from a letter written to me three months afterwards by my brother-in-law, Stephan von Breuning, in which he said: 'Beethoven tells me at least once a week that he means to write to you; but I believe his *intended marriage is broken off*; he therefore feels no ardent inclination to thank you for having procured his baptismal certificate.'"]

[Footnote 2: Beethoven was mistaken; Wegeler had only supplied other music to the words of Matthisson's *Opfer Lied*.]

65.
TO ZMESKALL.

July 9, 1810.

DEAR Z.,--

You are about to travel, and so am I on account of my health. In the mean time all goes topsy-turvy with me. The *Herr*[1] wants to have me with him, and Art is not less urgent in her claims. I am partly in Schönbrunn and partly here; every day assailed by messages from strangers and new acquaintances, and even as regards art I am often driven nearly distracted by my undeserved fame. Fortune seeks me, and for that very reason I almost dread some new calamity. As for your "Iphigénie," the facts are these. I have not seen it for the last two years and a half, and have no doubt lent it to some one; but to whom?--that is the question. I have sent in all directions, and have not yet discovered it, but hope still to find it. If lost, you shall be indemnified. Farewell, my dear Z. I trust that when we meet again you will find that my art has made some progress in the interim.

Ever remain my friend, as much as I am yours,

BEETHOVEN.

[Footnote 1: The "Herr" is his pupil, the Archduke Rudolph.]

66.
TO BETTINA BRENTANO.[1]

Vienna, August 11, 1810.

MY DEAREST FRIEND,--

Never was there a lovelier spring than this year; I say so, and feel it too, because it was then I first knew you. You have yourself seen that in society I am like a fish on the sand, which writhes and writhes, but cannot get away till some benevolent Galatea casts it back into the mighty ocean. I was indeed fairly stranded, dearest friend, when surprised by you at a moment in which moroseness had entirely mastered me; but how quickly it vanished at your aspect! I was at once conscious that you came from another sphere than this absurd world, where, with the best inclinations, I cannot open my ears. I am a wretched creature, and yet I complain of others!! You will forgive this from the goodness of heart that beams in your eyes, and the good sense manifested by your ears; at least they understand how to flatter, by the mode in which they listen. My ears are, alas! a partition-wall, through which I can with difficulty hold any intercourse with my fellow-creatures. Otherwise, perhaps, I might have felt more assured with you; but I was only conscious of the full, intelligent glance from your eyes, which affected me so deeply that never can I forget it. My dear friend! dearest girl!--Art! who comprehends it? with whom can I discuss this mighty goddess? How precious to me were the few days when we talked together, or, I should rather say, corresponded! I have carefully preserved the little notes with your clever, charming, most charming answers; so I have to thank my defective hearing for the greater part of our fugitive intercourse being written down. Since you left this I have had some unhappy hours,--hours of the deepest gloom, when I could do nothing. I wandered for three hours in the Schönbrunn Allée after you left us, but no *angel* met me there to take possession of me as you did. Pray forgive, my dear friend, this deviation from the original key, but I must have such intervals as a relief to my heart. You have no doubt written to Goethe about me? I would gladly bury my head in a sack, so that I might neither see nor hear what goes on in the world, because I shall meet you there no more; but I shall get a letter from you? Hope sustains me, as it does half the world; through life she has been my close companion, or what would have become of me? I send you "Kennst Du das Land," written with my own hand, as a remembrance of the hour when I first knew you; I send you also another that I composed since I bade you farewell, my dearest, fairest sweetheart!

Herz, mein Herz, was soll das geben,
Was bedränget dich so sehr;
Welch ein neues fremdes Leben,
Ich erkenne dich nicht mehr.

Now answer me, my dearest friend, and say what is to become of me since my heart has turned such a rebel. Write to your most faithful friend,

BEETHOVEN.

[Footnote 1: The celebrated letters to Bettina are given here exactly as published in her book, *Ilius Pamphilius und die Ambrosia* (Berlin, Arnim, 1857) in two volumes. I never myself had any doubts of their being genuine (with the exception of perhaps some words in the middle of the third letter), nor can any one now distrust them, especially after the publication of *Beethoven's Letters*. But for the sake of those for whom the weight of innate conviction is not sufficient proof, I may here mention that in December, 1864, Professor Moritz Carrière, in Munich, when conversing with me about *Beethoven's Letters*, expressly assured me that these three letters were genuine, and that he had seen them in Berlin at Bettina v. Arnim's in 1839, and read them most attentively and with the deepest interest. From their important contents, he urged their immediate publication; and when this shortly after ensued, no change whatever struck him as having been made in the original text; on the contrary, he still perfectly remembered that the much-disputed phraseology (and especially the incident with Goethe) was precisely the same as in the originals. This testimony seems to me the more weighty, as M. Carrière must not in such matters be looked on as a novice, but as a competent judge, who has carefully studied all that concerns our literary heroes, and who would not permit anything to be falsely imputed to Beethoven any more than to Goethe. Beethoven's biography is, however, the proper place to discuss more closely such things, especially his character and his conduct in this particular case. At present we only refer in general terms to the first chapter of *Beethoven's Jugend*, which gives all the facts connected with these letters to Bettina and the following ones--a characteristic likeness of Beethoven thus impressed itself on the mind of the biographer, and was reproduced in a few bold outlines in his *Biography*. These letters could not, however, possibly be given *in extenso* in a general introduction to a comprehensive biography.]

67.
TO BETTINA BRENTANO.

Vienna, Feb. 10, 1811.

DEAR AND BELOVED FRIEND,--

I have now received two letters from you, while those to Tonie show that you still remember me, and even too kindly. I carried your letter about with me the whole summer, and it often made me feel very happy; though I do not frequently write to you, and you never see me, still I write you letters by thousands in my thoughts. I can easily imagine what you feel at Berlin in witnessing all the noxious frivolity of the world's rabble,[1] even had you not written it to me yourself. Such prating about art, and yet no results!!! The best description of this is to be found in Schiller's poem "Die Flüsse," where the river Spree is supposed to speak. You are going to be married, my dear friend, or are already so, and I have had no chance of seeing you even once previously. May all the felicity that marriage ever bestowed on husband and wife attend you both! What can I say to you of myself? I can only exclaim with Johanna, "Compassionate my fate!" If I am spared for some years to come, I will thank the Omniscient, the Omnipotent, for the boon, as I do for all other weal and woe. If you mention me when you write to Goethe, strive to find words expressive of my deep reverence and admiration. I am about to write to him myself with regard to "Egmont," for which I have written some music solely from my love for his poetry, which always delights me. Who can be sufficiently grateful to a great poet,--the most precious jewel of a nation! Now no more, my dear sweet friend! I only came home this morning at four o'clock from an orgy, where I laughed heartily, but to-day I feel as if I could weep as sadly; turbulent pleasures always violently recoil on my spirits. As for Clemens [Brentano, her brother], pray thank him for his complaisance; with regard to the Cantata, the subject is not important enough for us here--it is very different in Berlin; and as for my affection, the sister engrosses so large a share, that little remains for the brother. Will he be content with this?

Now farewell, my dear, dear friend; I imprint a sorrowful kiss on your forehead, thus impressing my thoughts on it as with a seal. Write soon, very soon, to your brother,

BEETHOVEN.

[Footnote 1: An expression which, as well as many others, he no doubt borrowed from Bettina, and introduced to please her.]

68.
TO ZMESKALL.

1811.

I am disposed to engage a man who has just offered me his services,--a music-copyist. His parents live in Vienna, which might be convenient in many respects, but I first wish to speak to you about the terms; and as you are disengaged to-morrow, which I,

BEETHOVEN.

69.
TO ZMESKALL.

1811.

MOST HIGH-BORN OF MEN!--

We beg you to confer some goose-quills on us; we will in return send you a whole bunch of the same sort, that you may not be obliged to pluck out your own. It is just possible that you may yet receive the Grand Cross of the Order of the Violoncello. We remain your gracious and most friendly of all friends,

BEETHOVEN.

70.
TO THE ARCHDUKE RUDOLPH.[1]

The Spring of 1811.

YOUR ROYAL HIGHNESS,--

As in spite of every effort I can find no copyist to write in my house, I send you my own manuscript; all you have to do is to desire Schlemmer to get you an efficient copyist, who must, however, write out the Trio in your palace, otherwise there would be no security against piracy. I am better, and hope to have the honor of waiting on you in the course of a few days, when we must strive to make up for lost time. I always feel anxious and uneasy when I do not attend your Royal Highness as often or as assiduously as I wish. It is certainly the truth when I say that the loss is mine, but I trust I shall not soon again be so unwell. Be graciously pleased to remember me; the time may yet come when I shall be able to show you doubly and trebly that I deserve this more than ever.

I am your Royal Highness's devoted servant,
LUDWIG V. BEETHOVEN.

[Footnote 1: Schlemmer was for many years Beethoven's copyist.]

71.

MY DEAR FRIEND,--[1]

I have taken this trouble only that I might figure correctly, and thus be able sometimes to lead others. As for mistakes, I scarcely ever required to have them pointed out to me, having had from my childhood such a quick perception, that I exercised it unconscious that it ought to be so, or in fact could be otherwise.

[Footnote 1: Written on a sheet of music-paper (oblong folio) numbered 22, and evidently torn out of a large book. On the other side (21) is written, in Beethoven's hand, instructions on the use of the fourth in retardations, with five musical examples. The leaf is no doubt torn from one of the books that Beethoven had compiled from various text-books, for the instruction of the Archduke Rudolph. I have therefore placed Beethoven's remark here.]

72.
TO THE DRAMATIC POET TREITSCHKE.

June 6, 1811.

DEAR TREITSCHKE,--

Have you read the book, and may I venture to hope that you will be persuaded to undertake it? Be so good as to give me an answer, as I am prevented going to you myself. If you have already read it, then send it back to me, that I may also look over it again before you begin to work at it. Above all, if it be your good pleasure that I should soar to the skies on the wings of your poetry, I entreat you to effect this as soon as possible.

Your obedient servant,
L. V. BEETHOVEN.

73.
TO ZMESKALL.

Sept. 10, 1811.

DEAR ZMESKALL,--

Let the rehearsal stand over for the present. I must see my doctor again to-day, of whose bungling I begin to tire. Thanks for your metronome; let us try whether we can measure Time into Eternity with it, for it is so *simple* and *easily managed* that there seems to be no impediment to this! In the mean time we will have a conference on the subject. The mathematical precision of clockwork is of course greater; yet formerly, in watching the little experiments you made in my presence, I thought there was something worthy of notice in your metronome, and I hope we shall soon succeed in *setting it thoroughly right*. Ere long I hope to see you.

Your friend,
BEETHOVEN.

74.
TO ZMESKALL.

Oct. 26, 1811.

I shall be at the "Swan" to-day, and hope to meet you there *to a certainty*, but don't come too late. My foot is better; the author of so many poetical *feet* promises the *head* author a sound foot within a week's time.

75.
TO ZMESKALL.

Nov. 20, 1811.

We are deucedly obliged to you. We beg you to be careful not to lose your well-earned fame. You are exhorted to pursue the same course, and we remain once more your deucedly attached

LUDWIG VAN BEETHOVEN.

76.
TO ZMESKALL.

Jan. 19, 1812.

I shall be at the "Swan" to-day, dear Z. I have, alas! *too much* leisure, and you *none*! Your

BEETHOVEN.

77.
TO ZMESKALL.[1]

1812.

CONFOUNDED LITTLE QUONDAM MUSICAL COUNT!

What the deuce has become of you? Are you to be at the "Swan" to-day? No? ... Yes! See from this enclosure what I have done for Hungary. When a German undertakes a thing, even without pledging his word, he acts very differently from one of those Hungarian Counts, such as B. [Brunswick], who allowed me to travel by myself--from what paltry, miserable motive who can tell?--and kept me waiting, though he did not wait for me!

My excellent little quondam musical Count,

I am now, as ever, your attached

BEETHÖVERL.

Return the enclosure, for we wish to bring it, and something else, pretty forcibly under the notice of the Count.

[Footnote 1: The date of this and the following note is decided by the allusion to his compositions written for Hungary (Pesth). See the subsequent letter to Varenna.]

78.
TO ZMESKALL.

You are summoned to appear to-day at the "Swan;" Brunswick also comes. If you do not appear, you are henceforth excluded from all that concerns us. Excuses *per excellentiam* cannot be accepted. Obedience is enjoined, knowing that we are acting for your benefit, and that our motive is to guard you against temptations and faithlessness *per excellentiam--dixi*.

BEETHOVEN.

79.
TO ZMESKALL.

DEAR ZMESKALL,--

The well-known watchmaker who lives close to the Freiung is to call on you. I want a first-rate repeater, for which he asks forty ducats. As you like that kind of thing, I beg you will exert yourself on my behalf, and select a really good watch for me.

With the most enthusiastic admiration for a man like yourself, who is soon to give me an opportunity of displaying in his favor my particular knowledge of horn-playing, I am your

LUDWIG VAN BEETHOVEN.

80.
TO KAMMERPROCURATOR VARENNA,--GRATZ.[1]

1812.

If the wish to benefit the poor were not so evident in your letter, I should have felt not a little offended by your accompanying your request to me by the offer of payment. From my childhood, whenever my art could be serviceable to poor suffering humanity, I have never allowed any other motive to influence me, and never required anything beyond the heartfelt gratification that it always caused me. With this you will receive an Oratorio--(A), the performance of which occupies half an evening, also an Overture and a Fantasia with Chorus--(B). If in your benevolent institution you possess a *dépôt* for such things, I beg you will deposit these three works there, as a mark of my sympathy for the destitute; to be considered as their property, and to be given at any concerts intended for their sole benefit. In addition to these, you will receive an Introduction to the "Ruins of Athens," the score of which shall be written out for you as soon as possible. Likewise a Grand Overture to "Ungarn's erste Wohlthäter" [Hungary's First Benefactors].

Both form part of two works that I wrote for the Hungarians at the opening of their new theatre [in Pesth]. Pray give me, however, your written assurance that these works shall not be performed elsewhere, as they are not published, nor likely to be so for some time to come. You shall receive the latter Grand Overture as soon as it is returned to me from Hungary, which it will be in the course of a few days.

The engraved Fantasia with Chorus could no doubt be executed by a lady, an amateur, mentioned to me here by Professor Schneller.[2] The words after the Chorus No. 4, in C major, were altered by the publishers, and are now quite contrary to the musical expression; those written in *pencil*, therefore, on the music must be sung. If you can make use of the Oratorio, I can send you *all the parts written out*, so that the outlay may be less for the poor. Write to me about this.

Your obedient
LUDWIG VAN BEETHOVEN.

[Footnote 1: The correspondence with Varenna, consisting of fourteen letters and four notes, was purchased some years ago by a collector of autographs in Leipzig, and sold again by public auction, probably to different persons. It would be like pursuing leaves scattered by the wind to try to recover these letters. Those here given have for the most part appeared in newspapers; I cannot, therefore, be responsible for the text, farther than their publication goes, which, however, has evidently been conducted by a clever hand. The date of the first letter is to be gleaned from the second, and we also learn from them that *The Ruins of Athens* and *King Stephen* (or at all events the Overture) were already finished in January, 1812.]

[Footnote 2: This *dilettante* was Mdlle. Marie Koschak, subsequently the wife of Dr. Pachler, an advocate in Gratz, from whom two letters are given by Schindler of the dates of August 15th, 1825, and November 5th, 1826, in which she invites Beethoven to visit her in Gratz. Schindler considers as applicable to this lady the words of a note in Beethoven's writing of which he has given a fac-simile in his *Biography*, I. 95; the date 1817 or 1818. They are as follows:--"Love alone, yes! love alone can make your life happier. O God! grant that I may at last find her who can strengthen me in virtue, whom I can legitimately call my own. On July 27th, when she drove past me in Baden, she seemed to gaze at me." This lady also plays a friendly part in Franz Schubert's *Life*. See her *Biography* by Dr. Kreissle.]

81.
TO ZMESKALL.

Feb. 2, 1812.

By no means *extraordinary*, but *very ordinary* mender of pens! whose talent has failed on this occasion (for those I send require to be fresh mended), when do you intend at last to cast off your fetters?--when? You never for a moment think of me; accursed to me is life amid this Austrian barbarism. I shall go now chiefly to the "Swan," as in other taverns I cannot defend myself against intrusion. Farewell! that is, *fare as well* as I wish you to do without

> Your friend,
> BEETHOVEN.

Most wonderful of men! We beg that your servant will engage a person to fit up my apartment; as he is acquainted with the lodgings, he can fix the proper price at once. Do this soon, you Carnival scamp!!!!!!!

The enclosed note is at least a week old.

82.
TO ZMESKALL.

Feb. 8, 1812.

Most extraordinary and first and foremost man of the pendulum in the world, and without a lever too!!!

I am much indebted to you for having imparted to me some share of your motive power. I wish to express my gratitude in person, and therefore invite you this morning to come to the "Swan,"--a tavern, the name of which itself shows that it is a fitting place when such a subject is in question,

> Yours ever,
> BEETHOVEN.

83.
TO VARENNA,--GRATZ.

Vienna, Feb. 8, 1812.

Herr Rettich has already got the parts of the Oratorio, and when you no longer require them I beg you will send them back to me. It is not probable that anything is wanting, but even in that case, as you have the score, you can easily remedy this. I only yesterday received the Overtures from Hungary, and shall have them copied and forwarded to you as soon as possible. I likewise send a March with a vocal Chorus, also from the "Ruins of Athens." Altogether you will now have sufficient to fill up the time.

As these pieces are only in manuscript, I shall let you know at the time I send them what precautions I wish you to take with regard to the Overtures and the March with Chorus.

As I do not publish any new work until a year after its composition, and, when I do so, am obliged invariably to give a written assurance to the publisher that no one is in possession of it, you can yourself perceive that I must carefully guard against any possible contingency or casualty as to these pieces. I must, however, assure you that I shall always be disposed to show the warmest zeal in aid of your charity, and I here pledge myself to send you every year works that exist solely in manuscript, or compositions written expressly for this charitable purpose. I beg you will also let me know what your future plans are with regard to your institution, that I may act accordingly.

Farewell! I remain, with the highest consideration,

> Your obedient
> LUDWIG VAN BEETHOVEN.

84.
TO ZMESKALL.[1]

Feb. 19, 1812.

DEAR Z.,--

I only yesterday received the written information that the Archduke pays his share in the new paper-money of the full value [*Einlösungsschein*]. I beg you will write out for me, as nearly as you can, the substance of what you said on Sunday, and which we thought it advisable to send to the other two. I am offered a certificate that the Archduke is to pay in *Einlösungsschein*, but I think this unnecessary, more especially as the people about Court, in spite of all their apparent friendship for me, declare that my demands are *not just*!!!! O Heaven! aid me in enduring this! I am no Hercules, to help Atlas in carrying the world, or to strive to do so in his place. It was only yesterday that I heard the particulars of the handsome manner in which Baron von Kraft had judged and spoken of me to Zisius! But never mind, dear Z.! My endurance of these shameful attacks cannot continue much longer; persecuted art will everywhere find an asylum--Daedalus, though imprisoned in a labyrinth, found wings to carry him aloft. Oh! I too shall find wings!

Yours ever,
BEETHOVEN.

If you have time, send me this morning the draft of the memorial;--probably for nothing, and to receive nothing! so much time is already lost, and only to be kept in suspense by civil words!

[Footnote 1: The Finance Patent appeared in Austria in 1811, by which the value of money was depreciated by a fifth. This also affected the salary that Beethoven drew from the Archduke Rudolph, Prince Kinsky, and Prince Lobkowitz. The first of these gentlemen paid his full share in *Einlösungsschein*. Lobkowitz, at the request of Beethoven, soon after did the same; with Kinsky's share alone difficulties arose subsequently, owing to his death.]

85.
TO VARENNA.

Lent, 1812.

In spite of my anxiety to serve the cause of your charity, I have been quite unable to do so. I have no copyist of my own to write for me as formerly, and the limited time renders it impossible for me to do so myself; thus I am obliged to have recourse to strangers as copyists. One of these promised to write out the Overtures, &c., &c., for you; but Passion Week intervening, when there are so many concerts, prevented his being able to keep his word, in spite of every effort on my part. Even if the Overtures and the March with Chorus were transcribed, it would not be possible to send them by this post, and if we wait for the next, the music will arrive too late for Easter Sunday. Let me know if there are any means you could adopt to gain a little more time, or any chance opportunity of sending these works to you, and I will do all that lies in my power to aid the cause of your charity.

I am, with esteem, yours obediently,
LUDWIG VAN BEETHOVEN.

86.
TO THE ARCHDUKE RUDOLPH.[1]

1812.

YOUR IMPERIAL HIGHNESS,--

I was much vexed not to receive Y.I.H.'s message to come to you till very late yesterday evening--indeed nearly at eleven o'clock. Contrary to my usual custom, I did not go home at all during the afternoon, the fine weather having tempted me to spend the whole afternoon in walking, and the evening at the Banda, "auf der Wieden," and thus I was not aware of your wish till I returned home. In the mean time, whenever Y.I.H. desires it, I am ready at any hour or moment to place myself at your disposal. I therefore await your gracious commands.

I am your Imperial Highness's most obedient
LUDWIG VAN BEETHOVEN.

[Footnote 1: The date 1812 is marked on the sheet by another hand, and the close of the second note proves that it was at the commencement of this year.]

87.
TO THE ARCHDUKE RUDOLPH.

1812.

YOUR IMPERIAL HIGHNESS,--

I was unable till to-day, when I leave my bed for the first time, to answer your gracious letter. It will be impossible for me to wait on you to-morrow, but perhaps the day after. I have suffered much during the last few days, and I may say two-fold from not being in a condition to devote a great part of my time to you, according to my heartfelt wish. I hope now, however, to have cleared off all scores for spring and summer (I mean as to health).

I am your Imperial Highness's most obedient servant,

LUDWIG VAN BEETHOVEN.

88.
TO VARENNA,--GRATZ.

Vienna, May 8, 1812.

SIR,--

Being still far from well, and much occupied, I have been unable to reply to your letters. How in the world did such an unfounded idea ever occur to you as that I was displeased? It would certainly have been better had you returned the music as soon as it had been performed; for at that period I could have produced it here, whereas now, unluckily, it comes too late; but I only say *unluckily* because it prevents my being able to spare the worthy ladies the expenses of copying. At any other time I would on no account have allowed them to pay for writing out the works, but it so happens that at this moment I am visited with every kind of *contretemps*, so I cannot avoid doing so. Possibly Herr O., although with the best intentions, has delayed informing you of this, which obliged me to apply to him for repayment of the expenses of copying; perhaps, too, in my haste, I did not express myself distinctly. You can now, esteemed sir, have the Overture and the Chorus again if you require them.

I feel convinced that in any event you will prevent my confidence being abused; in the mean time you may keep the Overture on the conditions I have stated. If I find that I am able to pay for the copying, I will redeem it for my own use.

The score of the Oratorio is a gift, and also the Overture to "Egmont." Keep the parts of the Oratorio beside you till you can have it performed.

Select whatever you choose for the concert which I hear you now intend to give, and if you decide on the Chorus and the Overture, they shall be forwarded to you at once. For the future concert, for the benefit of the venerable Ursulines, I promise you an entirely new symphony at all events, and perhaps also a work of some importance for voices, and as I have now a favorable opportunity, the copying shall not cost you a farthing. My joy would be beyond all bounds if the concert were to be successful, and I could spare you all expense;--at all events, take my good-will for granted.

Remember me to the admirable teachers of the children, and say to them that I shed tears of joy at the happy result of my poor good-will, and that so far as my humble capabilities can serve them, they shall always find in me the warmest sympathy.

My cordial thanks for your invitation; I would fain become acquainted with the interesting scenery of Styria, and possibly I may one day enjoy that pleasure. Farewell! I heartily rejoice in having found in you a friend to the poor and needy, and am always yours to command.

LUDWIG VAN BEETHOVEN, M.P.

89.
TO JOSEPH FREIHERR VON SCHWEIGER, CHAMBERLAIN OF THE ARCHDUKE RUDOLPH.[1]

1812.

The most insignificant of mortals has just been to wait on his gracious master, when he found everything closed; so he came here, where indeed all was *open*, but no one to be found except the trusty servant. I had a heavy packet of music with me, in order to ensure a good musical evening before we parted; but in vain. Malfatti[2] is resolved that I shall go to Töplitz, which is anything but agreeable to me. As, however, I must obey, I hope at least that my gracious master will not enjoy himself quite so much without me. *O vanitas!* for it is nothing else. Before I set off for Töplitz I will either go to Baden to see you or write. Farewell! Pray present my homage to my gracious master, and continue your regard for

Your friend,
[K.] BEETHOVEN.

[Footnote 1: The journey to Töplitz took place in the year 1812.]
[Footnote 2: A very celebrated physician in Vienna at that time, consulted by Beethoven.]

90.
TO VARENNA,--GRATZ.

Töplitz, July 19, 1812.

My thanks have been too long delayed for all the dainties which the worthy ladies sent for my enjoyment; being constantly ill in Vienna, I was at last forced to take refuge here.

However, better late than never; so I beg you will say all sorts of kind things in my name to the admirable Ursuline ladies, though I did not deserve so much gratitude; indeed it is rather for me to thank Him who enables me to render my art occasionally useful to others. When you next wish to make use of my poor abilities for the benefit of the venerable ladies, you have only to write to me.

A new symphony is now ready for you, and as the Archduke Rudolph has had it copied out, it will cost you nothing. Perhaps I may one of these days be able to send you something vocal. I only wish and hope that you will not ascribe my anxiety to serve these venerable ladies to a certain degree of vanity or desire for fame, as this would grieve me exceedingly. If these good ladies wish to do me any service in return, I beg they will include me with their pupils in their pious orisons. I remain, with esteem,

Your friend,
LUDWIG VAN BEETHOVEN.

I shall remain here for some weeks; so if there is any occasion to write, address to me here.

91.
WRITTEN IN THE ALBUM OF THE SINGER, MDME. AUGUSTE SEBALD.

Töplitz, August 8, 1812.
LUDWIG VAN BEETHOVEN,

Who even if you would,
Forget you never should.

92.
TO H.R. HIGHNESS THE ARCHDUKE RUDOLPH.

Franzensbrunn, Aug. 12, 1812.

It was my bounden duty long ago to have recalled myself to Y.R.H.'s recollection, but partly my occupations and the state of my health, as well as my own insignificance, made me reluctant to do so. I missed Y.R.H. by one night only in Prague; for when proceeding to pay my respects to you in the morning, I found you had set off the very night before. In Töplitz I heard a military band four times a day,--the only musical report which I can give you. I was a great deal with Goethe.[1] My physician Staudenheim, however, ordered me off to Carlsbad,[2] and from thence here, and probably I shall have to go back to Töplitz from this. What flights! And yet it seems very doubtful whether any improvement in my condition has hitherto taken place. I receive the best accounts of Y.R.H.'s health, and also of the persistent devotion you exhibit towards the musical Muse. Y.R.H. has no doubt heard of a concert that I gave for the benefit of the sufferers by fire in the Stadt Baden,[3] assisted by Herr Polledro.[4] The receipts were nearly 1000 florins W.W., and if I had not been restricted in my arrangements we might easily have taken 2000 florins. It was literally a *poor concert for the poor*. I could only find at the publisher's here some of my earlier sonatas with violin accompaniments, and as Polledro had set his heart on these, I was obliged to content myself with playing an old Sonata.[5] The entire concert consisted of a trio, in which Polledro played, my Sonata with violin, then again something was played by Polledro, and, lastly, I extemporized. Meanwhile I do sincerely rejoice that by this means something has fallen to the share of the poor *Badeners*. Pray deign to accept my best wishes for your welfare, and my entreaty that you will sometimes think of me.

[K.]

[Footnote 1: Beethoven speaks very briefly of his meeting with Goethe. Goethe in his *Tag- und Jahrschriften* of 1812 makes no allusion to Beethoven during his stay at Töplitz. It does not, therefore, appear that either of these master-minds found any particular pleasure in each other when they met personally. Beethoven, indeed, dedicated to "the immortal Goethe" (1812) his composition the *Meeresstille und glückliche Fahrt*, but only wrote once to him in 1823 to obtain a subscription from the Grand Duke of Weimar for his Grand Mass, and received no answer from Goethe. In the complete edition of Goethe's works Beethoven's name is only once mentioned by Goethe, when he refers to his funeral obsequies.]

[Footnote 2: Dr. Staudenheim was, like Malfatti, one of the most celebrated physicians in Vienna. Beethoven, too, was well acquainted with Staudenheim, but in his regimen he neither followed the prescriptions of Staudenheim nor of Malfatti.]

[Footnote 3: The Stadt Baden, near Vienna, had been visited on July 16th by a most destructive conflagration.]

[Footnote 4: Giov. Batt. Polledro, Kapellmeister in Turin, born 1776, travelled through Germany as a violinist from 1809 to 1812. He gave a concert in Vienna in March, 1812.]

[Footnote 5: The violin Sonata with pianoforte was probably Op. 47 (composed in 1803 and published in 1805, according to Thayer, No. 111), or one of his earlier compositions, Op. 30, or 24, or 23.]

93.
TO BETTINA VON ARNIM.

Töplitz, August 15, 1812.

MY MOST DEAR KIND FRIEND,--

Kings and princes can indeed create professors and privy-councillors, and confer titles and decorations, but they cannot make great men,--spirits that soar above the base turmoil of this world. There their powers fail, and this it is that forces them to respect us.[1] When two persons like Goethe and myself meet, these grandees cannot fail to perceive what such as we consider great. Yesterday, on our way home, we met the whole Imperial family; we saw them coming some way off, when Goethe withdrew his arm from mine, in order to stand aside; and, say what I would, I could not prevail on him to make another step in advance. I pressed down my hat more firmly on my head, buttoned up my great-coat, and, crossing my arms behind me, I made my way through the thickest portion of the crowd. Princes and courtiers formed a lane for me; Archduke Rudolph took off his hat, and the Empress bowed to me first. These great ones of the earth *know me*. To my infinite amusement, I saw the procession defile past Goethe, who stood aside with his hat off, bowing profoundly. I afterwards took him sharply to task for this; I gave him no quarter, and upbraided him with all his sins, especially towards you, my dear friend, as we had just been speaking of you. Heavens! if I could have lived with you as *he* did, believe me I should have produced far greater things. A musician is also a poet, he too can feel himself transported into a brighter world by a pair of fine eyes, where loftier spirits sport with him and impose heavy tasks on him. What thoughts rushed into my mind when I first saw you in the Observatory during a refreshing May shower, so fertilizing to me also![2] The most beautiful themes stole from your eyes into my heart, which shall yet enchant the world when Beethoven no longer *directs*. If God vouchsafes to grant me a few more years of life, I must then see you once more, my dear, most dear friend, for the voice within, to which I always listen, demands this. Spirits may love one another, and I shall ever woo yours. Your approval is dearer to me than all else in the world. I told Goethe my sentiments as to the influence praise has over men like us, and that we desire our equals to listen to us with their understanding. Emotion suits women only; (forgive me!) music ought to strike fire from the soul of a man. Ah! my dear girl, how long have our feelings been identical on all points!!! The sole real good is some bright kindly spirit to sympathize with us, whom we thoroughly comprehend, and from whom we need not hide our thoughts. *He who wishes to appear something, must in reality be something*. The world must acknowledge us, it is not always unjust; but for this I care not, having a higher purpose in view. I hope to get a letter from you in Vienna; write to me soon and fully, for a week hence I shall be there. The Court leaves this to-morrow, and to-day they have another performance. The Empress has studied her part thoroughly. The Emperor and the Duke wished me to play some of my own music, but I refused, for they are both infatuated with *Chinese porcelain*. A little indulgence is required, for reason seems to have lost its empire; but I do not choose to minister to such perverse folly--I will not be a party to such absurd doings to please those princes who are constantly guilty of eccentricities of this sort. Adieu! adieu! dear one; your letter lay all night next my heart, and cheered me. Musicians permit themselves great license. *Heavens! how I love you!* Your most faithful friend and deaf brother,

BEETHOVEN.

[Footnote 1: Fräulein Giannatasio del Rio, in the journal she sent to the *Grenz Boten* in 1857, states that Beethoven once declared, "It is very pleasant to associate with the great of the earth, but one must possess some quality which inspires them with respect."]

[Footnote 2: According to Bettina (see *Goethe's Correspondence with a Child*, II. 193), their first acquaintance was made in Beethoven's apartments.]

94.
TO PRINCESS KINSKY,--PRAGUE

Vienna, Dec. 30, 1812.

YOUR HIGHNESS,--

The dreadful event which deprived you of your husband, Prince von Kinsky, snatching him from his father-land and from all those who love him,[1] as well as from many whom he generously supported, filling every heart capable of appreciating goodness and greatness with the deepest sorrow, affected me also in the most profound and painful degree. The stern duty of self-interest compels me to lay before your Highness a humble petition, the reasonable purport of which may, I hope, plead my excuse for intruding on your Highness at a time when so many affairs of importance claim your attention. Permit me to state the matter to your Highness.

Y.H. is no doubt aware that when I received a summons to Westphalia in the year 1809, his Highness Prince von Kinsky, your late husband, together with his I.H. Archduke Rudolph and H.H. the Prince von Lobkowitz, offered to settle on me for life an annual income of 4000 gulden, provided I declined the proposal in question, and determined to remain in Austria. Although this sum was by no means in proportion to that secured to me in Westphalia, still my predilection for Austria, as well as my sense of this most generous proposal, induced me to accept it without hesitation. The share contributed by H.H. Prince Kinsky consisted of 1800 florins, which I have received by quarterly instalments since 1809 from the Prince's privy purse. Though subsequent occurrences partially diminished this sum, I rested satisfied, till the appearance of the Finance Patent, reducing bank-notes into *Einlösung Schein*. I applied to H.I.H. the Archduke Rudolph to request that the portion of the annuity contributed by H.I.H. should in future be paid in *Einlösung Schein*. This was at once granted, and I received a written assurance to that effect from H.I.H. Prince von Lobkowitz agreed to the same with regard to his share,--700 florins [see No. 84]. H.H. Prince von Kinsky being at that time in Prague, I addressed my respectful petition to him last May, through Herr Varnhagen von Ense, an officer in the Vogelsang Regiment, that his Highness's contribution to my salary--1800 florins--should be paid like the rest in *Einlösung Schein*. Herr von Varnhagen wrote as follows, and the original of the letter is still extant:--

"I had yesterday the desired interview with Prince Kinsky. With the highest praise of Beethoven, he at once acceded to his demand, and is prepared to pay up the arrears, and also all future sums from the date of the *Einlösung Schein*, in that currency. The cashier here has received the necessary instructions, and Beethoven can draw for the whole sum on his way through Prague, or, if he prefers it, in Vienna, as soon as the Prince returns there.

"Prague, June 9, 1812."

When passing through Prague some weeks afterwards, I took the opportunity of waiting on the Prince, and received from him the fullest confirmation of this promise. H.H. likewise assured me that he entirely admitted the propriety of my demand, and considered it quite reasonable. As I could not remain in Prague till this affair was finally settled, H.H. was so kind as to make me a payment of sixty ducats on account, which, according to H.H.'s calculation, were good for 600 florins Vienna currency. The arrears were to be paid up on my return to Vienna, and an order given to the cashier to pay my salary in future in *Einlösung Schein*. Such was H.H.'s pleasure. My illness increasing in Töplitz, I was obliged to remain there longer than I originally intended. In the month of September I therefore addressed to H.H., who was then in Vienna, through one of my friends here, Herr Oliva, a written memorial, claiming his promise, when H.H. graciously repeated to this friend the assurance he had already given me, adding that in the course of a few days he would give the necessary instructions on the subject to his cashier.

A short time afterwards he left Vienna. When I arrived there, I inquired from the Prince's secretary whether H.H. had given directions about my salary before leaving Vienna, when, to my surprise, I was told that H.H. had done nothing in the matter.

My title to the liquidation of my claim is proved by the testimony of the Herren von Varnhagen and Oliva, to whom H.H. spoke on the subject, reiterating his consent. I feel convinced that the illustrious heirs and family of this prince will in the same spirit of benevolence and generosity strive to fulfil his intentions. I therefore confidently place in Y.H.'s hands my respectful petition, viz., "to pay up the arrears of my salary in *Einlösung Schein*, and to instruct your cashier to transmit me the amount in future, in the same currency." Relying on your sense of justice according me a favorable decision, I remain Y.H.'s

Most obedient servant,
LUDWIG VAN BEETHOVEN.

[Footnote 1: Prince Josef Ferdinand Kinsky, born December, 1781, and killed by a fall from his horse, November 3, 1812.]

95.
TO THE ARCHDUKE RUDOLPH.

1813.[1]

I have been far from well since last Sunday, but have suffered more in mind than in body. I beg your forgiveness a thousand times for not having sooner sent my apologies; each day I had the strongest inclination to wait on you, but Heaven knows that in spite of the best will that I always entertain for the best of masters I was unable to do so, distressing as it is to me not to have it in my power to sacrifice all to him for whom I cherish the highest esteem, love, and veneration. Y.R.H. would perhaps act wisely in making a pause at present with the Lobkowitz concerts; even the most brilliant talent may lose its effect by too great familiarity.

[K.]

[Footnote 1: Prince Franz Josef Lobkowitz died December 25th, 1816. His musical meetings were certainly continued till 1813, or longer.]

96.
TO THE ARCHDUKE RUDOLPH.

1813.[1]

At early dawn to-morrow the copyist shall begin the last movement. As I am in the mean time writing several other works, I did not hurry myself much with this last movement merely for the sake of punctuality, especially as I must write this more deliberately, with a view to Rode's[2] playing; we like quick, full-toned passages in our *Finales*, which do not suit R., and this rather cramps me. At all events, all is sure to go well next Tuesday. I very much doubt whether I shall be able to present myself at Y.R.H.'s on that evening, in spite of my zeal in your service; but to make up for this, I mean to come to you to-morrow forenoon and to-morrow afternoon, that I may entirely fulfil the wishes of my illustrious pupil.

[K.]

[Footnote 1: 1813. January--February.]

[Footnote 2: Pierre Rode, the violinist, arrived in Vienna in January, 1813, and gave a concert in the Redoutensaal on February 6th, but did not give universal satisfaction (*A.M.Z.*, 1813, p. 114), and a second concert that he had projected does not appear to have taken place. He played in Gratz on February 20th and 27th. It seems that Rode was to play with Beethoven at the Archduke Rudolph's, for which occasion Beethoven prepared a composition for them both. Was this the Sonata for pianoforte and violin, Op. 36, which he afterwards dedicated to the Archduke? Thayer states that it was written by Beethoven in 1810, and sold to the music-publisher Steiner in Vienna in April, 1815. No other composition for the violin and pianoforte is so likely to be the one as this. It is, however, a mistake in the *Bibliothèque Universelle*, tome xxxvi. p. 210, to state that Beethoven during Rode's stay in Vienna composed the "délicieuse Romance" which was played with so much expression by De Baillot on the violin. There are only two Romances known for the violin by Beethoven, the one in G major, Op. 40, in the year 1803, and the second in F major, Op. 50, published in 1805. (Thayer, 102 and 104.)]

97.
TO THE ARCHDUKE RUDOLPH.

1813.

I had just gone out yesterday when your gracious letter reached me. As for my health, it is pretty much the same, particularly as moral causes affect it, which do not seem likely to be removed; particularly as I can have recourse to no one but myself for aid, and can find help in my own head alone; and more particularly still, because in these days neither words, nor honor, nor written pledges, seem binding on any one. As for my occupations, I have come to an end with some of them, and, even without your gracious invitation, I intended to appear at the usual hour to-day. With regard to Rode [see No. 96], I beg Y.R.H. to be so good as to let me have the part by the bearer of this, and I will send it to him at once, with a polite note from me. *He certainly will not take amiss my sending him the part. Oh! certainly not! Would to Heaven that I were obliged to ask his forgiveness on this account! for in that case things would really be in a better position.* Is it your pleasure that I should come to you this evening at five o'clock as usual, or does Y.R.H. desire another hour? I shall endeavor to arrange accordingly, and punctually to fulfil your wishes.

[K.]

98.
TO PRINCESS KINSKY.

Vienna, Feb. 12, 1813.

YOUR HIGHNESS!--

You were so gracious as to declare with regard to the salary settled on me by your deceased husband, that you saw the propriety of my receiving it in Vienna currency, but that the authority of the court of law which has assumed the guardianship of the estate must first be obtained. Under the conviction that the authorities who represent their princely wards could not fail to be influenced by the same motives that actuated the late Prince in his conduct towards me, I think I am justified in expecting the ratification of my claim from the aforesaid court, as I can prove, by the testimony of well-known, respectable, and upright men, the promise and intentions of H.H. in my behalf, which cannot fail to be binding on his heirs and children. If, therefore, the proofs submitted should even be found deficient in legal formality, I cannot doubt that this want will be supplied by the noble mode of thinking of this illustrious house, and by their own inclination to generous actions.

Possibly another question may at present arise from the condition of the inheritance, which is no doubt heavily burdened, both owing to the melancholy and sudden death of the late Prince, and by the state of the times, which renders it equally just and indispensable to husband carefully all possible resources. On this account it is far from my wish to claim more than is absolutely necessary for my own livelihood, and grounded on the contract itself,--the legality of such a claim on the heirs of the late Prince not being in any way disputed.

I beg, then, that Y.H. will be pleased to direct the arrears of my salary, due since the 1st September, 1811, calculated in Vienna currency, in accordance with the scale of the contract, making in W.W. 1088 florins 42 kreuzers, to be paid, and *in the interim,* the question whether this salary ought to be paid in Vienna currency can be deferred until the affairs are settled, when the subject is again brought before the trustees, and my claims admitted to be just by their consent and authority. The late Prince having given me sixty ducats merely on account of my salary, which was to be paid by agreement in Vienna currency, and as this agreement (as every intelligent man will inform Y.H.) must be accepted to its full extent, or at all events not cause me loss, it follows as a matter of course that Y.H. will not object to my considering the sixty ducats as only an instalment of the arrears due to me beyond the usual scale of payment, agreed to be paid in Vienna currency, so that the amount must not be deducted from the sum still due to me.

I feel sure that Y.H.'s noble feelings will do justice to the equity of my proposal, and my wish to enter into every detail of this affair, so far as circumstances permit, and also my readiness to postpone my claims to suit your convenience. The same elevated sentiments which prompted you to fulfil the engagement entered into by the late Prince, will also make Y.H. apprehend the absolute necessity entailed on me by my position again to solicit immediate payment of the arrears of my salary, which are indispensable for my maintenance.

Anxiously hoping for a favorable answer to my petition, I have the honor to remain, with profound respect,

Y.R.H.'s obedient servant,
LUDWIG VAN BEETHOVEN.

99.
TO PRINCESS KINSKY.

HIGHLY HONORED PRINCESS!--

As the Prince's counsel declared that my claim could not be heard till the choice of a guardian had been made, and as I now hear that Y.H. has been graciously pleased yourself to assume that office, but decline receiving any one, I present my humble petition in writing, requesting at the same time your early consideration; for you can easily understand that, relying on a thing as a certainty, it is painful to be so long deprived of it, especially as I am obliged entirely to support an unfortunate sickly brother and his whole family,[1] which (not computing my own wants) has entirely exhausted my resources, having expected to provide for myself by the payment of my salary. You may perceive the justice of my claims from the fact of my faithfully naming the receipt of the sixty ducats, advanced to me by the late Prince in Prague, the Prince's counsel himself declaring that I might have said nothing about this sum, the late Prince not having mentioned it either to him or to his cashier.

Forgive my being obliged to intrude this affair on you, but necessity compels me to do so. Some days hence I shall take the liberty of making inquiries on the subject from the Prince's counsel, or from any one Y.H. may appoint.

I remain, most esteemed and illustrious Princess,

Your devoted servant,
LUDWIG VAN BEETHOVEN.

[Footnote 1: See a letter to Ries, Nov. 22d, 1815:--"He was consumptive for some years, and, in order to make his life easier, I can safely compute what I gave him at 10,000 florins W.W."]

100.
TO ZMESKALL.

DEAR Z.,--

Forward the accompanying letter to-day without fail to Brunswick, that it may arrive as soon and as safely as possible. Excuse the trouble I give you. I have been again applied to, to send some of my works to Gratz, in Styria, for a concert to be given in aid of the Ursuline convent and its schools: last year they had very large receipts by this means. Including this concert, and one I gave in Carlsbad for the benefit of the sufferers from fire at Baden, three concerts have been given by me, and through me, for benevolent purposes in one year; and yet if I ask a favor, people are as deaf as a post. Your

BEETHOVEN.

I. Letter to Sclowonowitsch (Maître des bureaux des postes) in Cassel. I can no longer do without the books of Tiedge and Frau von der Recke, as I am expected to give some opinion about them.

101.
TO HERR JOSEPH VARENNA,--GRATZ.

MY GOOD SIR,--

Rode was not quite correct in all that he said of me; my health is not particularly good, and from no fault of my own,--my present condition being the most unfortunate of my life. But neither this nor anything in the world shall prevent me from assisting, so far as it lies in my power, the innocent and distressed ladies of your convent by my poor works. I therefore place at your disposal two new symphonies, a bass aria with chorus, and several minor choruses; if you desire again to perform "Hungaria's Benefactors," which you gave last year, it is also at your service. Among the choruses you will find a "Dervise Chorus," a capital bait for a mixed public.

In my opinion, your best plan would be to select a day when you could give the "Mount of Olives," which has been everywhere performed. This would occupy one half of the concert, and the other half might consist of a new symphony, the overtures, and various choruses, and likewise the above-named bass aria and chorus; thus the evening would not be devoid of variety. But you can settle all this more satisfactorily with the aid of your own musical authorities. I think I can guess what you mean about a gratuity for me from a *third person*. Were I in the same position as formerly, I would at once say, "Beethoven never accepts anything *where the benefit of humanity is concerned*;" but owing to my own too great benevolence I am reduced to a low ebb, the cause of which, however, does not put me to shame, being combined with other circumstances for which men devoid of honor and principle are alone to blame; so I do not hesitate to say that I would not refuse the contribution of the rich man to whom you allude.[1] But there is no question here of any *claim*. If, however, the affair with the *third person* comes to nothing, pray rest assured that I shall be equally disposed to confer the same benefit as last year on my friends the respected Ursuline ladies, and shall at all times be ready to succor the poor and needy so long as I live. And now farewell! Write soon, and I will zealously strive to make all necessary arrangements. My best wishes for the convent.

I am, with esteem, your friend,
LUDWIG VAN BEETHOVEN.

[Footnote 1: Reichardt, on the 1st March, 1809, writes in his *Vertraute Briefe*,--"Beethoven, by 'a rich third person,' as the following letter proves, meant Louis Bonaparte, who, after abdicating the Dutch throne, lived in Gratz."]

102.
TO VARENNA.

MY EXCELLENT V. [VARENNA],--

I received your letter with much pleasure, but with much displeasure the 100 florins allotted to me by our poor convent ladies; in the mean time I will apply part of this sum to pay the copyists--the surplus and the accounts for copying shall be sent to these good ladies.

I never accept anything for such a purpose. I thought that perhaps the *third person* to whom you alluded might be the Ex-King of Holland, in which case I should have had no scruples, under my present circumstances, in accepting a gratuity from him, who has no doubt taken enough from the Dutch in a less legitimate way; but as it is, I must decline (though in all friendship) any renewal of this subject.

Let me know whether, were I to come myself to Gratz, I could give a concert, and what the receipts would probably be; for Vienna, alas! can no longer continue my place of abode. Perhaps it is now too late? but any information from you on the point will be very welcome.

The works are being copied, and you shall have them as soon as possible. You may do just what you please with the Oratorio; where it will be of most use it will best fulfil my intentions.

I am, with esteem, your obedient
BEETHOVEN.

P.S. Say all that is kind from me to the worthy Ursuline ladies. I rejoice in being able to serve them.

103.
TO ZMESKALL.

Confounded, invited guest! *Domanowetz!*--not musical Count, but gobbling Count! dinner Count! supper Count! &c., &c. The Quartet is to be tried over to-day at ten o'clock or half-past, at Lobkowitz's.[1] His Highness, whose wits are generally astray, is not yet arrived; so pray join us, if you can escape from your Chancery jailer. Herzog is to see you to-day. He intends to take the post of my man-servant; you may agree to give him thirty florins, with his wife *obbligata*. Firing, light, and morning livery found. I must have some one who knows how to cook, for if my food continues as bad as it now is, I shall always be ill. I dine at home to-day, because I get better wine. If you will only order what you like, I very much wish you to come to me. You shall have the wine *gratis*, and of far better quality than what you get at the scoundrelly "Swan."

Your very insignificant
BEETHOVEN.

[Footnote 1: Reichardt, in his *Vertraute Briefe*, writes: "The beautiful quartets and evening concerts for the Archduke Rudolph still continue at Prince von Lobkowitz's, although the Prince himself is about to join his battalion in Bohemia." Reichardt, Vol. I. p. 182, calls Lobkowitz "an indefatigable, insatiable, genuine enthusiast for art."]

104.
TO ZMESKALL.

Feb. 25, 1813.

I have been constantly indisposed, dear Zmeskall, since I last saw you; in the mean time the servant who lived with you before your present one has applied for my situation. I do not recollect him, but he told me he had been with you, and that you had nothing to say against him, except that he did not dress your hair as you wished. I gave him earnest-money, though only a florin. Supposing you have no other fault to find with the man (and if so I beg you will candidly mention it), I intend to engage him, for you know that it is no object with me to have my hair dressed; it would be more to the purpose if my finances could be dressed, or *re-dressed*. I hope to get an answer from you to day. If there is no one to open the door to your servant, let him leave the note in the entrance to the left, and should he find no one there either, he must give it to the porter's wife below stairs. May Heaven prosper you in your musical undertakings! Your

BEETHOVEN,
Miserabilis.

105.
TO ZMESKALL.

Feb. 28, 1813.

Let us leave things as they are for to-day, dear Z., till we meet [and so on about the servant].

Farewell! Carefully guard the fortresses of the realm, which, as you know, are no longer virgins, and have already received many a shot.

Your friend,
BEETHOVEN.

106.
TO ZMESKALL.

MOST WORTHY COUNSELLOR, OWNER OF MINES AND LORD OF FASTNESSES IN BURGUNDY AND BUDA!--

Be so good as to let me know how matters stand, as this afternoon at latest I shall take advantage of your reply to my question, by giving my servant warning for this day fortnight. His wages, &c., &c. [The rest relates to his servant.]

107.
TO ZMESKALL.

April 19, 1813.

MY DEAR ZMESKALL,--

I have been refused the University Hall. I heard this two days since; but being indisposed yesterday I could not go to see you, nor can I to-day either. We have no resource now but the Kärnthnerthor Theatre, or the one "an der Wien." I believe there will only be one concert. If both these fail, we must then have recourse to the Augarten, in which case we ought certainly to give two concerts. Reflect on this, my dear friend, and let me have your opinion. To-morrow the symphonies may perhaps be tried over at the Archduke's if I am able to go out, of which I will apprise you.

Your friend,
BEETHOVEN.

108.
TO ZMESKALL.

April 23, 1813.

DEAR Z.,--

All will go right, the Archduke being resolved to take this Prince *Fizlypuzly* roundly to task. Let me know if you are to dine at the tavern to-day, or where? Pray tell me if "Sentivany" is properly spelt, as I wish to write to him at the same time about the Chorus. We must also consult together what day to choose. By the by, be cautious not to mention the intercession of the Archduke, for Prince *Fizlypuzly* is not to be with him till Sunday, and if that evil-minded creditor had any previous hint of the affair, he would still try to evade us.

Yours ever,
BEETHOVEN.

109.
TO ZMESKALL.

April 26, 1813.

Lobkowitz will give me a day on the 15th of May, or after that period, which seems to me scarcely better than none at all; so I am almost disposed to give up all idea of a concert. But the Almighty will no doubt prevent my being utterly ruined.

Yours,
BEETHOVEN.

110.
TO THE ARCHDUKE RUDOLPH.

Baden, May 27, 1813.

I have the honor to inform you of my arrival in Baden, which is indeed still very empty of human beings, but with all the greater luxuriance and full lustre does Nature shine in her enchanting loveliness. Where I fail, or ever have failed, be graciously indulgent towards me, for so many trying occurrences, succeeding each other so closely, have really almost bewildered me; still I am convinced that the resplendent beauties of Nature here, and the charming environs, will gradually restore my spirits, and a double share of tranquillity be my portion, as by my stay here I likewise fulfil the wishes of Y.R.H. Would that my desire soon to hear that Y.R.H. is fully restored were equally fulfilled! This is indeed my warmest wish, and how much I grieve that I cannot at this moment contribute to your recovery by means of *my* art! This is reserved for the goddess Hygeia alone, and I, alas! am only a poor mortal, who commends himself to Y.R.H., and sincerely hopes soon to be permitted to wait on you.

[K.]

111.
TO THE ARCHDUKE RUDOLPH.

Vienna, July 24, 1813.

From day to day I have been expecting to return to Baden; in the mean time, the discords that detain me here may possibly be resolved by the end of the ensuing week. To me a residence in a town during the summer is misery, and when I also remember that I am thus prevented waiting on Y.R.H., it is still more vexatious and annoying. It is, in fact, the Lobkowitz and Kinsky affairs that keep me here. Instead of pondering over a number of bars, I am obliged constantly to reflect on the number of peregrinations I am forced to make; but for this, I could scarcely endure to the end. Y.R.H. has no doubt heard of Lobkowitz's misfortunes,[1] which are much to be regretted; but after all, to be rich is no such great happiness! It is said that Count Fries alone paid 1900 gold ducats to Duport, for which he had the security of the ancient Lobkowitz house. The details are beyond all belief. I hear that Count Rasumowsky[2] intends to go to Baden, and to take his Quartet with him, which is really very pretty, and I have no doubt that Y.R.H. will be much pleased with it. I know no more charming enjoyment in the country than quartet music. I beg Y.R.H. will accept my heartfelt wishes for your health, and also compassionate me for being obliged to pass my time here under such disagreeable circumstances. But I will strive to compensate twofold in Baden for what you have lost.

[K.]

[Footnote 1: Prince Lobkowitz's "misfortunes" probably refer to the great pecuniary difficulties which befell this music and pomp loving Prince several years before his death. Beethoven seems to have made various attempts to induce the Prince to continue the payment of his share of the salary agreed on, though these efforts were long fruitless. The subject, however, appears to have been again renewed in 1816, for on the 8th of March in this year Beethoven writes to Ries to say that his salary consists of 3400 florins E.S., and this sum he received till his death.]

[Footnote 2: Those who played in Count Rasumowsky's Quartets, to whom Beethoven dedicated various compositions, were the *virtuosi* Schuppanzigh (1st), Sina (2d violin), Linke (violoncello), Weiss (violin).]

112.
TO THE ARCHDUKE RUDOLPH.

1813.[1]

I beg to inquire whether, being in some degree restored, I am to wait on you this evening? I at the same time take the liberty to make a humble request. I was in hopes that by this time, at all events, my melancholy circumstances would have brightened, but all continues in its old state, so I must determine on giving two concerts.[2] I find that I am compelled to give up my former resolution never to give any except for benevolent purposes; as self-maintenance demands that I should do so. The hall of the University would be the most advantageous and distinguished for my present object, and my humble request consists in entreating Y.R.H. to be so gracious as to send a line to the present *Rector Magnificus* of the University, through Baron Schweiger, which would certainly ensure my getting the hall. In the hope of a favorable answer, I remain, &c., &c.

[K.]

[Footnote 1: Late in the autumn of 1813.]

[Footnote 2: The concerts here referred to were given in the University Hall on the 8th and 12th December, 1813, when the *Battle of Vittoria* and the A major Symphony were performed for the first time. Beethoven himself conducted.]

113.
TO FREIHERR JOSEF VON SCHWEIGER.

Late in the Autumn of 1813.

MY DEAR FRIEND,--

I have to-day applied (by letter) to my gracious master to interest himself in procuring the University Hall for two concerts which I think of giving, and in fact must give, for all remains as it was. Always considering you, both in good and evil fortune, my best friend, I suggested to the Duke that you should apply in his name for this favor to the present Rector of the University. Whatever may be the result, let me know H.R.H.'s decision as soon as possible, that I may make further efforts to extricate myself from a position so detrimental to me and to my art. I am coming this evening to the Archduke.

Your friend,
BEETHOVEN.

[K.]

114.
TO HERR VON BAUMEISTER.[1]

DEAR SIR,--

I request you will send me the parts of the Symphony in A, and likewise my score. His I.H. can have the MS. again, but I require it at present for the music in the Augarten to-morrow. I have just received two tickets, which I send to you, and beg you will make use of them.

I am, with esteem, yours,
L. V. BEETHOVEN.

[Footnote 1: Private Secretary to the Archduke Rudolph.]

115.
TO ZMESKALL.

Oct. 9, 1813.

MY DEAR GOOD Z.,--

Don't be indignant with me for asking you to address the enclosed letter properly; the person for whom it is intended is constantly complaining that he gets no letters from me. Yesterday I took one myself to the post-office, when I was asked where the letter was meant to go. I see, therefore, that my writing seems to be as little understood as myself. Thence my request to you. Your

BEETHOVEN.

116.
LETTER OF THANKS.

I esteem it my duty to express my gratitude for the great zeal shown by all those artists who so kindly coöperated on the 8th and 12th December [1813] in the concerts given for the benefit of the Austrian and Bavarian soldiers wounded at the battle of Hanau. It was a rare combination of eminent artists, where all were inspired by the wish to be of use to their father-land, and to contribute by the exercise of their talents to the fulfilment of the undertaking, while, regardless of all precedence, they gladly accepted subordinate places.[1] While an artist like Herr Schuppanzigh was at the head of the first violins, and by his fiery and expressive mode of conducting kindled the zeal of the whole orchestra, Herr Kapellmeister Salieri did not scruple to give the time to the drums and cannonades; Herr Spohr and Herr Mayseder, each worthy from his talents to fill the highest post, played in the second and third rank. Herr Siboni and Herr Giuliani also filled subordinate places. The conducting of the whole was only assigned to me from the music being my own composition; had it been that of any one else, I would willingly, like Herr Hummel, have taken my place at the big drum, as the only feeling that pervaded all our hearts was true love for our father-land, and the wish cheerfully to devote our powers to those who had sacrificed so much for us. Particular thanks are due to Herr Maelzel, inasmuch as he first suggested the idea of this concert, and the most troublesome part of the enterprise, the requisite arrangements, management, and regulations, devolved on him. I more especially thank him for giving me an opportunity by this concert of fulfilling a wish I have long cherished, to compose for such a benevolent object (exclusive of the works already made over to him) a comprehensive work more adapted to the present times, to be laid on the altar of my father-land.[2] As a notice is to be published of all those who assisted on this occasion, the public will be enabled to judge of the noble self-denial exercised by a mass of the greatest artists, working together with the same benevolent object in view.

LUDWIG VAN BEETHOVEN.

[Footnote 1: The A major Symphony and *Wellington's Victory at Vittoria* were performed.]
[Footnote 2: "Obsolete" is written in pencil by Beethoven.]

117.
TO THE ARCHDUKE RUDOLPH.[1]

1814.

I beg you will send me the score of the "Final Chorus"[2] for half a day, as the theatrical score is so badly written.

[K.]

[Footnote 1: The spring of 1814.]
[Footnote 2: The *Schlusschor*, the score of which Beethoven requests the Archduke to send him, is in all probability the Finale *Germania! Germania!* intended for Treitschke's Operetta *Die gute Nachricht*, which refers to the taking of Paris by the Allies, and was performed for the first time at Vienna in the Kärnthnerthor Theatre on the 11th April, 1814. The same *Final Chorus* was substituted for another of Beethoven's (*Es ist vollbracht*) in Treitschke's Operetta *Die Ehrenpforten*, first given on the 15th July, 1815, in the Kärnthnerthor Theatre. Both these choruses are printed in score in Breitkopf & Härtel's edition of Beethoven's works.]

118.
TO THE ARCHDUKE RUDOLPH.

1814.

Having only so recently received the score of the "Final Chorus," I must ask you to excuse your getting it back so late. The best thing H.R.H. can do is to have it transcribed, for in its present form the score is of no use. I would have brought it myself, but I have been laid up with a cold since last Sunday, which is most severe, and obliges me to be very careful, being so much indisposed. I never feel greater satisfaction than when Y.R.H. derives any pleasure through me. I hope very soon to be able to wait on you myself, and in the mean time I pray that you will keep me in remembrance.

[K.]

119.
TO THE ARCHDUKE RUDOLPH.

1814.

The song "Germania" belongs to the whole world who sympathize with the subject, and to you beyond all others, just as I myself am wholly yours. I wish you a good journey to Palermo.

[K.]

120.
TO TREITSCHKE.

March, 1814.

MY DEAR, WORTHY T.,--

I have read with the greatest satisfaction your amendments of the Opera ["Fidelio" which was about to be again performed]. It has decided me once more to rebuild the desolate ruins of an ancient fortress.

Your friend,
BEETHOVEN.

121.
TO TREITSCHKE.

The affair of the Opera is the most troublesome in the world, and there is scarcely one part of it which quite satisfies me now, and that I have not been obliged to *amend by something more satisfactory*. But what a difference between this, and giving one's self up to freely flowing thought and inspiration!

122.
TO TREITSCHKE.

1814.

I request, my dear T., that you will send me the score of the song [in "Fidelio," *Geld ist eine schöne Sache*], that the interpolated notes may be transcribed in all the instrumental parts; though I shall not take it at all amiss if you prefer that Girowetz or any other person, perhaps Weinmüller [who sang the part of Rocco], should do so. This I have nothing to say against, but I will not suffer my composition to be altered by any one whatever, be he who he may.

I am, with high consideration,
Your obedient
BEETHOVEN.

123.
TO COUNT MORITZ LICHNOWSKY.[1]

MY DEAR COUNT,--

If you wish to attend our council [about the alterations in "Fidelio"], I beg to inform you that it assembles this afternoon at half-past three o'clock, in the Spielmann Haus, auf dem Graben, No. 188, 4th Etage, at Herr Weinmüller's. I shall be very glad if you have leisure to be present.

[Footnote 1: The mention of Weinmüller decides the date of this note, as it was in the spring of 1814 that he, together with the singers Saal and Vogl, brought about the revival of *Fidelio*.]

124.
TO COUNT MORITZ LICHNOWSKY.[1]

My dear, victorious, and yet sometimes nonplussed (?) Count! I hope that you rested well, most precious and charming of all Counts! Oh! most beloved and unparalleled Count! most fascinating and prodigious Count!

(*To be repeated at pleasure.*)

At what hour shall we call on Walter to-day? My going or not depends entirely on you. Your

BEETHOVEN.

[Footnote 1: In Schindler's *Beethoven's Nachlass* there is also an autograph Canon of Beethoven's in F major, 6/8, on Count Lichnowsky, on the words, *Bester Herr Graf, Sie sind ein Schaf*, written (according to Schindler) Feb. 20th, 1823, in the coffee-house "Die Goldne Birne," in the Landstrasse, where Beethoven usually went every evening, though he generally slipped in by the backdoor.]

125.
TO THE ARCHDUKE RUDOLPH.

1814.

I hope you forgive me for not having come to you. Your displeasure would be totally undeserved, and I will amply compensate for lost time in a few days. My Opera of "Fidelio"[1] is again to be performed, which gives me a great deal to do; moreover, though I look well, I am not so in reality. The arrangements for my second concert[2] are partly completed. I must write something new for Mdlle. Milder.[3] Meanwhile it is a consolation to me to hear that Y.R.H. is so much better. I hope I am not too sanguine in thinking that I shall soon be able to contribute towards this. I have taken the liberty to apprise my Lord Falstaff[4] that he is ere long to have the honor of appearing before Y.R.H.

[K.]

[Footnote 1: Letters 125 and 126 refer to the revival of the Opera of *Fidelio*, which had not been given since 1806, and was not again produced on the stage till the 23d May, 1814, in the Kärnthnerthor Theatre. Beethoven's benefit took place on the 8th July, two newly composed pieces being inserted.]

[Footnote 2: Beethoven gave a concert on the 2d January, 1814, when *Wellington's Victory* was performed, and on the 26th March another for the benefit of the Theatrical Fund, at which the *Overture to Egmont* and *Wellingtons's Victory* were given, directed by Beethoven himself.]

[Footnote 3: Anna Milder, Royal Court opera singer, a pupil of Vogl's, who first sang the part of Leonore in *Fidelio*.]

[Footnote 4: By "my Lord Falstaff" he means the corpulent violinist Schuppanzigh.]

126.
TO THE ARCHDUKE RUDOLPH.

Vienna, July 14, 1814.

Whenever I inquire about you I hear nothing but good news. As for my own insignificant self, I have been hitherto hopelessly detained in Vienna, and unable to approach Y.R.H.; I am also thus deprived of the enjoyment of beautiful Nature, so dear to me. The directors of the theatre are so *conscientious*, that, contrary to their faithful promise, they have again given my Opera of "Fidelio," without thinking of giving me any share in the receipts. They would have exhibited the same commendable good faith a second time, had I not been on the watch like a French custom-house officer of other days. At last, after a great many troublesome discussions, it was settled that the Opera of "Fidelio" should be given on Monday the 18th of July, for my benefit. These *receipts* at this season of the year may more properly be called *deceits*; but if a work is in any degree successful it often becomes a little feast for the author. To this feast the master invites his illustrious pupil, and hopes-- yes! I hope that Y.R.H. will graciously consent to come, and thus add lustre to everything by your presence. It would be a great boon if Y.R.H. would endeavor to persuade the other members of the Imperial family to be present at the representation of my Opera, and I on my part will not fail to take the proper steps on the subject which duty commands. Vogl's illness[1] enabled me to satisfy my desire to give the part of Pizarro to Forti,[2] his voice being better suited to it; but owing to this there are daily rehearsals, which cannot fail to have a favorable effect on the performance, but which render it impossible for me to wait upon Y.R.H. before my benefit. Pray give this letter your favorable consideration, and think graciously of me.

[K.]

[Footnote 1: Joh. Mich. Vogl, born August 10th, 1768, was Court opera singer (tenor) in Vienna from 1794 to 1822; he died November 19th, 1840.]

[Footnote 2: Forti, born June 8th, 1790, a member of the Royal Court Theatre (a barytone), pensioned off in 1834.]

127.
DEPOSITION.

1814.

I voluntarily presented Maelzel *gratis* with a "Battle Symphony" for his panharmonica. After having kept it for some time, he brought me back the score, which he had already begun to engrave, saying that he wished it to be harmonized for a full orchestra. The idea of a battle had already occurred to me, which, however, could not be performed on his panharmonica. We agreed to select this and some more of my works [see No. 116] to be given at the concert for the benefit of disabled soldiers. At that very time I became involved in the most frightful pecuniary difficulties. Forsaken by every one in Vienna, and in daily expectation of remittances, &c., Maelzel offered me fifty gold ducats, which I accepted, saying that I would either repay them, or allow him to take the work to London, (provided I did not go there myself with him,) referring him to an English publisher for payment.

I got back from him the score written for the panharmonica. The concerts then took place, and during that time Herr Maelzel's designs and character were first fully revealed. Without my consent, he stated on the bills of the concert that the work was *his property*. Indignant at this, I insisted on his destroying these bills. He then stated that I had given it to him as a friendly act, because he was going to London. To this I did not object, believing that I had reserved the right to state the conditions on which the work should be his own. I remember that when the bills were being printed, I violently opposed them, but the time was too short, as I was still writing the work. In all the fire of inspiration, and absorbed in my composition, I scarcely thought at all on the subject. Immediately after the first concert in the University Hall, I was told on all sides, and by people on whom I could rely, that Maelzel had everywhere given out he had paid me 400 gold ducats for the Symphony. I sent what follows to a newspaper, but the editor would not insert it, as Maelzel stands well with them all. As soon as the first concert was over, I repaid Maelzel his fifty ducats, declaring that having discovered his real character, nothing should ever induce me to travel with him; justly indignant that, without consulting me, he had stated in the bills that all the arrangements for the concert were most defective. His own despicable want of patriotism too is proved by the following expressions: "I care nothing at all about L.; if it is only said in London that people have paid ten gulden for admission here, that is all I care about; the wounded are nothing to me." Moreover, I told him that he might take the work to London on certain conditions, which I would inform him of. He then asserted that it was a *friendly gift*, and made use of this phrase in the newspapers after the second concert, without giving me the most remote hint on the subject. As Maelzel is a rude, churlish man, entirely devoid of education or cultivation, it is easy to conceive the tenor of his conduct to me during this time, which still further irritated me. Who could bear to be forced to bestow a *friendly gift* on such a man? I was offered an opportunity to send the work to the Prince Regent, [afterwards George IV.] It was therefore quite impossible for me to *give away the work unconditionally*.

He then called on a mutual friend to make proposals. He was told on what day to return for an answer, but he never appeared, set off on his travels, and performed the work in Munich. How did he obtain it? He could not possibly *steal* it; but Herr Maelzel had several of the parts for some days in his house, and he caused the entire work to be harmonized by some obscure musical journeyman, and is now hawking it about the world. Herr Maelzel promised me ear-trumpets. I harmonized the "Battle Symphony" for his panharmonica from a wish to keep him to his word. The ear-trumpets came at last, but were not of the service to me that I expected. For this slight trouble Herr Maelzel, after my having arranged the "Battle Symphony" for a full orchestra, and composed a battle-piece in addition, declared that I ought to have made over these works to him as *his own exclusive property*. Even allowing that I am in some degree obliged to him for the ear-trumpets, this is entirely balanced by his having made at least 500 gulden in Munich by my mutilated or stolen battle-piece. He has therefore paid himself in full. He had actually the audacity to say here that he was in possession of the battle-piece; in fact he showed it, written out, to various persons. I did not believe this; and, in fact, with good reason, as the whole is not by me, but compiled by some one else. Indeed the credit he assumes for the work should alone be sufficient compensation.

The secretary at the War Office made no allusion whatever to me, and yet every work performed at both concerts was of my composition.

Herr Maelzel thinks fit to say that he has delayed his visit to London on account of the battle-piece, which is a mere subterfuge. He stayed to finish his patchwork, as the first attempt did not succeed.

BEETHOVEN.

128.
TO HERR J. KAUKA, DOCTOR OF LAWS IN PRAGUE, IN THE KINGDOM OF BOHEMIA.

The Summer of 1814.

A thousand thanks, my esteemed Kauka. At last I meet with a *legal representative* and a *man*, who can both write and think without using unmeaning formulas. You can scarcely imagine how I long for the end of this affair, as it not only interferes with my domestic expenditure, but is injurious to me in various ways. You know yourself that a sensitive spirit ought not to be fettered by miserable anxieties, and much that might render my life happy is thus abstracted from it. Even my inclination and the duty I assigned myself, to serve suffering humanity by means of my art, I have been obliged to limit, and must continue to do so.[1]

I write nothing about our monarchs and monarchies, for the newspapers give you every information on these subjects.[2] The intellectual realm is the most precious in my eyes, and far above all temporal and spiritual monarchies. Write to me, however, what you wish *for yourself* from my poor musical capabilities, that I may, in so far as it lies in my power, supply something for your own musical sense and feeling. Do you not require all the papers connected with the Kinsky case? If so I will send them to you, as they contain most important testimony, which, indeed, I believe you read when with me. Think of me and do not forget that you represent a disinterested artist in opposition to a niggardly family. How gladly do men withhold from the poor artist in one respect *what they pay him in another*, and there is no longer a Zeus with whom an artist can invite himself to feast on ambrosia. Strive, my dear friend, to accelerate the tardy steps of justice. Whenever I feel myself elevated high, and in happy moments revel in my artistic sphere, circumstances drag me down again, and none more than these two lawsuits. You too have your disagreeable moments, though with the views and capabilities I know you to possess, especially in your profession, I could scarcely have believed this; still I must recall your attention to myself. I have drunk to the dregs a cup of bitter sorrow, and already earned martyrdom in art through my beloved artistic disciples and colleagues. I beg you will think of me every day, and imagine it to be an *entire world*, for it is really asking rather too much of you to think of so humble an *individual* as myself.

I am, with the highest esteem and friendship,

Your obedient
LUDWIG VAN BEETHOVEN.

[Footnote 1: He supported a consumptive brother and his wife and child.]

[Footnote 2: At the Vienna Congress Beethoven was received with much distinction by the potentates present.]

129.
ADDRESS AND APPEAL TO LONDON ARTISTS BY L. VAN BEETHOVEN.

Vienna, July 25, 1814.

Herr Maelzel, now in London, on his way thither performed my "Battle Symphony" and "Wellington's Battle of Vittoria" in Munich, and no doubt he intends to produce them at London concerts, as he wished to do in Frankfort. This induces me to declare that I never in any way made over or transferred the said works to Herr Maelzel; that no one possesses a copy of them, and that the only one verified by me I sent to his Royal Highness the Prince Regent of England. The performance of these works, therefore, by Herr Maelzel is either an imposition on the public, as the above declaration proves that he does not possess them, or if he does, he has been guilty of a breach of faith towards me, inasmuch as he must have got them in a surreptitious manner.

But even in the latter case the public will still be deluded, for the works that Herr Maelzel performs under the titles of "Wellington's Battle of Vittoria" and "Battle Symphony" are beyond all doubt spurious and mutilated, as he never had any portion of either of these works of mine, except some of the parts for a few days.

This suspicion becomes a certainty from the testimony of various artists here, whose names I am authorized to give if necessary. These gentlemen state that Herr Maelzel, before he left Vienna, declared that he was in possession of these works, and showed various portions, which, however, as I have already proved, must be counterfeit. The question whether Herr Maelzel be capable of doing me such an injury is best solved by the following fact,--In the public papers he named himself as sole giver of the concert on behalf of our wounded soldiers, whereas my works alone were performed there, and yet he made no allusion whatsoever to me.

I therefore appeal to the London musicians not to permit such a grievous wrong to be done to their fellow-artist by Herr Maelzel's performance of the "Battle of Vittoria" and the "Battle Symphony," and also to prevent the London public being so shamefully imposed upon.

130.
TO DR. KAUKA.

Vienna, August 22, 1814.

You have shown a feeling for harmony, and you can resolve a great discord in my life, which causes me much discomfort, into more pleasing melody, if you will. I shortly expect to hear something of what you understand is likely to happen, as I eagerly anticipate the result of this most *unjust* affair with the Kinskys. When the Princess was here, she seemed to be well disposed towards me; still I do not know how it will end. In the mean time I must restrict myself in everything, and await with entire confidence what is *rightfully my own* and *legally devolves on me*; and though unforeseen occurrences caused changes in this matter, still two witnesses recently bore testimony to the wish of the deceased Prince that my appointed salary in *Banco Zettel* should be paid in *Einlösung Schein*, making up the original sum, and the Prince himself gave me sixty gold ducats *on account* of my claim.

Should the affair turn out badly for me by the conduct of the Kinsky family, I will publish it in every newspaper, to their disgrace. If there had been an heir, and the facts had been told to him *in all their truth*, just as I narrated them, I am convinced that he would at once have adopted the words and deeds of his predecessor. Has Dr. Wolf [the previous advocate] shown you the papers, or shall I make you acquainted with them? As I am by no means sure that this letter will reach you safely, I defer sending you the pianoforte arrangement of my opera "Fidelio," which is ready to be dispatched.

I hope, in accordance with your usual friendliness, soon to hear from you. I am also writing to Dr. Wolf (who certainly does not treat any one *wolfishly*), in order not to arouse his *passion*, so that he may have *compassion* on me, and neither take my purse nor my life.

I am, with esteem, your true friend,
LUDWIG VAN BEETHOVEN.

131.
TO COUNT MORITZ LICHNOWSKY.

Baden, Sept. 21, 1841.[1]

MOST ESTEEMED COUNT AND FRIEND,--

I unluckily only got your letter yesterday. A thousand thanks for your remembrance of me. Pray express my gratitude also to your charming Princess Christiane [wife of Prince Carl Lichnowsky]. I had a delightful walk yesterday with a friend in the Brühl, and in the course of our friendly chat you were particularly mentioned, and lo! and behold! on my return I found your kind letter. I see you are resolved to continue to load me with benefits.

As I am unwilling you should suppose that a step I have already taken is prompted by your recent favors, or by any motive of the sort, I must tell you that a sonata of mine [Op. 90] is about to appear, *dedicated to you*. I wished to give you a surprise, as this dedication has been long designed for you, but your letter of yesterday induces me to name the fact. I required no new motive thus publicly to testify my sense of your friendship and kindness. But as for anything approaching to a gift in return, you would only distress me, by thus totally misinterpreting my intentions, and I should at once decidedly refuse such a thing.

I beg to kiss the hand of the Princess for her kind message and all her goodness to me. *Never have I forgotten what I owe to you all*, though an unfortunate combination of circumstances prevented my testifying this as I could have wished.

From what you tell me about Lord Castlereagh, I think the matter in the best possible train. If I were to give an opinion on the subject, I should say that Lord Castlereagh ought to hear the work given here before writing to Wellington. I shall soon be in Vienna, when we can consult together about a grand concert. Nothing is to be effected at Court; I made the application, but--but--

Silentium!!!

Farewell, my esteemed friend; pray continue to esteem me worthy of your friendship. Yours,

A thousand compliments to the illustrious Princess.

BEETHOVEN.

[Footnote 1: The date reversed, as written by Beethoven, is here given.]

132.
TO THE ARCHDUKE RUDOLPH.

1814.

I perceive that Y.R.H. wishes to try the effect of my music even upon horses.[1] We shall see whether its influence will cause the riders to throw some clever summersets. Ha! ha! I can't help laughing at Y.R.H. thinking of me on such an occasion; for which I shall remain so long as I live, &c., &c., &c. The horse-music that Y.R.H. desires shall set off to you full gallop.

[K.]

[Footnote 1: A tournament was held on the 23d November, 1814, in the Royal Riding School. Beethoven was probably requested by the Archduke to compose some music for it, which, however, has not been traced.]

133.
TO THE ARCHDUKE RUDOLPH.

1814.

It is impossible for me to-day to wait on you, much as I wish it. I am dispatching the work on Wellington's victory[1] to London. Such matters have their appointed and fixed time, which cannot be delayed without final loss. To-morrow I hope to be able to call on Y.R.H.

[K.]

[Footnote 1: The Cantata *Der glorreiche Augenblick*, the poetry by Dr. Alois Weissenbach, set to music by Beethoven for chorus and orchestra (Op. 136), was first given in Vienna on the 29th November, 1814, and repeated on the 2d December.]

134.
TO THE ARCHDUKE RUDOLPH.

(In a different hand) Dec. 1814.

I really feel that I can never deserve your goodness towards me. I beg to offer my most respectful thanks for Y.R.H.'s gracious intervention in my affairs at Prague. I will punctually attend to the score of the Cantata.[1] I trust Y.R.H. will forgive my not having yet been to see you. After the concert for the poor, comes one in the theatre, equally for the benefit of the *impresario in angustia*, for they have felt some just shame, and have let me off with one third and one half of the usual charges. I have now some fresh work on hand, and then there is a new opera to be begun,[2] the subject of which I am about to decide on. Moreover, I am again far from well, but a few days hence I will wait on Y.R.H. If I could be of any service to Y.R.H., the most eager and anxious wish of my life would be fulfilled.

[K.]

[Footnote 1: What concert Beethoven alludes to I cannot discover, but no mention of it being made in the very exact *Allgemeine Leipziger Musikalische Zeitung*, it appears not to have taken place.]

[Footnote 2: The new opera, with the subject of which Beethoven was occupied, was no doubt Treitschke's *Romulus*.]

135.
TO THE ARCHDUKE RUDOLPH.

1814.

My warmest thanks for your present.[1] I only regret that you could not participate in the music. I have now the honor to send you the score of the Cantata [see No. 134]. Y.R.H. can keep it for some days, and afterwards I shall take care that it is copied for you as soon as possible.

I feel still quite exhausted from fatigue and worry, pleasure and delight!--all combined! I shall have the honor of waiting on you in the course of a few days. I hope to hear favorable accounts of

Y.R.H.'s health. How gladly would I sacrifice many nights, were it in my power to restore you entirely!

[K.]

[Footnote 1: The present he refers to was probably for the concert of November 29th, or December 2d, 1814.]

136.
TO THE ARCHDUKE RUDOLPH.

1814.[1]

I see with real pleasure that I may dismiss all fears for your well-being. As for myself, I hope (always feeling happy when able to give you any pleasure) that my health is also rapidly recruiting, when I intend forthwith to compensate both you and myself for the *pauses* that have occurred. As for Prince Lobkowitz, his *pauses* with me still continue, and I fear he will never again come in at the right place; and in Prague (good heavens! with regard to Prince Kinsky's affair) they scarcely as yet know what a figured bass is, for they sing in slow, long-drawn choral notes; some of these sustained through sixteen bars |======|. As all these discords seem likely to be very slowly resolved, it is best to bring forward only those which we can ourselves resolve, and to give up the rest to inevitable fate. Allow me once more to express my delight at the recovery of Y.R.H.

[K.]

[Footnote 1: 1814 or 1815. Prince Lobkowitz was still alive at that time (died December 21st, 1816).]

137.
TO THE ARCHDUKE RUDOLPH.

1814.

As you were so kind as to let me know through Count Troyer[1] that you would write a few lines on my affairs in Prague to the *Oberstburggraf* Count Kolowrat, I take the liberty to enclose my letter to Count K.; I do not believe that it contains anything to which Y.R.H. will take exception. There is no chance of my being allowed payment in *Einlösung Schein*, for, in spite of all the proofs, the guardians cannot be persuaded to consent to this; still it is to be hoped that by the friendly steps we have meanwhile had recourse to, *extra-judicially*, a more favorable result may be obtained,--as, for instance, the rate of the scale to be higher. If, however, Y.R.H. will either write a few words yourself, or cause it to be done in your name, the affair will certainly be *much accelerated*, which induces me earnestly to entreat Y.R.H. to perform your gracious promise to me. This affair has now gone on for three years, and is still--undecided.

[K.]

[Footnote 1: Count Ferdinand Troyer was one of the Archduke's chamberlains.]

138.
TO THE ARCHDUKE RUDOLPH.

1814.

I have again for a fortnight past been afflicted with severe headaches, though constantly hoping to get better, but in vain. Now, however, that the weather is improved, my physician promises me a speedy cure. Though as each day I expected to be the last of my suffering, I did not write to you on the subject; besides, I thought that Y.R.H. probably did not require me, as it is so long since Y.R.H. sent for me. During the festivities in honor of the Princess of Baden,[1] and the injury to Y.R.H.'s finger, I began to work very assiduously, and as the fruit of this, among others, is a new pianoforte trio.[2] Myself very much occupied, I had no idea that I had incurred the displeasure of Y.R.H., though I now begin almost to think this to be the case. In the mean time I hope soon to be able to present myself before your tribunal.

[K.]

[Footnote 1: The festivities in honor of the Princess of Baden were probably during the Congress, 1814.]

[Footnote 2: The new trio, if the one in B flat for the pianoforte, violin, and violoncello, Op. 97, was first performed on the 11th April, 1814, in the hall of the "Komischer Kaiser." Letter 139 also mentions this trio, composed in 1811 and published in July, 1816.]

139.
TO THE ARCHDUKE RUDOLPH.

1814.

I beg you will be so good as to let me have the Trio in B flat with all the parts, and also both parts of the violin Sonata in G,[1] as I must have them written out for myself with all speed, not being able to hunt out my own scores among so many others. I hope that this detestable weather has had no bad effect on Y.R.H.'s health; I must own that it rather deranges me. In three or four days at least I shall have the honor to restore both works to their proper place.

Do the musical pauses still continue?

[K.]

[Footnote 1: The Sonata for pianoforte and violin in G major, Op. 96, was purchased by Haslinger, April 1st, 1815, and published the end of July, 1816. It was composed in 1814--perhaps in 1813. Thayer thinks in 1810.]

140.
TO HERR KAUKA.

Vienna, Jan. 11, 1815.

MY GOOD, WORTHY K.,--

I received Baron Pasqualati's letter to-day, by which I perceive that you wish me to defer any fresh measures. In the mean time all the necessary papers are lodged with Pasqualati; so be so good as to inform him that he must delay taking any further steps. To-morrow a council is to be held here, and you and P. shall learn the result probably to-morrow evening. Meanwhile I wish you to look through the paper I sent to the Court through Pasqualati, and read the appendix carefully. You will then see that Wolf and others have not given you correct information.

One thing is certain, that there are sufficient proofs *for any one who wishes to be convinced*. How could it ever occur to me *to think of written legal testimony* with such a man as Kinsky, whose integrity and generosity were everywhere acknowledged? I remain, with the warmest affection and esteem,

In haste, your friend,
B.

141.
TO HERR KAUKA.

1815.

MY DEAR AND ESTEEMED K.,--

What can I think, or say, or feel? As for W. [Wolf], it seems to me that he not only showed *his weak points*, but gave himself no trouble to conceal them. It is impossible that he can have drawn up his statement in accordance with all the actual evidence he had. The order on the treasury about the rate of exchange was given by Kinsky previous to his consent to pay me my salary in *Einlösung Schein*, as the documents prove; indeed it is only necessary to examine the date to show this, so the first instruction is of importance. The *species facti* prove that I was more than six months absent from Vienna. As I was not anxious to get the money, I allowed the affair to stand over; so the Prince thus forgot to recall his former order to the treasury, but that he neither forgot his promise to me, nor to Varnhagen [an officer] in my behalf, is evident by the testimony of Herr von Oliva, to whom shortly before his departure from hence--and indeed into another world--he repeated his promise, making an appointment to see him when he should return to Vienna, in order to arrange the matter with the treasury, which of course was prevented by his untimely death.

The testimony of the officer Varnhagen is accompanied by a document (he being at present with the Russian army), in which he states that he is prepared to *take his oath* on the affair. The evidence of Herr Oliva is also to the effect that he is willing to confirm his evidence by oath before the Court.

As I have sent away the testimony of Col. Count Bentheim, I am not sure of its tenor, but I believe the Count also says that he is prepared at any time to make an affidavit on the matter in Court, and I am myself *ready to swear before the Court* that Prince Kinsky said to me in Prague, "he thought it only fair to me that my salary should be paid in *Einlösung Schein*." These were his own words.

He gave me himself sixty gold ducats in Prague, on account (good for about 600 florins), as, owing to my state of health, I could remain no longer, and set off for Töplitz. The Prince's word was *sacred* in my eyes, never having heard anything of him to induce me either to bring two witnesses with me or to ask him for any written pledge. I see from all this that Dr. Wolf has miserably mismanaged the business, and has not made you sufficiently acquainted with the papers.

Now as to the step I have just taken. The Archduke Rudolph asked me some time since whether the Kinsky affair was yet terminated, having probably heard something of it. I told him that it looked very bad, as I knew nothing, absolutely nothing, of the matter. He offered to write himself, but desired me to add a memorandum, and also to make him acquainted with all the papers connected with the Kinsky case. After having informed himself on the affair, he wrote to the *Oberstburggraf*, and enclosed my letter to him.

The *Oberstburggraf* answered both the Duke and myself immediately. In the letter to me he said "that I was to present a petition to the Provincial Court of Justice in Prague, along with all the proofs, whence it would be forwarded to him, and that he would do his utmost to further my cause." He also wrote in the most polite terms to the Archduke; indeed, he expressly said "that he was thoroughly cognizant of the late Prince Kinsky's intentions with regard to me and this affair, and that I might present a petition," &c. The Archduke instantly sent for me, and desired me to prepare the document and to show it to him; he also thought that I ought to solicit payment in *Einlösung Schein*, as there was ample proof, if not in strictly legal form, of the intentions of the Prince, and no one could doubt that if he had survived he would have adhered to his promise. If he [the Archduke] were this day the heir, *he would demand no other proofs than those already furnished*. I sent this paper to Baron Pasqualati, who is kindly to present it himself to the Court. Not till after the affair had gone so far did Dr. Adlersburg receive a letter from Dr. Wolf, in which he mentioned that he had made a claim for 1500 florins. As we have come so far as 1500 florins with the *Oberstburggraf*, we may possibly get on to 1800 florins. I do not esteem this any *favor*, for the late Prince was one of those who urged me most to refuse a salary of 600 gold ducats per annum, offered to me from Westphalia; and he said at the time "that he was resolved I should have no chance of eating hams in Westphalia." Another summons to Naples somewhat later I equally declined, and I am entitled to demand a fair compensation for the loss I incurred. If the salary were to be paid in bank-notes, what should I get? Not 400 florins in *Conventionsgeld*!!! in lieu of such a salary as 600 ducats! There are ample proofs for those who wish to act justly; and what does the *Einlösung Schein* now amount to??!!! It is even at this moment no equivalent for what I refused. This affair was pompously announced in all the newspapers while I was nearly reduced to beggary. The intentions of the Prince are evident, and in my opinion the family are bound to act in accordance with them unless they wish to be disgraced. Besides, the revenues have rather increased than diminished by the death of the Prince; so there is no sufficient ground for curtailing my salary.

I received your friendly letter yesterday, but am too weary at this moment to write all that I feel towards you. I can only commend my case to your sagacity. It appears that the *Oberstburggraf* is the chief person; so what he wrote to the Archduke must be kept a profound secret, for it might not be advisable that any one should know of it but you and Pasqualati. You have sufficient cause on looking through the papers to show how improperly Dr. Wolf has conducted the affair, and that another course of action is necessary. I rely on your friendship to act as you think best for my interests.

Rest assured of my warmest thanks, and pray excuse my writing more to-day, for a thing of this kind is very fatiguing,--more so than the greatest musical undertaking. My heart has found something for you to which yours will respond, and this you shall soon receive.

Do not forget me, poor tormented creature that I am! and *act for me* and *effect for me* all that is possible.

With high esteem, your true friend,
BEETHOVEN.

142.
TO HERR KAUKA.

Vienna, Jan. 14, 1815.

MY GOOD AND WORTHY K.,--

The long letter I enclose was written when we were disposed to claim the 1800 florins. Baron Pasqualati's last letter, however, again made me waver, and Dr. Adlersburg advised me to adhere to the steps already taken; but as Dr. Wolf writes that he has offered in your name to accept 1500 florins a year, I beg you will at least make every effort to get that sum. For this purpose I send you the long letter written before we received Baron P.'s dissuasive one, as you may discover in it many reasons for demanding *at least* the 1500 florins. The Archduke, too, has written a second time to the *Oberstburggraf*, and we may conclude from his previous reply that he will certainly exert himself, and that we shall at all events succeed in getting the 1500 florins.

Farewell! I cannot write another syllable; such things exhaust me. May your friendship accelerate this affair!--if it ends badly, then I must leave Vienna, because I could not possibly live on my income, for here things have come to such a pass that everything has risen to the highest price, and that price must be paid. The last two concerts I gave cost me 1508 florins, and had it not been for the Empress's munificent present I should scarcely have derived any profit whatever.

Your faithful friend,
BEETHOVEN.

143.[1]
TO THE HONORABLE MEMBERS OF THE LANDRECHT.

Vienna, 1815.

GENTLEMEN,--

Quite ignorant of law proceedings, and believing that all claims on an inheritance could not fail to be liquidated, I sent to my lawyer in Prague [Dr. Kauka] the contract signed by the Archduke Rudolph, Prince Lobkowitz, and Prince von Kinsky, in which these illustrious personages agreed to settle on me an annual allowance of 4000 florins. My constant efforts to obtain a settlement of my claim, and also, as I am bound to admit, my reproaches to Dr. Kauka for not conducting the affair properly (his application to the guardians having proved fruitless), no doubt prompted him to have recourse to law.

None but those who are fully aware of my esteem for the deceased Prince can tell how repugnant it is to my feelings to appear as a complainant against my benefactor.

Under these circumstances I have recourse to a shorter path, in the conviction that the guardians of the Prince's estate will be disposed to mark their appreciation of art, and also their desire to fulfil the engagements of the late Prince. According to the terms of the contract in question, the Archduke Rudolph, Prince Lobkowitz, and Prince v. Kinsky granted me these 4000 florins until I should obtain a situation of equal value; and further, if by misfortune or old age I was prevented exercising my art, these distinguished contracting parties secured this pension to me for life, while I, in return, pledged myself not to leave Vienna.

This promise was generous, and equally generous was its fulfilment, for no difficulty ever occurred, and I was in the peaceful enjoyment of my pension till the Imperial Finance Patent appeared. The consequent alteration in the currency made no difference in the payments of the Archduke Rudolph, for I received his share in *Einlösung Schein*, as I had previously done in bank-notes, without any reference to the new scale. The late illustrious Prince v. Kinsky also at once assured me that his share (1800 florins) should also be paid in *Einlösung Schein*. As however, he omitted giving the order to his cashier, difficulties arose on the subject. Although my circumstances are not brilliant, I would not have ventured to bring this claim before the notice of the guardians of the estate, if respectable, upright men had not received the same pledge from the late Prince's own lips, namely, that he would pay my past as well as my future claims in Vienna currency, which is proved by the papers B, C, D, appended to the pleas. Under these circumstances I leave the guardians to judge whether, after so implicitly relying on the promise of the deceased Prince, I have not cause to complain of my delicacy being wounded by the objection advanced by the curators to the witnesses, from their not having been present together at the time the promise was made, which is most distressing to my feelings.

In order to extricate myself from this most disagreeable lawsuit, I take the liberty to give an assurance to the guardians that I am prepared, both as to the past and the future, to be satisfied with the 1800 florins, Vienna currency; and I flatter myself that these gentlemen will admit that I on my part make thus no small sacrifice, as it was solely from my esteem for those illustrious Princes that I selected Vienna for my settled abode, at a time when the most advantageous offers were made to me elsewhere.

I therefore request the Court to submit this proposal to the guardians of the Kinsky estates for their opinion, and to be so good as to inform me of the result.

L. V. BEETHOVEN.

[Footnote 1: See No. 94. On the 18th January, 1815, the Court of Justice at Prague decreed that the trustees of Prince Kinsky's estate should pay to L. v. Beethoven the sum of 1200 florins W.W. from November 3d, 1812, instead of the original written agreement of 1800 florins. Dr. Constant, of Wurzbach, in his *Biographical Austrian Lexicon*, states that Beethoven dedicated his splendid song *An die Hoffnung*, Op. 94, to Princess Kinsky, wife of Prince Ferdinand Kinsky, who died in 1812.]

144.
TO BARON VON PASQUALATI.

January, 1815.

MY ESTEEMED FRIEND,--

I beg you will kindly send me by the bearer the proper form for the Kinsky receipt (*but sealed*) for 600 florins half-yearly from the month of April. I intend to send the receipt forthwith to Dr. Kauka in Prague,[1] who on a former occasion procured the money for me so quickly. I will deduct your debt from this, but if it be possible to get the money here before the remittance arrives from Prague, I will bring it at once to you myself.

I remain, with the most profound esteem,

Your sincere friend,
BEETHOVEN

[Footnote 1: This man, now ninety-four years of age and quite blind, was at that time Beethoven's counsel in Prague. Pasqualati was that benefactor of Beethoven's who always kept rooms for him in his house on the Mölker Bastei, and whose kind aid never deserted him to the close of his life.]

145.
TO HERR KAUKA.

Vienna, Feb. 24, 1815.

MY MUCH ESTEEMED K.,--

I have repeatedly thanked you through Baron Pasqualati for your friendly exertions on my behalf, and I now beg to express one thousand thanks myself. The intervention of the Archduke could not be very palatable to you, and perhaps has prejudiced you against me. You had already done all that was possible when the Archduke interfered. If this had been the case sooner, and we had not employed that one-sided, or many-sided, or weak-sided Dr. Wolf, then, according to the assurances of the *Oberstburggraf* himself, the affair might have had a still more favorable result. I shall therefore ever and always be grateful to you for your services. The Court now deduct the sixty ducats I mentioned of my own accord, and to which the late Prince never alluded either to his treasurer or any one else. Where truth could injure me it has been accepted, so why reject it when it could have benefited me? How unfair! Baron Pasqualati requires information from you on various points.

I am again very tired to-day, having been obliged to discuss many things with poor P.; such matters exhaust me more than the greatest efforts in composition. It is a new field, the soil of which I ought not to be required to till. This painful business has cost me many tears and much sorrow. The time draws near when Princess Kinsky must be written to. Now I must conclude. How rejoiced shall I be when I can write you the pure effusions of my heart once more; and this I mean to do as soon as I am extricated from all these troubles. Pray accept again my heartfelt thanks for all that you have done for me, and continue your regard for

Your attached friend,
BEETHOVEN.

146.
TO THE ARCHDUKE RUDOLPH.

1815.

I heard yesterday, and it was indeed confirmed by meeting Count Troyer, that Y.R.H. is now here. I therefore send the dedication of the Trio [in B flat] to Y.R.H., whose name is inscribed on it; but all my works on which I place any value, though the name does not appear, are equally designed for Y.R.H. I trust, however, that you will not think I have a motive in saying this,--men of high rank being apt to suspect self-interest in such expressions,--and I mean on this occasion to risk the imputation so far as *appearances* go, by at once asking a favor of Y.R.H. My well-grounded reasons for so doing you will no doubt at once perceive, and graciously vouchsafe to grant my request. I have been very much indisposed in Baden since the beginning of last October; indeed, from the 5th of October I have been entirely confined to my bed, or to my room, till about a week ago. I had a very serious inflammatory cold, and am still able to go out very little, which has also been the cause of my not writing to Y.R.H. in Kremsir. May all the blessings that Heaven can shower upon earth attend you.

[K.]

SECOND PART.

LIFE'S MISSION.
1815 TO 1822.

147.
WRITTEN IN SPOHR'S ALBUM.[1]

Vienna, March 3, 1815.

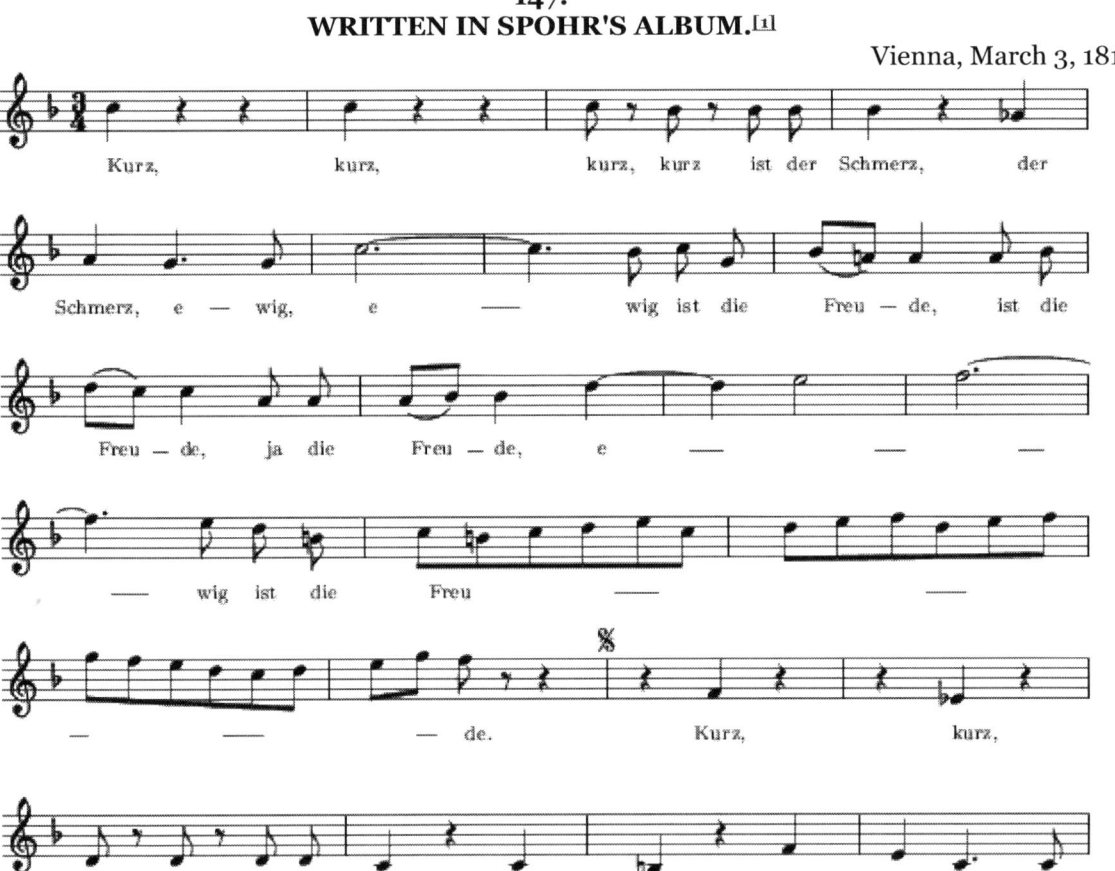

Whenever, dear Spohr, you chance to find true art and true artists, may you kindly remember

Your friend,
LUDWIG VAN BEETHOVEN.

[Footnote 1: From the fac-simile in Spohr's *Autobiography*, Vol. I.]

148.
TO HERR KAUKA.

Vienna, April 8, 1815.

It seems scarcely admissible to be on the friendly terms on which I consider myself with you, and yet to be on such unfriendly ones that we should live close to each other and never meet!!!!![1] You write "*tout à vous*." Oh! you humbug! said I. No! no! it is really too bad. I should like to thank you 9000 times for all your efforts on my behalf, and to reproach you 20,000 that you came and went as you did. So all is a delusion! friendship, kingdom, empire; all is only a vapor which every breeze wafts into a different form!! Perhaps I may go to Töplitz, but it is not certain. I might take advantage of that opportunity to let the people of Prague hear something--what think you? if *indeed you still think of me at all*! As the affair with Lobkowitz is now also come to a close, we may write *Finis*, though it far from *fine is* for me.

Baron Pasqualati will no doubt soon call on you again; he also has taken much trouble on my account. Yes, indeed! it is easy to talk of *justice*, but to obtain it from others is *no easy matter*. In what way can I be of service to you in my own art? Say whether you prefer my celebrating the monologue of a fugitive king, or the perjury of a usurper--or the true friends, who, though near neighbors, never saw each other? In the hope of soon hearing from you--for being now so far asunder it is easier to hold intercourse than when nearer!--I remain, with highest esteem,

Your ever-devoted friend,
LUDWIG VAN BEETHOVEN.

[Footnote 1: Kauka evidently had been recently in Vienna without visiting Beethoven.]

149.
TO HERR KAUKA.

1815.

MY DEAR AND WORTHY K.,--

I have just received from the Syndic Baier in R. the good news that you told him yourself about Prince F.K. As for the rest, you shall be perfectly satisfied.

I take the liberty to ask you again to look after my interests with the Kinsky family, and I subjoin the necessary receipt for this purpose [see No. 144]. Perhaps some other way may be found, though it does not as yet occur to me, by means of which I need not importune you in future. On the 15th October [1815] I was attacked by an inflammatory cold, from the consequences of which I still suffer, and my art likewise; but it is to be hoped that I shall now gradually recover, and at all events be able once more to display the riches of my little realm of sweet sounds. Yet I am very poor in all else-- owing to the times? to poverty of spirit? or what???? Farewell! Everything around disposes us to *profound silence*; but this shall not be the case as to the bond of friendship and soul that unites us. I loudly proclaim myself, now as ever,

Your loving friend and admirer,
BEETHOVEN.

150.
TO HERR KAUKA.

1815.

MY MOST WORTHY FRIEND,--

My second letter follows that of yesterday, May 2d. Pasqualati tells me to-day, after the lapse of a month and six days, that the house of Ballabene is too *high and mighty* to assist me in this matter. I must therefore appeal to your *insignificance* (as I myself do not hesitate to be so mean as to serve other people). My house-rent amounts to 550 florins, and must be paid out of the sum in question.

As soon as the newly engraved pianoforte pieces appear, you shall receive copies, and also of the "Battle," &c., &c. Forgive me, forgive me, my generous friend; some other means must be found to forward this affair with due promptitude.

In haste, your friend and admirer,
BEETHOVEN.

151.
TO MR. SALOMON,--LONDON.[1]

Vienna, June 1, 1815.

MY GOOD FELLOW-COUNTRYMAN,--

I always hoped to meet you one day in London, but many obstacles have intervened to prevent the fulfilment of this wish, and as there seems now no chance of such a thing, I hope you will not refuse a request of mine, which is that you will be so obliging as to apply to some London publisher, and offer him the following works of mine. Grand Trio for piano, violin, and violoncello [Op. 97], 80 ducats. Pianoforte Sonata, with violin accompaniment [Op. 96], 60 ducats. Grand Symphony in A (one of my very best); a short Symphony in F [the 8th]; Quartet for two violins, viola, and violoncello in F minor [Op. 95]; Grand Opera in score, 30 ducats. Cantata with Choruses and Solos ["The Glorious Moment"], 30 ducats. Score of the "Battle of Vittoria" and "Wellington's Victory," 80 ducats; also the pianoforte arrangement of the same, if not already published, which, I am told here, is the case. I have named the prices of some of these works, on a scale which I hold to be suitable for England, but I leave it to you to say what sum should be asked both for these and the others. I hear, indeed, that

Cramer [John, whose pianoforte-playing was highly estimated by Beethoven] is also a publisher, but my scholar Ries lately wrote to me that Cramer not long since *publicly expressed his disapproval of my works*: I trust from no motive but that of *being of service to art*, and if so I have no right to object to his doing this. If, however, Cramer should wish to possess any of my *pernicious* works, I shall be as well satisfied with him as with any other publisher; but I reserve the right to give these works to be published here, so that they may appear at the same moment in London and Vienna.

Perhaps you may also be able to point out to me in what way I can recover from the Prince Regent [afterwards George IV.] the expenses of transcribing the "Battle Symphony" on Wellington's victory at Vittoria, to be dedicated to him, for I have long ago given up all hope of receiving anything from that quarter. I have not even been deemed worthy of an answer, whether I am to be authorized to dedicate the work to the Prince Regent; and when at last I propose to publish it here, I am informed that it has already appeared in London. What a fatality for an author!!! While the English and German papers are filled with accounts of the success of the work, as performed at Drury Lane, and that theatre drawing great receipts from it, the author has not one friendly line to show, not even payment for the cost of copying the work, and is thus deprived of all profit.[2] For if it be true that the pianoforte arrangement is soon to be published by a German publisher, copied from the London one, then I lose both my fame and my *honorarium*. The well-known generosity of your character leads me to hope that you will take some interest in the matter, and actively exert yourself on my behalf.

The inferior paper-money of this country is now reduced to one fifth of its value, and I am paid according to this scale. After many struggles and considerable loss, I at length succeeded in obtaining the full value; but at this moment the old paper-money has again risen far beyond the fifth part, so that it is evident my salary becomes for the second time almost *nil*, and there is no hope of any compensation. My whole income is derived from my works. If I could rely on a good sale in England, it would doubtless be very beneficial to me. Pray be assured of my boundless gratitude. I hope soon, very soon, to hear from you.

I am, with esteem, your sincere friend,
LUDWIG VAN BEETHOVEN.

[Footnote 1: J.P. Salomon was likewise a native of Bonn, and one of the most distinguished violin-players of his time. He had been Kapellmeister to Prince Heinrich of Prussia, and then went to London, where he was very active in the introduction of German music. It was through his agency that Beethoven's connection with Birchall, the music publisher, first commenced, to whom a number of his letters are addressed.]

[Footnote 2: Undoubtedly the true reading of these last words, which in the copy before me are marked as "difficult to decipher."]

152.
TO THE ARCHDUKE RUDOLPH.

1815.

Pray forgive my asking Y.R.H. to send me the two Sonatas with violin *obbligato*[1] which I caused to be transcribed for Y.R.H. I require them only for a few days, when I will immediately return them.

[K.]

[Footnote 1: If by the two Sonatas for the pianoforte with violoncello *obbligato*, Op. 102 is meant, they were composed in July-August, 1815, and appeared on Jan. 13th, 1819. The date of the letter appears also to be 1815.]

153.
TO THE ARCHDUKE RUDOLPH.

1815.

I beg you will kindly send me the Sonata in E minor,[1] as I wish to correct it. On Monday I shall inquire for Y.R.H. in person. *Recent occurrences*[2] render it indispensable to complete many works of mine about to be engraved as quickly as possible; besides, my health is only partially restored. I earnestly entreat Y.R.H. to desire *some one* to write me a few lines as to the state of your own health. I trust I shall hear a better--nay, the best report of it.

[K.]

[Footnote 1: The letters 152 and 153 speak sometimes expressly of the pianoforte Sonata in E minor, Op. 90, these being engraved or under revision, and sometimes only indicate them. This Sonata, dedicated to Count Lichnowsky, was composed on August 14th, 1814, and published in June, 1815.]

[Footnote 2: What "recent occurrences" Beethoven alludes to, unless indeed his well-known misfortunes as to his salary and guardianship we cannot discover.]

154.
TO THE ARCHDUKE RUDOLPH.

1815.

You must almost think my illness a mere fiction, but that is assuredly not the case. I am obliged always to come home early in the evening. The first time that Y.R.H. was graciously pleased to send for me, I came home immediately afterwards, but feeling much better since then, I made an attempt the evening before last to stay out a little later. If Y.R.H. does not countermand me, I intend to have the honor of waiting on you this evening at five o'clock. I will bring the new Sonata with me, merely for to-day, for it is so soon to be engraved that it is not worth while to have it written out.

[K.]

155.
TO THE ARCHDUKE RUDOLPH.

1815.

I intended to have given you this letter myself, but my personal attendance might possibly be an intrusion; so I take the liberty once more to urge on Y.R.H. the request it contains. I should also be glad if Y.R.H. would send me back my last MS. Sonata, for as I *must* publish it, it would be labor lost to have it transcribed, and I shall soon have the pleasure of presenting it to you engraved. I will call again in a few days. I trust these joyous times may have a happy influence on your precious health.

[K.]

156.
TO THE ARCHDUKE RUDOLPH.

Vienna, July 23, 1815.

When you were recently in town, the enclosed Chorus[1] occurred to me. I hurried home to write it down, but was detained longer in doing so than I at first expected, and thus, to my great sorrow, I missed Y.R.H. The bad custom I have followed from childhood, instantly to write down my first thoughts, otherwise they not unfrequently go astray, has been an injury to me on this occasion. I therefore send Y.R.H. my impeachment and my justification, and trust I may find grace in your eyes. I hope soon to present myself before Y.R.H., and to inquire after a health so precious to us all.

[K.]

[Footnote 1: In 1815 the Chorus of *Die Meeresstille* was composed by Beethoven. Was this the chorus which occurred to him? The style of the letter leaves his meaning quite obscure.]

157.
TO THE ARCHDUKE RUDOLPH.

1815.

It is neither presumption, nor the pretension of advocating any one's cause, still less from the wish of arrogating to myself the enjoyment of any especial favor with Y.R.H., that induces me to make a suggestion which is in itself very simple. Old Kraft[1] was with me yesterday; he wished to know if it were possible for him to be lodged in your palace, in return for which he would be at Y.R.H.'s service as often as you please it. He has lived for twenty years in the house of Prince Lobkowitz, and during a great part of that time he received no salary; he is now obliged to vacate his rooms without receiving any compensation whatever. The position of the poor deserving old man is hard, and I should have considered myself equally hard, had I not ventured to lay his case before you. Count Troyer will request an answer from Y.R.H. As the object in view is to brighten the lot of a fellow-creature, pray forgive your, &c., &c.

[K.]

[Footnote 1: Old Kraft was a clever violoncello-player who had an appointment in Prince Lobkowitz's band, but when the financial crisis occurred in the Prince's affairs he lost his situation, and was obliged to give up his lodging.]

158.
WRITTEN IN ENGLISH TO MR. BIRCHALL, MUSIC PUBLISHER, LONDON.

Mr. Beethoven send word to Mr. Birchall that it is severall days past that he has sent for London Wellington's Battel Sinphonie and that Mr. B[irchall] may send for it at Thomas Coutts. Mr. Beethoven wish Mr. B. would make ingrave the sayd Sinphonie so soon as possible and send him word in time the day it will be published that he may prevend in time the Publisher in Vienna.

In regard the 3. Sonata which Mr. Birchall receive afterwerths there is not wanted such a g't hurry and Mr. B. will take the liberty to fixe the day when the are to be published.

Mr. B[irchall] sayd that Mr. Salomon has a good many tings to say concerning the Synphonie in G [? A].

Mr. B[eethoven] wish for a answer so soon as possible concerning the days of the publication.

159.
TO ZMESKALL.

October 16, 1815.

I only wish to let you know that I am *here*, and not *elsewhere*, and wish in return to hear if you are *elsewhere* or *here*. I should be glad to speak to you for a few minutes when I know that you are at home and alone. *Farewell*--but not *too well*--sublime Commandant Pacha of various mouldering fortresses!!!

In haste, your friend,
BEETHOVEN.

160.
TO THE ARCHDUKE RUDOLPH.

Nov. 16, 1815.

Since yesterday afternoon I have been lying in a state of exhaustion, owing to my great distress of mind caused by the sudden death of my unhappy brother. It was impossible for me to send an answer to Y.R.H. yesterday, and I trust you will graciously receive my present explanation. I expect, however, certainly to wait on Y.R.H. to-morrow.

[K.]

161.
TO THE MESSRS. BIRCHALL,--LONDON.

Vienna, Nov. 22, 1815.

You will herewith receive the pianoforte arrangement of the Symphony in A. "Wellington's Battle Symphony," and "Victory at Vittoria" were sent a month since, through Herr Neumann, to the care of Messrs. Coutts; so you have no doubt received them long ere this.

In the course of a fortnight you shall have the Trio and Sonata, when you are requested to pay into the hands of Messrs. Coutts the sum of 130 gold ducats. I beg you will make no delay in bringing out these works, and likewise let me know on what day the "Wellington Symphony" is to appear, so that I may take my measures here accordingly. I am, with esteem,

Your obedient
LUDWIG VAN BEETHOVEN.

162.
TO RIES.

Vienna, Wednesday, Nov. 22, 1815.

MY DEAR RIES,--

I hasten to apprise you that I have to-day forwarded by post the pianoforte arrangement of the Symphony in A, to the care of Messrs Coutts. As the Court is absent, few, indeed almost no couriers go from here; moreover, the post is the safest way. The Symphony ought to be brought out about March; the precise day I will fix myself. So much time has already been lost on this occasion that I could not give an earlier notice of the period of publication. The Trio in [??] and the violin Sonata may be allowed more time, and both will be in London a few weeks hence. I earnestly entreat you, dear Ries, to take charge of these matters, and also to see that I get the money; I require it, and it costs me a good deal before all is sent off.

I have lost 600 florins of my yearly salary; at the time of the *bank-notes* there was no loss, but then came the *Einlösungsscheine* [reduced paper-money], which deprives me of these 600 florins, after entailing on me several years of annoyance, and now the total loss of my salary. We are at present arrived at a point when the *Einlösungsscheine* are even lower than the *bank-notes* ever were. I pay 1000 florins for house-rent: you may thus conceive all the misery caused by paper-money.

My poor unhappy brother [Carl v. Beethoven, a cashier in Vienna] is just dead [Nov. 15th, 1815]; he had a bad wife. For some years past he has been suffering from consumption, and from my wish to make his life less irksome I may compute what I gave him at 10,000 florins (*Wiener Währung*). This indeed does not seem much to an Englishman, but it is a great deal for a poor German, or rather Austrian. The unhappy man was latterly much changed, and I must say I lament him from my heart, though I rejoice to think I left nothing undone that could contribute to his comfort.

Tell Mr. Birchall that he is to repay the postage of my letters to you and Mr. Salomon, and also yours to me; he may deduct this from the sum he owes me; I am anxious that those who work for me should lose as little as possible by it. "Wellington's Victory at Vittoria"[1] must have arrived long ago through the Messrs. Coutts. Mr. Birchall need not send payment till he is in possession of all the works; only do not delay letting me know when the day is fixed for the publication of the pianoforte arrangement. For to-day, I only further earnestly recommend my affairs to your care; I shall be equally at your service at any time. Farewell, dear Ries.

Your friend,
BEETHOVEN.

[Footnote 1: "This is also to be the title of the pianoforte arrangement." (Note by Beethoven.)]

163.
TO ZMESKALL.

Jan. 1816.

MY GOOD ZMESKALL,--

I was shocked to discover to-day that I had omitted replying to a proposal from the "Society of Friends to Music in the Austrian States" to write an Oratorio for them.

The death of my brother two months ago, which, owing to the guardianship of my nephew having devolved on me, has involved me in all sorts of annoyances and perplexities, has caused this delay in my answer. In the mean time, the poem of Herr van Seyfried is already begun, and I purpose shortly to set it to music. I need not tell you how very flattering I consider such a commission, for how could I think otherwise? and I shall endeavor to acquit myself as honorably as my poor talents will admit of.

With regard to our artistic resources, when the time for the performance arrives I shall certainly take into consideration those usually at our disposal, without, however, strictly limiting myself to them. I hope I have made myself clearly understood on this point. As I am urged to say what gratuity I require in return, I beg to know whether the Society will consider 400 gold ducats a proper remuneration for such a work? I once more entreat the forgiveness of the Society for the delay in my answer, but I am in some degree relieved by knowing that, at all events, you, my dear friend, have already verbally apprised the Society of my readiness to write a work of the kind.[1]

Ever, my worthy Z., your
BEETHOVEN.

[Footnote 1: In the *Fischof'sche Handschrift* we are told:--"The allusion to 'our artistic resources' requires some explanation. Herr v. Zmeskall had at that time received instructions to give a hint to the great composer (who paid little regard to the difficulty of executing his works) that he must absolutely take into consideration the size of the orchestra, which at grand concerts amounted to 700 performers. The Society only stipulated for the exclusive right to the work for one year, and did not purchase the copyright; they undertook the gratuity for the poem also, so they were obliged to consult their pecuniary resources, and informed the composer that they were prepared to give him 200 gold ducats for the use of the work for a year, as they had proposed. Beethoven was quite satisfied, and made no objection whatever; he received an advance on this sum according to his own wish, the receipt of which he acknowledged in 1819. Beethoven rejected the first poem selected, and desired to have another. The Society left his choice quite free. Herr Bernhard undertook to supply a new one. Beethoven and he consulted together in choosing the subject, but Herr Bernhard, overburdened by other business, could only send the poem bit by bit. Beethoven, however, would not begin till the whole was in his hands."]

164.
TO MDLLE. MILDER-HAUPTMANN.[1]

Vienna, Jan. 6, 1816.

MY HIGHLY VALUED MDLLE. MILDER, MY DEAR FRIEND,--

I have too long delayed writing to you. How gladly would I personally participate in the enthusiasm you excite at Berlin in "Fidelio!" A thousand thanks on my part for having so faithfully adhered to *my* "Fidelio." If you will ask Baron de la Motte-Fouqué, in my name, to discover a good subject for an opera, and one suitable likewise to yourself, you will do a real service both to me and to the German stage; it is also my wish to write it expressly for the *Berlin Theatre*, as no new opera can ever succeed in being properly given here under this very penurious direction. Answer me soon, very soon--quickly, very quickly--as quickly as possible--as quick as lightning--and say whether such a thing is practicable. Herr Kapellmeister B. praised you up to the skies to me, and he is right; well may he esteem himself happy who has the privilege of enjoying your muse, your genius, and all your splendid endowments and talents;--it is thus I feel. Be this as it may, those around can only call themselves your fellow-creatures [Nebenmann], whereas I alone have a right to claim the honored name of captain [*Hauptmann*].

In my secret heart, your true friend and admirer,
BEETHOVEN.

My poor unfortunate brother is dead, which has been the cause of my long silence. As soon as you have replied to this letter, I will write myself to Baron de la Motte-Fouqué. No doubt your influence in Berlin will easily obtain for me a commission to write a grand opera (in which you shall be especially studied) on favorable terms; but do answer me soon, that I may arrange my other occupations accordingly.

Away with all other false *Hauptmänner*! [captains.]

[Footnote 1: Mdlle. Milder married Hauptmann, a jeweller in Munich, in 1810, travelled in 1812, and was engaged at Berlin in 1816.]

165.
TO RIES

Vienna, Jan. 20, 1816.

DEAR RIES,--

The Symphony is to be dedicated to the Empress of Russia. The pianoforte score of the Symphony in A must not, however, appear before June, for the publisher here cannot be ready sooner. Pray, dear Ries, inform Mr. Birchall of this at once. The Sonata with violin accompaniment, which will be sent from here by the next post, can likewise be published in London in May, but the Trio at a later date (it follows by the next post); I will myself name the time for its publication. And now, dear Ries, pray receive my heartfelt thanks for your kindness, and especially for the corrections of the proofs. May Heaven bless you more and more, and promote your progress, in which I take the most sincere interest. My kind regards to your wife. Now as ever,

Your sincere friend,
LUDWIG VAN BEETHOVEN.

166.
TO MR. BIRCHALL,--LONDON.

Vienne, le 3. Febr. den 1816

VOUS RECEUES CI JOINT--

Le grand Trio p. Pf. V. et Vllo. Sonata pour Pf. et Violin--qui form le reste de ce qu'il vous a plus à me comettre. Je vous prie de vouloir payer la some de 130 Ducats d'Holland come le poste lettre a Mr. Th. Cutts et Co. de votre ville e de me croire avec toute l'estime et consideration

Votre tres humble Serviteur,
LOUIS VAN BEETHOVEN.

167.
TO CZERNY.[1]

MY DEAR CZERNY,--

Pray give the enclosed to your parents for the dinners the boy had recently at your house; I positively will not accept these *gratis*. Moreover, I am very far from wishing that your lessons should remain without remuneration,--even those already given must be reckoned up and paid for; only I beg you to have a little patience for a time, as nothing can be *demanded* from the widow, and I had and still have heavy expenses to defray;--but I *borrow* from you for the moment only. The boy is to be with you to-day, and I shall come later.

Your friend,
BEETHOVEN.

[Footnote 1: Carl Czerny, the celebrated pianist and composer, for whom Beethoven wrote a testimonial in 1805 (see No. 42). He gave lessons to Beethoven's nephew in 1815, and naturally protested against any payment, which gave rise to the expressions on the subject in many of his notes to Czerny, of which there appear to be a great number.]

168.
TO CZERNY.[1]

Vienna, Feb. 12, 1816.

DEAR CZERNY,--

I cannot see you to-day, but I will call to-morrow being desirous to talk to you. I spoke out so bluntly yesterday that I much regretted it afterwards. But you must forgive this on the part of an author, who would have preferred hearing his work as he wrote it, however charmingly you played it. I will, however, *amply* atone for this by the violoncello Sonata.[2]

Rest assured that I cherish the greatest regard for you as an artist, and I shall always endeavor to prove this.

Your true friend,
BEETHOVEN.

[Footnote 1: Czerny, in the *A.M. Zeitung*, 1845, relates:--"On one occasion (in 1812), at Schuppanzigh's concert, when playing Beethoven's quintet with wind-instruments, I took the liberty, in my youthful levity, to make many alterations,--such as introducing difficulties into the passages, making use of the upper octaves, &c., &c. Beethoven sternly and deservedly reproached me for this, in the presence of Schuppanzigh, Linke, and the other performers."]

[Footnote 2: Opera 69, which Czerny (see *A.M. Zeitung*) was to perform with Linke the following week.]

169.
TO RIES,--LONDON.

Vienna, Feb. 28, 1816.

... For some time past I have been far from well; the loss of my brother affected both my spirits and my works. Salomon's death grieves me much, as he was an excellent man whom I have known from my childhood. You are his executor by will, while I am the guardian of my late poor brother's child. You can scarcely have had as much vexation from Salomon's death as I have had from that of my brother!--but I have the sweet consolation of having rescued a poor innocent child from the hands of an unworthy mother. Farewell, dear Ries; if I can in any way serve you, look on me as

Your true friend,
BEETHOVEN.

170.
TO GIANNATASIO DEL RIO,--VIENNA.

Feb. 1816.

SIR,--

I have great pleasure in saying that at last I intend to-morrow to place under your care the dear pledge intrusted to me. But I must impress on you not to permit any influence on the mother's part to decide when and where she is to see her son. We can, however, discuss all this more minutely to-morrow.... You must keep a watchful eye on your servant, for mine was *bribed by her* on one occasion. More as to this verbally, though it is a subject on which I would fain be silent; but the future welfare of the youth you are to train renders this unpleasant communication necessary. I remain, with esteem,

Your faithful servant and friend,
BEETHOVEN.

171.
TO G. DEL RIO.

1816.

Your estimable lady, Mdme. A.G. [Giannatasio] is politely requested to let the undersigned know as soon as possible (that I may not be obliged to keep it all in my head) how many pairs of stockings, trousers, shoes, and drawers are required, and how many yards of kerseymere to make a pair of black trousers for my tall nephew; and for the sake of the "Castalian Spring" I beg, without any further reminders on my part, that I may receive an answer to this.

As for the Lady Abbess [a nickname for their only daughter], there shall be a conference held on Carl's affair to-night, viz., if things are to continue as they are.

Your well (and ill) born
BEETHOVEN.

172.
TO G. DEL RIO.

1816.

I heard yesterday evening, unluckily at too late an hour, that you had something to give me; had it not been for this, I would have called on you. I beg, however, that you will send it, as I have no doubt it is a letter for me from the "Queen of the Night."[1] Although you gave me permission to fetch Carl twice already, I must ask you to let him come to me when I send for him at eleven o'clock to-morrow, as I wish to take him with me to hear some interesting music. It is also my intention to make him play to me to-morrow, as it is now some time since I heard him. I hope you will urge him to study more closely than usual to-day, that he may in some degree make up for his holiday. I embrace you cordially, and remain,

Yours truly,
LUDWIG VAN BEETHOVEN.

[Footnote 1: The "Queen of the Night" was the name given to Carl's mother by Beethoven. She was a person of great levity of conduct and bad reputation, and every effort was made by Beethoven to withdraw her son from her influence, on which account he at once removed him from her care, and placed him in this institution. She consequently appealed to the law against him,--the first step in a long course of legal proceedings of the most painful nature.]

173.
TO G. DEL RIO.[1]

1816.

I send you, dear sir, the cloak, and also a school-book of my Carl's, and request you will make out a list of his clothes and effects, that I may have it copied for myself, being obliged, as his guardian, to look carefully after his property. I intend to call for Carl to-morrow about half-past twelve o'clock, to take him to a little concert, and wish him to dine with me afterwards, and shall bring him back myself. With respect to his mother, I desire that *under the pretext* of the boy being *so busy*, you will not let her see him; no man on earth can know or judge of this matter better than myself, and by any other line of conduct all my well-matured plans for the welfare of the child might be materially injured. I will myself discuss with you when the mother is henceforth to have access to Carl, for I am anxious on every account to prevent the occurrence of yesterday ever being repeated. I take all the responsibility on myself; indeed, so far as I am concerned, the Court conferred on me full powers, and the authority at once to counteract anything adverse to the welfare of the boy. If they could have looked on her in the light of an estimable mother, they assuredly would not have excluded her from the guardianship of her child. Whatever she may think fit to assert, nothing has been done in a clandestine manner against her. There was but one voice in the whole council on the subject. I hope to have no further trouble in this matter, for the burden is already heavy enough.

From a conversation I had yesterday with Adlersburg [his lawyer], it would appear that a long time must yet elapse before the Court can decide what really belongs to the child. In addition to all these anxieties am I also to endure a persecution such as I have recently experienced, and from which I thought I *was entirely rescued by your Institution*? Farewell!

I am, with esteem, your obedient
L. V. BEETHOVEN.

[Footnote 1: Beethoven's arbitrary authority had been previously sanctioned by a decree of the Court, and the mother deprived of all power over her son.]

174.
TO FERDINAND RIES,--LONDON.

Vienna, March 8, 1816.

My answer has been too long delayed; but I was ill, and had a great press of business. Not a single farthing is yet come of the ten gold ducats, and I now almost begin to think that the English are only liberal when in foreign countries. It is the same with the Prince Regent, who has not even sent me the cost of copying my "Battle Symphony," nor one verbal or written expression of thanks. My whole income consists of 3400 florins in paper-money. I pay 1100 for house-rent, and 900 to my servant and his wife; so you may reckon for yourself what remains. Besides this, the entire maintenance of my young nephew devolves on me. At present he is at school, which costs 1100 florins, and is by no means a good one; so that I must arrange a proper household and have him with me. How much money must be made to live at all here! and yet there seems no end to it--because!--because!--because!--but you know well what I mean.

Some commissions from the Philharmonic would be very acceptable to me, besides, the concert. Now let me say that my dear scholar Ries must set to work and dedicate something valuable to me, to which his master may respond, and repay him in his own coin. How can I send you my portrait? My kind regards to your wife. I, alas! have none. One alone I wished to possess, but never shall I call her mine![1] This, however, has not made me a woman-hater.

Your true friend,
BEETHOVEN.

[Footnote 1: See the statement of Fräulein del Rio in the *Grenzboten*. We read:--"My father's idea was that marriage alone could remedy the sad condition of Beethoven's household matters; so he asked him whether he knew any one, &c., &c. Our long-existing presentiment was then realized." His love was unfortunate. Five years ago he had become acquainted with a person with whom he would have esteemed it the highest felicity of his life to have entered into closer ties; but it was vain to think of it, being almost an impossibility! a chimera! and yet his feelings remained the same as the very first day he had seen her! He added, "that never before had he found such harmony! but no declaration had ever been made, not being able to prevail on himself to do so." This conversation took place in Sept. 1816, at Helenenthal, in Baden, and the person to whom he alluded was undoubtedly Marie L. Pachler-Koschak in Gratz. (See No. 80.)]

175.
TO F. RIES.

Vienna, April 3, 1816.

Neate[1] is no doubt in London by this time. He took several of my works with him, and promised to do the best he could for me.

The Archduke Rudolph [Beethoven's pupil, see No. 70] also plays your works with me, my dear Ries; of these "Il Sogno" especially pleased us. Farewell! Remember me to your charming wife, and to any fair English ladies who care to receive my greetings.

Your true friend,
BEETHOVEN.

[Footnote 1: Charles Neate, a London artist, as Schindler styles him in his *Biography* (II. 254), was on several different occasions for some time resident in Vienna, and very intimate with Beethoven, whom he tried to persuade to come to London. He also was of great service in promoting the sale of his works. A number of Neate's letters, preserved in the Berlin State Library, testify his faithful and active devotion and attachment to the master.]

176.
POWER OF ATTORNEY.

Vienna, May 2, 1816.

I authorize Herr v. Kauka, Doctor of Laws in the kingdom of Bohemia, relying on his friendship, to obtain for me the receipt of 600 florins W.W., payable at the treasury of Prince Kinsky, from the house of Ballabene in Prague, and after having drawn the money to transmit the same to me as soon as possible.

Witness my hand and seal.
LUDWIG VAN BEETHOVEN.

177.
TO F. RIES.

Vienna, June 11, 1816.

MY DEAR RIES,--

I regret much to put you to the expense of postage on my account; gladly as I assist and serve every one, I am always unwilling myself to have recourse to others. I have as yet seen nothing of the ten ducats, whence I draw the inference that in England, just as with us, there are idle talkers who prove false to their word. I do not at all blame you in this matter. I have not heard a syllable from Neate; so I do wish you would ask him whether he has disposed of the F minor Concerto. I am almost ashamed to allude to the other works I intrusted to him, and equally so of myself, for having given them to him so confidingly, devoid of all conditions save those suggested by his own friendship and zeal for my interests.

A translation has been sent to me of an article in the "Morning Chronicle" on the performance of the Symphony. Probably it will be the same as to this and all the other works Neate took with him as with the "Battle Symphony;" the only profit I shall derive will be reading a notice of their performance in the newspapers.

178.
TO G. DEL RIO.

1816.

MY WORTHY G.,--

I beg you will send Carl to me with the bearer of this letter; otherwise I shall not be able to see him all day, which would be contrary to his own interest, as my influence seems to be required; in the same view, I beg you will give him a few lines with a report of his conduct, so that I may enter at once on any point where improvement is necessary.

I am going to the country to-day, and shall not return till rather late at night; being always unwilling to infringe your rules, I beg you will send some night-things with Carl, so that if we return too late to bring him to you to-day, I can keep him all night, and take him back to you myself early next morning.

In haste, always yours,
L. V. BEETHOVEN.

179.
TO G. DEL RIO.

1816.

I must apologize to you, my good friend, for Carl having come home at so late an hour. We were obliged to wait for a person who arrived so late that it detained us, but I will not soon repeat this breach of your rules. As to Carl's mother, I have now decided that your wish not to see her again in your house shall be acceded to. This course is far more safe and judicious for our dear Carl, experience having taught me that every visit from his mother leaves a root of bitterness in the boy's heart, which may injure, but never can benefit him. I shall strive to arrange occasional meetings at my house, which is likely to result in everything being entirely broken off with her. As we thoroughly agree on the subject of Carl's mother, we can mutually decide on the mode of his education.

Your true friend,
BEETHOVEN.

180.
TO THE ARCHDUKE RUDOLPH.

Vienna, July 11, 1816.

Your kindness towards me induces me to hope that you will not attribute to any *selfish* design on my part the somewhat audacious (though only as to the surprise) dedication annexed. The work[1] was written for Y.R.H., or rather, it owes its existence to you, and this the world (the musical world) ought to know. I shall soon have the honor of waiting on Y.R.H. in Baden. Notwithstanding all the efforts of my physician, who will not allow me to leave this, the weakness in my chest is no better, though my general health is improved. I hope to hear all that is cheering of your own health, about which I am always so much interested.

[K.]

[Footnote 1: Does Beethoven here allude to the dedication of the Sonata for pianoforte and violin in G major, Op. 96, which, though sold to a publisher in April, 1815, was designated as quite new in the *Allgemeine Zeitung* on July, 29, 1816?]

181.
WRITTEN IN ENGLISH TO MR. BIRCHALL.

1816.

Received, March, 1816, of Mr. Robert Birchall, music-seller, 133 New Bond Street, London, the sum of one hundred and thirty gold Dutch ducats, value in English currency sixty-five pounds, for all my copyright and interest, present and future, vested or contingent, or otherwise within the United kingdom of Great Britain and Ireland in the four following compositions or pieces of music composed or arranged by me, viz.:--

1st. A Grand Battle Sinfonia, descriptive of the battle and victory at Vittoria, adapted for the pianoforte and dedicated to his Royal Highness the Prince Regent--40 ducats.

2d. A Grand Symphony in the key of A, adapted to the pianoforte and dedicated to--

3d. A Grand Trio for the pianoforte, violin, and violoncello in the key of B.

4th. A Sonata for the pianoforte, with an accompaniment for the violin in the key of G, dedicated to--

And, in consideration of such payment I hereby, for myself, my executors, and administrators, promise and engage to execute a proper anignment thereof to him, his executors and administrators or anignees, at his or their request and costs, as he or they shall direct. And I likewise promise and engage as above, that none of the above shall be published in any foreign country, before the time and day fixed and agreed on for such publication between R. Birchall and myself shall arrive.

L. VAN BEETHOVEN.

182.
WRITTEN IN FRENCH TO MR. BIRCHALL,--LONDON.

Vienne 22. Juilliet, 1816.

MONSIEUR,--

J'ai reçu la déclaration de proprieté de mes Oeuvres entierement cedé a Vous pour y adjoindre ma Signature. Je suis tout a fait disposer a seconder vos voeux si tôt, que cette affaire sera entierement en ordre, en egard de la petite somme de 10 # d'or la quelle me vient encore pour le fieux de la Copieture de poste de lettre etc. comme j'avois l'honneur de vous expliquier dans une note detaillé sur ses objectes. Je vous invite donc Monsieur de bien vouloir me remettre ces petits objects, pour me mettre dans l'état de pouvoir vous envoyer le Document susdit. Agrées Monsieur l'assurance de l'estime la plus parfait avec la quelle j'ai l'honneur de me dire

LOUIS VAN BEETHOVEN.

```
Copying   ....    1. 10. 0.
Postage to Amsterdam 1. 0. 0.
 ---- Trio ...    2. 10. --
                 -----------
                  £5. 0. 0.
```

183.
TO G. DEL RIO.

July 28, 1816.

MY GOOD FRIEND,--

Various circumstances compel me to take charge of Carl myself; with this view permit me to enclose you the amount due at the approaching quarter, at the expiry of which Carl is to leave you. Do not, I beg, ascribe this to anything derogatory either to yourself or to your respected institution, but to other pressing motives connected with Carl's welfare. It is only an experiment, and when it is actually carried out I shall beg you to fortify me by your advice, and also to permit Carl sometimes to visit your institution. I shall always feel the most sincere gratitude to you, and never can forget your solicitude, and the kind care of your excellent wife, which has fully equalled that of the best of mothers. I would send you at least four times the sum I now do, if my position admitted of it; but at all events I shall avail myself at a future and, I hope, a brighter day, of every opportunity to acknowledge and to do justice to the foundation *you* have laid for the moral and physical good of my Carl. With regard to the "Queen of the Night," our system must continue the same; and as Carl is about to undergo an operation in your house which will cause him to feel indisposed, and consequently make him irritable and susceptible, you must be more careful than ever to prevent her having access to him; otherwise she might easily contrive to revive all those impressions in his mind which we are so anxious to avoid. What confidence can be placed in any promise to reform on her part, the impertinent scrawl I enclose will best prove [in reference, no doubt, to an enclosed note]. I send it merely to show you how fully I am justified in the precautions I have already adopted with regard to her. On this occasion, however, I did not answer like a Sarastro, but like a Sultan. I would gladly spare you the anxiety of the operation on Carl, but as it must take place in your house, I beg you will inform me of the outlay caused by the affair, and the expenses consequent on it, which I will thankfully repay. Now farewell! Say all that is kind from me to your dear children and your excellent wife, to whose continued care I commend my Carl. I leave Vienna to-morrow at five o'clock A.M., but shall frequently come in from Baden.

Ever, with sincere esteem, your
L. V. BEETHOVEN.

184.
TO G. DEL RIO.

Mdme. A.G. is requested to order several pairs of good linen drawers for Carl. I intrust Carl to her kindness, and entirely rely on her motherly care.

185.
TO ZMESKALL.

Baden, September 5, 1816.

DEAR Z.,--

I don't know whether you received a note that I recently left on the threshold of your door, for the time was too short to enable me to see you. I must therefore repeat my request about another servant, as the conduct of my present one is such that I cannot possibly keep him.[1] He was engaged on the 25th of April, so on the 25th of September he will have been five months with me, and he received 50 florins on account. The money for his boots will be reckoned from the third month (in my service), and from that time at the rate of 40 florins per annum; his livery also from the third month. From the very first I resolved not to keep him, but delayed discharging him, as I wished to get back the value of my florins. In the mean time if I can procure another, I will let this one leave my service on the 15th of the month, and also give him 20 florins for boot money, and 5 florins a month for livery (both reckoned from the third month), making altogether 35 florins. I ought therefore still to receive 15 florins, but these I am willing to give up; in this way I shall at all events receive some equivalent for my 50 florins. If you can find a suitable person, I will give him 2 florins a day while I am in Baden, and if he knows how to cook he can use my firewood in the kitchen. (I have a kitchen, though I do not cook in it.) If not, I will add a few kreutzers to his wages. As soon as I am settled in Vienna, he shall have 40 florins a month, and board and livery as usual, reckoned from the third month in my service, like other servants. It would be a good thing if he understood a little tailoring. So now you have my proposals, and I beg for an answer by the 10th of this month at the latest, that I may discharge my present servant on the 2d, with the usual fortnight's warning; otherwise I shall be obliged to keep him for another month, and every moment I wish to get rid of him. As for the new one, you know pretty well what I require,--*good, steady conduct*, a *good character*, and *not to be of a bloodthirsty nature*, that I may feel my life to be safe, as, for the sake of various scamps in this world, I should like to live a little longer. By the 10th, therefore, I shall expect to hear from you on this affair. If you don't run restive, I will soon send you my treatise on the four violoncello strings, very profoundly handled; the first chapter devoted exclusively to entrails in general, the second to catgut in particular. I need scarcely give you any further warnings, as you seem to be quite on your guard against wounds inflicted before certain fortresses. The most *profound peace* everywhere prevails!!! Farewell, my good *Zmeskällchen*! I am, as ever, *un povero musico* and your friend,

BEETHOVEN.

N.B. I shall probably only require my new servant for some months, as, for the sake of my Carl, I must shortly engage a housekeeper.

[Footnote 1: During a quarrel, the servant scratched Beethoven's face.]

186.
TO HERR KAUKA.

Baden, Sept. 6, 1816.

MY WORTHY K.,--

I send you herewith the receipt, according to your request, and beg that you will kindly arrange that I should have the money by the 1st October, and without any deduction, which has hitherto been the case; I also particularly beg *you will not assign the money to Baron P.* (I will tell you why when we meet; for the present let this remain between ourselves.) Send it either direct to myself, or, if it must come through another person, do not let it be Baron P. It would be best for the future, as the house-rent is paid here for the great house belonging to Kinsky, that my money should be paid at the same time. This is only my own idea. The Terzet you heard of will soon be engraved, which is infinitely preferable to all written music; you shall therefore receive an engraved copy, and likewise some more of my unruly offspring. In the mean time I beg that you will see only what is truly good in them, and look with an indulgent eye on the human frailties of these poor innocents. Besides, I am full of cares, being in reality father to my late brother's child; indeed I might have ushered into the world a second part of the "Flauto Magico," having also been brought into contact with a "Queen of the Night." I embrace you from my heart, and hope soon in so far to succeed that you may owe some thanks to my Muse. My dear, worthy Kauka, I ever am your truly attached friend,

BEETHOVEN.

187.
QUERY?

What would be the result were I to leave this, and indeed the kingdom of Austria altogether? Would the life-certificate, if signed by the authorities of a non-Austrian place, still be valid?

A tergo.

I beg you will let me know the postage all my letters have cost you.

188.
TO G. DEL RIO.

Sunday, September 22, 1816.

Certain things can never be fully expressed. Of this nature are my feelings, and especially my gratitude, on hearing the details of the operation on Carl from you. You will excuse my attempting even remotely to shape these into words. I feel certain, however, that you will not decline the tribute I gladly pay you; but I say no more. You can easily imagine my anxiety to hear how my dear son is going on; do not omit to give me your exact address, that I may write to you direct. After you left this I wrote to Bernhard [Bernard], to make inquiries at your house, but have not yet got an answer; so possibly you may have thought me a kind of half-reckless barbarian, as no doubt Herr B. has neglected to call on you, as well as to write to me. I can have no uneasiness about Carl when your admirable wife is with him: that is quite out of the question. You can well understand how much it grieves me not to be able to take part in the sufferings of my Carl, and that I at least wish to hear frequently of his progress. As I have renounced such an unfeeling, unsympathizing friend as Herr B. [Bernard], I must have recourse to your friendship and complaisance on this point also, and shall hope soon to receive a few lines from you. I beg to send my best regards and a thousand thanks to your admirable wife.

In haste, your
BEETHOVEN.

I wish you to express to Smetana [the surgeon] my esteem and high consideration.

189.
TO G. DEL RIO.

If you do not object, I beg you will allow Carl to come to me with the bearer of this. I forgot, in my haste, to say that all the love and goodness which Mdme. A.G. [Giannatasio] showed my Carl during his illness are inscribed in the list of my obligations, and I hope one day to show that they are ever present in my mind. Perhaps I may see you to-day with Carl.

In haste, your sincere friend,
L. V. BEETHOVEN.

190.
TO WEGELER.

I take the opportunity through J. Simrock to remind you of myself. I hope you received the engraving of me [by Letronne], and likewise the Bohemian glass. When I next make a pilgrimage through Bohemia you shall have something more of the same kind. Farewell! You are a husband and a father; so am I, but without a wife. My love to your dear ones--to *our* dear ones.

Your friend,
L. V. BEETHOVEN.

191.
WRITTEN IN ENGLISH TO MR. BIRCHALL, MUSIC SELLER, LONDON.

Vienna, 1. Oct. 1816.

MY DEAR SIR,--

I have duly received the £5 and thought previously you would non increase the number of Englishmen neglecting their word and honor, as I had the misfortune of meeting with two of this sort. In replic to the other topics of your favor, I have no objection to write variations according to your plan, and I hope you will not find £30 too much, the Accompaniment will be a Flute or Violin or a Violoncello; you'll either decide it when you send me the approbation of the price, or you'll leave it to me. I expect to receive the songs or poetry--the sooner the better, and you'll favor me also with the probable number of Works of Variations you are inclined to receive of me. The Sonata in G with the accompan't of a Violin to his Imperial Highnesse Archduke Rodolph of Austria--it is Op'a 96. The Trio in Bb is dedicated to the same and is Op. 97. The Piano arrangement of the Symphony in A is dedicated to the Empress of the Russians--meaning the Wife of the Emp'r Alexander--Op. 98.

Concerning the expences of copying and packing it is not possible to fix him before hand, they are at any rate not considerable, and you'll please to consider that you have to deal with a man of honor, who will not charge one 6p. more than he is charged for himself. Messrs. Fries & Co. will account with Messrs. Coutts & Co.--The postage may be lessened as I have been told. I offer you of my Works the following new ones. A Grand Sonata for the Pianoforte alone £40. A Trio for the Piano with accomp't of Violin and Violoncello for £50. It is possible that somebody will offer you other works of mine to purchase, for ex. the score of the Grand Symphony in A.--With regard to the arrangement of this Symphony for the Piano I beg you not to forget that you are not to publish it until I have appointed the day of its publication here in Vienna. This cannot be otherwise without making myself guilty of a dishonorable act--but the Sonata with the Violin and the Trio in B fl. may be published without any delay.

With all the *new works*, which you will have of me or which I offer you, it rests with you to name the day of their publication at your own choice: I entreat you to honor me as soon as possible with an answer having many ordres for compositions and that you may not be delayed. My address or direction is

Monsieur Louis van Beethoven

No. 1055 & 1056 Sailerstette 3d. Stock. Vienna.

You may send your letter, if you please, direct to your most humble servant

LUDWIG VAN BEETHOVEN.

192.
TO ZMESKALL.

Oct. 24, 1816.

WELL BORN, AND YET EVIL BORN! (AS WE ALL ARE!)

We are in Baden to-day, and intend to bring the celebrated naturalist Ribini a collection of dead leaves. To-morrow we purpose paying you not only a *visit* but a *visitation*.

Your devoted
LUDWIG VAN BEETHOVEN.

193.
TO THE ARCHDUKE RUDOLPH.

November, 1816.[1]

I have been again much worse, so that I can only venture to go out a little in the daytime; I am, however, getting better, and hope now to have the honor of waiting on Y.R.H. three times a week.

Meanwhile, I have many and great cares in these terrible times (which surpass anything we have ever experienced), and which are further augmented by having become the father since last November of a poor orphan. All this tends to retard my entire restoration to health. I wish Y.R.H. all imaginable good and happiness, and beg you will graciously receive and not misinterpret

Your, &c., &c.
[K.]

[Footnote 1: A year after Carl von Beethoven's death (Nov. 15, 1815).]

194.
TO FREIHERR VON SCHWEIGER.

BEST!
MOST AMIABLE!
FIRST AND FOREMOST TURNER MEISTER OF EUROPE!

The bearer of this is a poor devil! (like many another!!!) You could assist him by asking your gracious master whether he is disposed to purchase one of his small but neat pianos. I also beg you will recommend him to any of the Chamberlains or Adjutants of the Archduke Carl, to see whether it is possible that H.R.H. would buy one of these instruments for his Duchess. We therefore request an introduction from the illustrious *Turner Meister* for this poor devil[1] to the Chamberlains and Adjutants of the household.

Likewise
1
poor devil,
[K.] L. V. BEETHOVEN.

[Footnote 1: A name cannot now be found for the "poor devil."]

195.
TO G. DEL RIO.

Nov. 16, 1816.

MY DEAR FRIEND,--

My household seems about to make shipwreck, or something very like it. You know that I was duped into taking this house on false pretexts; besides, my health does not seem likely to improve in a hurry. To engage a tutor under such circumstances, whose character and whose very exterior even are unknown to me, and thus to intrust my Carl's education to hap-hazard, is quite out of the question, no matter how great the sacrifices which I shall be again called on to make. I beg you, therefore, to keep Carl for the ensuing quarter, commencing on the 9th. I will in so far comply with your proposal as to the cultivation of the science of music, that Carl may come to me two or three times a week, leaving you at six o'clock in the evening and staying with me till the following morning, when he can return to you by eight o'clock. It would be too fatiguing for Carl to come every day, and indeed too great an effort and tie for me likewise, as the lessons must be given at the same fixed hour.

During this quarter we can discuss more minutely the most suitable plan for Carl, taking into consideration both his interests and my own. I must, alas! mention my own also in these times, which are daily getting worse. If your garden residence had agreed with my health, everything might have been easily adjusted. With regard to my debt to you for the present quarter, I beg you will be so obliging as to call on me, that I may discharge it; the bearer of this has the good fortune to be endowed by Providence with a vast amount of stupidity, which I by no means grudge him the benefit of, provided others do not suffer by it. As to the remaining expenses incurred for Carl, either during his illness or connected with it, I must, for a few days only, request your indulgence, having great calls on me at present from all quarters. I wish also to know what fee I ought to give Smetana for the successful operation he performed; were I rich, or not in the same sad position in which all are who have linked their fate to this country (always excepting *Austrian usurers*), I would make no inquiries on the subject; and I only wish you to give me a rough estimate of the proper fee. Farewell! I cordially embrace you, and shall always look on you as a friend of mine and of Carl's.

I am, with esteem, your
L. V. BEETHOVEN.

196.
TO G. DEL RIO.

Though I would gladly spare you all needless disagreeable trouble, I cannot, unluckily, do so on this occasion. Yesterday, in searching for some papers, I found this pile, which has been sent to me respecting Carl. I do not quite understand them, and you would oblige me much by employing some one to make out a regular statement of all your outlay for Carl, so that I may send for it to-morrow. I hope you did not misunderstand me when I yesterday alluded to *magnanimity*, which certainly was not meant for you, but solely for the "Queen of the Night," who is never weary of hoisting the sails of her vindictiveness against me; so on this account I require vouchers, more for the satisfaction of others than for her sake (as I never will submit to render her any account of my actions). No stamp is required, and the sum alone for each quarter need be specified, for I believe most of the accounts are forthcoming; so all you have to do is to append them to your *prospectus* [the conclusion illegible].

L. V. BEETHOVEN.

197.
TO G. DEL RIO.

Nov. 14, 1816.

MY GOOD FRIEND,--

I beg you will allow Carl to come to me to-morrow, as it is the anniversary of his father's death [Nov. 15th], and we wish to visit his grave together. I shall probably come to fetch him between twelve and one o'clock. I wish to know the effect of my treatment of Carl, after your recent complaints. In the mean time, it touched me exceedingly to find him so susceptible as to his honor. Before we left your house I gave him some hints on his want of industry, and while walking together in a graver mood than usual, he pressed my hand vehemently, but met with no response from me. At dinner he scarcely eat anything, and said that he felt very melancholy, the cause of which I could not extract from him. At last, in the course of our walk, he owned that *he was vexed because he had not been so industrious as usual*. I said what I ought on the subject, but in a kinder manner than before. This, however, proves a certain delicacy of feeling, and such *traits* lead me to augur all that is good. If I cannot come to you to-morrow, I hope you will let me know by a few lines the result of my conference with Carl.

I once more beg you to let me have the account due for the last quarter. I thought that you had misunderstood my letter, or even worse than that. I warmly commend my poor orphan to your good heart, and, with kind regards to all, I remain

Your friend,
L. V. BEETHOVEN.

198.
TO G. DEL RIO.

MY GOOD FRIEND,--

Pray forgive me for having allowed the enclosed sum to be ready for you during the last twelve days or more, and not having sent it. I have been very much occupied, and am only beginning to recover, though indeed the word *recovery* has not yet been pronounced.

In haste, with much esteem, ever yours,
L. V. BEETHOVEN.

199.
TO HERR TSCHISCHKA.

SIR,--

It is certainly of some moment to me *not to appear in a false light*, which must account for the accompanying statement being so prolix. As to the future system of education, I can at all events congratulate myself on having done all that I could possibly effect at present *for the best*, and trust *that the future may be in accordance with it*. But if the welfare of my nephew demands a *change*, I shall be the first not only to propose such a step, but *to carry it out*. I am no self-interested guardian, but I wish to establish a new monument to my name through my nephew. I *have no need of my nephew*, but he has need of me. Idle talk and calumnies are beneath the dignity of a man with proper self-respect, and what can be said when these extend even to the subject of linen!!! This might cause me great annoyance, *but a just man ought to be able to bear injustice* without in the *most remote degree* deviating from the path of *right*. In this conviction I will stand fast, and nothing shall make me flinch. To deprive me of my nephew would indeed entail a heavy responsibility. As a matter of *policy* as well as of morality, such a step would be productive of evil results to my nephew. *I urgently recommend his interests to you.* As for me, *my actions* for *his* benefit (not for my *own*) must speak for me.

I remain, with esteem,
Your obedient
BEETHOVEN.

Being very busy, and rather indisposed, I must claim your indulgence for the writing of the memorial.

200.
WRITTEN IN ENGLISH TO MR. BIRCHALL,--LONDON.

Vienna 14. December 1816--1055 Sailerstette.

DEAR SIR,--

I give you my word of honor that I have signed and delivered the receipt to the home Fries and Co. some day last August, who as they say have transmitted it to Messrs. Coutts and Co. where you'll have the goodness to apply. Some error might have taken place that instead of Messrs. C. sending it to you they have been directed to keep it till fetched. Excuse this irregularity, but it is not my fault, nor had I ever the idea of withholding it from the circumstance of the £5 not being included. Should the receipt not come forth as Messrs. C., I am ready to sign any other, and you shall have it directly with return of post.

If you find Variations--in my style--too dear at £30, I will abate for the sake of your friendship one third--and you have the offer of such Variations as fixed in our former lettres for £20 each Air.

Please to publish the Symphony in A immediately--as well as the Sonata--and the Trio--they being ready here. The Grand Opera Fidelio is my work. The arrangement for the Pianoforte has been published here under my care, but the score of the Opera itself is not yet published. I have given a copy of the score to Mr. Neate under the seal of friendship and whom I shall direct to treat for my account in case an offer should present.

I anxiously hope your health is improving, give me leave to subscribe myself

Dear Sir
Your very obedient Serv.
LUDWIG VAN BEETHOVEN.

201.
TO ZMESKALL.

Dec. 16, 1816.

With this, dear Zmeskall, you will receive my friendly dedication [a stringed quartet, Op. 95], which may, I hope, serve as a pleasant memorial of our long-enduring friendship here; pray accept it as a proof of my esteem, and not merely as the extreme end of a thread long since spun out (for you are one of my earliest friends in Vienna).

Farewell! Beware of mouldering fortresses! for an attack on them will be more trying than on those in a better state of preservation! As ever,

Your friend,
BEETHOVEN.

N.B. When you have a moment's leisure, let me know the probable cost of a livery, without linen, but including hat and boots. Strange changes have come to pass in my house. The man is off to the devil, I am thankful to say, whereas his wife seems the more resolved to take root here.

202.
TO FRAU VON STREICHER--NÉE STEIN.

Dec. 28, 1816.

N---- ought to have given you the New Year's tickets yesterday, but it seems she did not do so. The day before I was occupied with Maelzel, whose business was pressing, as he leaves this so soon; otherwise you may be sure that I would have hurried up again to see you. Your dear kind daughter was with me yesterday, but I scarcely ever remember being so ill; my *precious servants* were occupied from seven o'clock till ten at night in trying to heat the stove. The bitter cold, particularly in my room, caused me a chill, and the whole of yesterday I could scarcely move a limb. All day I was coughing, and had the most severe headache I ever had in my life; so by six o'clock in the evening I was obliged to go to bed, where I still am, though feeling somewhat better. Your brother dined with me yesterday, and has shown me great kindness. You are aware that on the same day, the 27th of December, I discharged B. [Baberl]. I cannot endure either of these vile creatures; I wonder if Nany will behave rather better from the departure of her colleague? I doubt it--but in that case I shall send her *packing* without any ceremony. She is too uneducated for a housekeeper, indeed quite a *beast*; but the other, in spite of her pretty face, is even *lower than the beasts*. As the New Year draws near, I think five florins will be enough for Nany; I have not paid her the charge for *making her spencer*, on account of her *bad behavior to you*. The other certainly *deserves no New Year's gift*; besides, she has nine florins of mine on hand, and when she leaves I don't expect to receive more than four or five florins of that sum. I wish to have *your opinion about all this*. Pray accept my best wishes for your welfare, which are offered in all sincerity. I am your debtor in so many ways, that I really often feel quite ashamed. Farewell; I trust I may always retain your friendship.

Now, as ever, your friend,
L. V. BEETHOVEN.

203.
TO FRAU VON STREICHER.

I thank you for the interest you take in me. I am rather better, though to-day again I have been obliged to endure a great deal from Nany; but I shied half a dozen books at her head by way of a New Year's gift. We have stripped off the leaves (by sending off Baberl) and lopped off the branches, but we must extirpate the *roots*, till nothing is left but the actual soil.

204.
TO FRAU VON STREICHER.

Nany is not strictly *honest*, and an odiously stupid *animal* into the bargain. Such people must be managed not by *love* but by *fear*. I now see this clearly. Her account-book alone cannot show you everything clearly; you must often drop in unexpectedly at dinner-time, like an avenging angel, to see with your own eyes *what* we actually have. I never dine at home now, *unless* I have some friend as my guest, for I have no wish to pay as much for one person as would serve for four. I shall *now soon* have my dear son Carl with me, so economy is more necessary than ever. I cannot prevail on myself to go to you; I know you will forgive this. I am very sensitive, and not used to such things, so the less ought I to expose myself to them. In addition to twelve kreutzers for bread, Nany has a roll of white bread every morning. Is this usual?--and it is the same with the cook. A daily roll for breakfast comes to eighteen florins a year. *Farewell*, and *work well* for me. Mdlle. Nany is wonderfully changed for the better since I sent the half-dozen books at her head. Probably they chanced to come in collision with her *dull brain* or her *bad heart*; at all events, she now plays the part of a penitent swindler!!!

In haste, yours,
BEETHOVEN.

205.
TO FRAU VON STREICHER.

Nany yesterday took me to task in the vulgar manner usual with people of her *low class*, about my complaining to you; so she evidently knew that I had written to you on the subject. All the devilry began again yesterday morning, but I made short work of it by throwing the heavy arm-chair beside my bed at B.'s head, which procured me peace for the rest of the day. They always take their revenge on me when I write to you, or when they discover any communication between us.

I do thank Heaven that I everywhere find men who interest themselves in me; one of the *most distinguished Professors* in this University has in the kindest manner undertaken *all that concerns Carl's education*. If you happen to meet any of the Giannatasios at Czerny's, you had better *know nothing of what is going on about Carl*, and say that it is *contrary* to my *usual habit to disclose my plans, as when a project is told to others it is no longer exclusively your own*. They would like to interfere in the matter, and I do not choose that these *commonplace people should do so, both for* my *own sake and Carl's*. Over their portico is inscribed, in golden letters, "Educational Institution," whereas "*Non*-Educational Institution" would be more appropriate.

As for the servants, there is only *one voice* about their immorality, to which *all* the other annoyances here may be ascribed.

Pray receive my benediction in place of that of the Klosterneuburgers.[1]

In haste, your friend,
BEETHOVEN.

[Footnote 1: Frau von Streicher was at that time in Klosterneuburg.]

206.
TO FRAU VON STREICHER.

Judgment was executed to-day on the notorious criminal! She bore it nearly in the same spirit as Caesar did Brutus's dagger, except that in the former case truth formed the basis, while in hers only wicked malice. The kitchen-maid seems more handy than the former *ill-conducted beauty*; she no longer shows herself,--a sign that she does not expect a *good character* from me, though I really had some thoughts of giving her one. The kitchen-maid at first made rather a wry face about carrying wood, &c.

207.
TO THE ARCHDUKE RUDOLPH.

Last day of December, 1816.

I have been again obliged to keep my room ever since the Burgher concert,[1] and some time must no doubt elapse before I shall be able to dismiss all precautions as to my health. The year is about to close; and with this new year my warmest wishes are renewed for the welfare of Y.R.H.; but indeed these have neither beginning nor end with me, for every day I cherish the same aspirations for Y.R.H. If I may venture to add a wish for myself to the foregoing, it is, that I may daily thrive and prosper more in Y.R.H.'s good graces. The master will always strive not to be unworthy of the favor of his illustrious master and pupil.

[K.]

[Footnote 1: Beethoven directed his A major Symphony in the Burgher concert in the Royal Redoutensaal on the 25th December, 1816.]

208.
TO G. DEL RIO.

... As to his mother, she urgently requested to see Carl in my house. You have sometimes seen me tempted to place more confidence in her, and my feelings would lead me to guard against harshness towards her, especially as it is not in her power to injure Carl. But you may well imagine that to one usually so independent of others, the annoyances to which I am exposed through Carl are often utterly insupportable, and above all with regard to his mother; I am only too glad to hear nothing of her, which is the cause of my avoiding her name. With respect to Carl, I beg you will enforce the strictest discipline on him, and if he refuses to obey your orders or to do his duty, I trust you will at once *punish* him. Treat him as if he were your own child rather than a *mere pupil*, for I already told you that during his father's lifetime he only submitted to the discipline of blows, which was a bad system; still, such was the fact, and we must not forget it.

If you do not see much of me, pray ascribe it solely to the little inclination I have for society, which is sometimes more developed and sometimes less; and this you might attribute to a change in my feelings, but it is not so. What is good alone lives in my memory, and not what is painful. Pray impute therefore solely to these hard times my not more practically showing my gratitude to you on account of Carl. God, however, directs all things; so my position may undergo a favorable change, when I shall hasten to show you how truly I am, with sincere esteem, your grateful friend,

L. V. BEETHOVEN.

I beg you will read this letter to Carl.

209.
TO G. DEL RIO.

Carl must be at H.B.'s to-day before four o'clock; I must request you therefore to ask his professor to dismiss him at half-past three o'clock; if this cannot be managed he must not go into school at all. In the latter case, I will come myself and fetch him; in the former, I will meet him in the passage of the University. To avoid all confusion, I beg for an explicit answer as to what you settle. As you have been loudly accused of showing great party feeling, I will take Carl myself. If you do not see me, attribute it to my distress of mind, for I am now only beginning to feel the full force of this terrible incident.[1]

In haste, your
BEETHOVEN.

[Footnote 1: Probably the reversal of the first decree in the lawsuit with Carl's mother, who in order to procure a verdict more favorable to her claims, pointed out to the Austrian "Landrecht," where the lawsuit had been hitherto carried on, an error in their proceedings, the "Van," prefixed to Beethoven's name, having been considered by them a sign of nobility. Beethoven was cited to appear, and on the appointed day, pointing to his head and his heart, he said, "My nobility is here, and here." The proceedings were then transferred to the "magistrate," who was in universal bad odor from his mode of conducting his business.]

210.
TO G. DEL RIO.

The assertions of this wicked woman have made such a painful impression on me, that I cannot possibly answer every point to-day; to-morrow you shall have a detailed account of it all; but on no pretext whatever allow her to have access to Carl, and adhere to your rule that she is only to see him once a month. As she has been once this month already, she cannot come again till the next.

In haste, your
BEETHOVEN.

211.
TO HOFRATH VON MOSEL.

1817.

SIR,--

I sincerely rejoice that we take the same view as to the terms in use to denote the proper time in music which have descended to us from barbarous times. For example, what can be more irrational than the general term *allegro*, which only means *lively*; and how far we often are from comprehending the real time, so that the piece itself *contradicts the designation*. As for the four chief movements,--which are, indeed, far from possessing the truth or accuracy of the four cardinal points,--we readily agree *to dispense with them*, but it is quite another matter as to the words that indicate the character of the music; these we cannot consent to do away with, for while the time is, as it were, part and parcel of the piece, the *words denote the spirit in which it is conceived*.

So far as I am myself concerned, I have long purposed giving up those inconsistent terms *allegro, andante, adagio,* and *presto*; and Maelzel's metronome furnishes us with the best opportunity of doing so. I here *pledge* myself *no longer* to make use of them in any of my new compositions. It is another question whether we can by this means attain the necessary universal use of the metronome. I scarcely think we shall! I make no doubt that we shall be loudly proclaimed as *despots*; but if the cause itself were to derive benefit from this, it would at least be better than to incur the reproach of Feudalism! In our country, where music has become a national requirement, and where the use of the metronome must be enjoined on every village schoolmaster, the best plan would be for Maelzel to endeavor to sell a certain number of metronomes by subscription, at the present higher prices, and as soon as the number covers his expenses, he can sell the metronomes demanded by the national requirements at so cheap a rate, that we may certainly anticipate their *universal use* and *circulation*. Of course some persons must take the lead in giving an impetus to the undertaking. You may safely rely on my doing what is in my power, and I shall be glad to hear what post you mean to assign to me in the affair.

I am, sir, with esteem, your obedient
LUDWIG VAN BEETHOVEN.

212.
TO S.A. STEINER, MUSIC PUBLISHER,--VIENNA.

HIGHEST BORN! MOST ADMIRABLE! AND MARVELLOUS LIEUTENANT-GENERAL![1]

We beg you to give us bank-notes for twenty-four gold ducats at yesterday's rate of exchange, and to send them to us this evening or to-morrow, in order that we may forthwith *remit* and *transmit* them. I should be glad and happy if your trustworthy Adjutant were to bring me these, as I have something particular to say to him. He must forget all his resentment, like a good Christian; we acknowledge his merits and do not contest his demerits. In short, and once for all, we wish to see him. This evening would suit us best.

We have the honor to remain, most astounding Lieutenant-General! your devoted

GENERALISSIMUS.

[Footnote 1: Beethoven styled himself "Generalissimus," Herr A. Steiner "Lieutenant-General," and his partner, Tobias Haslinger, "Adjutant" and "Adjutant-General."]

213.
TO LIEUTENANT-GENERAL VON STEINER.--PRIVATE.

PUBLICANDUM,--

After due consideration, and by the advice of our Council, we have determined and decreed that henceforth on all our works published with German titles, the word *Pianoforte* is to be replaced by that of *Hammer Clavier*, and our worthy Lieutenant-General, his Adjutant, and all whom it may concern, are charged with the execution of this order.

Instead of Pianoforte--*Hammer Clavier*.

Such is our will and pleasure.

Given on the 23d of January, 1817, by the *Generalissimus*.

Manu propria.

214.
TO STEINER.

The following dedication occurred to me of my new Sonata:--

"Sonata for the Pianoforte,
or
Hammer Clavier.
Composed and dedicated to Frau Baronin Dorothea
Ertmann--née Graumann,
by
Ludwig van Beethoven."

If the title is already engraved, I have the two following proposals to make; viz., that I pay for one title--I mean that it should be at my expense, or reserved for another new sonata of mine, for which purpose the mines of the Lieutenant-General (or *pleno titulo*, Lieutenant-General and First Councillor of State) must be opened to usher it into the light of day; the title to be previously shown to a good linguist. *Hammer Clavier* is certainly German, and so is the device. Honor to whom honor is due! How is it, then, that I have as yet received no reports of the carrying out of my orders, which, however, have no doubt been attended to?

Ever and always your attached
Amicus
ad Amicum
de Amico.

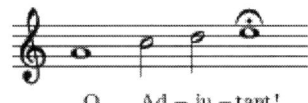

N.B. I beg you will observe the most profound silence about the dedication, as I wish it to be a surprise!

215.
TO ZMESKALL.

Jan. 30, 1817.

DEAR Z.,--

You seem to place me on a level with Schuppanzigh, &c., and have distorted the plain and simple meaning of my words. You are not my debtor, but I am yours, and now you make me so more than ever. I cannot express to you the pain your gift has caused me, and I must candidly say that I cannot give you one friendly glance *in return*. Although you confine yourself to the practice of music, still you have often recourse to the power of imagination, and it seems to me that this not unfrequently leads to uncalled-for caprice on your part; at least, so it appeared to me from your letter after my dedication. Loving as my sentiments are towards you, and much as I prize all your goodness, still I feel provoked!--much provoked!--terribly provoked!

Your debtor afresh,
Who will, however, contrive to have his revenge,
L. VAN BEETHOVEN.

VOL. II

BEETHOVEN'S LETTERS.

216.
TO STEINER & CO.

The Adjutant's innocence is admitted, and there is an end of it!

We beg you to be so good as to send us two copies in score of the Symphony in A. We likewise wish to know when we may expect a copy of the Sonata for Baroness von Ertmann, as she leaves this, most probably, the day after to-morrow.

No. 3--I mean the enclosed note--is from a musical friend in Silesia, not a rich man, for whom I have frequently had my scores written out. He wishes to have these works of Mozart in his library; as my servant, however, has the good fortune, by the grace of God, to be one of the greatest blockheads in the world (which is saying a good deal), I cannot make use of him for this purpose. Be so kind therefore as to send to Herr ---- (for the *Generalissimus* can have no dealings with a petty tradesman), and desire him to *write down the price of each work* and send it to me with my two scores in A, and also an answer to my injunction about Ertmann, as early to-day as you can (*presto, prestissimo!*)--*nota bene*, the *finale* to be *a march in double-quick time*. I recommend the best execution of these orders, so that no further obstacle may intervene to my recovery.

L. VAN BEETHOVEN,
The best *generalissimus* for the good,
But the devil himself for the bad!

217.
TO STEINER.

The Lieutenant-General is requested to send his *Diabolum*, that I may tell him myself my opinion of the "Battle," which is *printed in the vilest manner*. There is much to be altered.

THE G----S.

218.
TO TOBIAS HASLINGER.

MY GOOD ADJUTANT,--

Best of all little fellows! Do see again about that house, and get it for me. I am very anxious also to procure *the treatise on education*. It is of some importance to me to be able to compare my own opinions on this subject with those of others, and thus still further improve them. As for our juvenile Adjutant, I think I shall soon have hit on the right system for his education. Your

CONTRA FA,
Manu propria.

219.
TO THE HIGH-BORN HERR HASLINGER, HONORARY MEMBER OF THE HÖFEN GRABENS AND PATER NOSTER GÄSSCHEN.

BEST OF ALL PRINTERS AND ENGRAVERS,--

Be kinder than kind, and throw off a hundred impressions of the accompanying small plate.[1] I will repay you threefold and fourfold. Farewell!

Your

BEETHOVEN.

[Footnote 1: This is possibly the humorous visiting-card that Beethoven sometimes sent to his friends, with the inscription *Wir bleiben die Alten* ("We are the same as ever"), and on reversing the card, a couple of asses stared them in the face! Frau Eyloff told me of a similar card that her brother Schindler once got from Beethoven on a New Year's day.]

220.
TO BARONESS DOROTHEA VON ERTMANN.[1]

Feb. 23, 1817.

MY DEAR AND VALUED DOROTHEA CECILIA,--

You have no doubt often misjudged me, from my apparently forbidding manner; much of this arose from circumstances, especially in earlier days, when my nature was less understood than at present. You know the manifestations of those self-elected apostles who promote their interests by means very different from those of the true Gospel. I did not wish to be included in that number. Receive now what has been long intended for you,[2] and may it serve as a proof of my admiration of your artistic talent, and likewise of yourself! My not having heard you recently at Cz---- [Czerny's] was owing to indisposition, which at last appears to be giving way to returning health.

I hope soon to hear how you get on at St. Polten [where her husband's regiment was at that time quartered], and whether you still think of your admirer and friend,

L. VAN BEETHOVEN.

My kindest regards to your excellent husband.

[Footnote 1: It was admitted that she played Beethoven's compositions with the most admirable taste and feeling. Mendelssohn thought so in 1830 at Milan, and mentions it in his *Letters from Italy and Switzerland*.]

[Footnote 2: Undoubtedly the Sonata dedicated to her, Op. 101.]

221.
TO ZMESKALL.

DEAR Z.,--

I introduce to your notice the bearer of this, young Bocklet, who is a very clever violin-player. If you can be of any service to him through your acquaintances, do your best for him, especially as he is warmly recommended to me from Prague.[1]

As ever, your true friend,

BEETHOVEN.

[Footnote 1: Carl Maria Bocklet, a well-known and distinguished pianist in Vienna. He told me himself that he came for the first time to Vienna in 1817, where he stayed six weeks. On April 8th he gave a violin concert in the *Kleine Redoutensaale*. He brought a letter of introduction to Beethoven, from his friend Dr. Berger in Prague.]

222.
TO STEINER & CO.

The Lieutenant-General is desired to afford all aid and help to the young artist Bocklet from Prague. He is the bearer of this note, and a virtuoso on the violin. We hope that our command will be obeyed, especially as we subscribe ourselves, with the most vehement regard, your

GENERALISSIMUS.

223.
TO G. DEL RIO.

I only yesterday read your letter attentively at home. I am prepared to give up Carl to you at any moment, although I think it best not to do so till after the examination on Monday; but I will send him sooner if you wish it. At all events it would be advisable afterwards to remove him from here, and to send him to Mölk, or some place where he will neither see nor hear anything more of his abominable mother. When he is in the midst of strangers, he will meet with less support, and find that he can only gain the love and esteem of others by his own merits.

In haste, your
BEETHOVEN.

224.
TO G. DEL RIO.

I request you, my dear friend, to inquire whether in any of the houses in your vicinity there are lodgings to be had at Michaelmas, consisting of a few rooms. You must not fail to do this for me to-day or to-morrow.

Your friend,
L. VAN BEETHOVEN.

P.S.--N.B. Though I would gladly profit by your kind offer of living in your garden-house, various circumstances render this impossible. My kind regards to all your family.

225.
TO G. DEL RIO.

HOUSE OF GIANNATASIO!--

The treatise on the piano is a general one,--that is, it is a kind of compendium. Besides, I am pleased with the Swiss [probably Weber, a young musician who had been recommended to him], but the "Guaden" is no longer the fashion.

In haste, the devoted servant and friend of the Giannatasio family,

BEETHOVEN.

226.
TO G. DEL RIO.

You herewith receive through Carl, my dear friend, the ensuing quarter due to you. I beg you will attend more to the cultivation of his feelings and kindness of heart, as the latter in particular is the lever of all that is good; and no matter how a man's kindly feeling may be ridiculed or depreciated, still our greatest authors, such as Goethe and others, consider it an admirable quality; indeed, many maintain that without it no man can ever be very distinguished, nor can any depth of character exist.

My time is too limited to say more, but we can discuss verbally how in my opinion Carl ought to be treated on this point.

Your friend and servant,
L. VAN BEETHOVEN.

Alser Vorstadt--Beim Apfel, 2ter Étage,
No. 12, Leiberz, Dressmaker.

227.
TO G. DEL RIO.

This is at any rate the first time that it has been necessary to remind me of an agreeable duty; very pressing business connected with my art, as well as other causes, made me totally forget the account, but this shall not occur again. As for my servant bringing home Carl in the evening, the arrangement is already made. In the mean time I thank you for having been so obliging as to send your servant for him yesterday, as I knew nothing about it, so that Carl probably must otherwise have remained at Czerny's. Carl's boots are too small, and he has repeatedly complained of this; indeed, they are so bad that he can scarcely walk, and it will take some time before they can be altered to fit him. This kind of thing ruins the feet, so I beg you will not allow him to wear them again till they are made larger.

With regard to his pianoforte studies, I beg you will keep him strictly to them; otherwise his music-master would be of no use. Yesterday Carl could not play the whole day, I have repeatedly wished to hear him play over his lessons, but have been obliged to come away without doing so.

"La musica merita d'esser studiata."

Besides, the couple of hours now appointed for his music lessons are quite insufficient. I must therefore the more earnestly urge on you their being strictly adhered to. It is by no means unusual that this point should be attended to in an institute; an intimate friend of mine has also a boy at school, who is to become a professor of music, where every facility for study is afforded him; indeed, I was rather struck by finding the boy quite alone in a distant room practising, neither disturbing others, nor being himself disturbed.

I beg you will allow me to send for Carl to-morrow about half-past ten o'clock, as I wish to see what progress he has made, and to take him with me to some musicians.

I am, with all possible esteem, your friend,

L. VAN BEETHOVEN.

228.
TO CZERNY.

DEAR CZERNY,--

I beg you will treat Carl with as much patience as possible; for though he does not as yet get on quite as you and I could wish, still I fear he will soon do even less, because (though I do not want him to know it) he is over-fatigued by the injudicious distribution of his lesson hours. Unluckily it is not easy to alter this; so pray, however strict you may be, show him every indulgence, which will, I am sure, have also a better effect on Carl under such unfavorable circumstances.

With respect to his playing with you, when he has finally acquired the proper mode of fingering, and plays in right time, and gives the notes with tolerable correctness, you must only then first direct his attention to the mode of execution; and when he is sufficiently advanced, do not stop his playing on account of little mistakes, but only point them out at the end of the piece. Although I have myself given very little instruction, I have always followed this system, which quickly forms a *musician*; and this is, after all, one of the first objects of art, and less fatiguing both to master and scholar. In certain passages, like the following,--

I wish all the fingers to be used; and also in similar ones, such as these,--

so that they may go very smoothly; such passages can indeed be made to sound very *perlés*, or like a pearl, played by fewer fingers, but sometimes we wish for a different kind of jewel.[1] More as to this some other time. I hope that you will receive these suggestions in the same kindly spirit in which they are offered and intended. In any event I am, and ever must remain, your debtor. May my candor serve as a pledge of my wish to discharge this debt at some future day!

Your true friend,
BEETHOVEN.

[Footnote 1: Carl Czerny relates in the Vienna *A.M. Zeitung* of 1845, No. 113, as follows:-- "Beethoven came to me usually every day himself with the boy, and used to say to me, 'You must not think that you please me by making Carl play my works; I am not so childish as to wish anything of the kind. Give him whatever you think best.' I named Clementi. 'Yes, yes,' said he, 'Clementi is very good indeed;' and, added he, laughing, 'Give Carl occasionally what is *according to rule*, that he may hereafter come to what is *contrary to rule*.' After a hit of this sort, which he introduced into almost every speech, he used to burst into a loud peal of laughter. Having in the earlier part of his career been often reproached by the critics with his *irregularities*, he was in the habit of alluding to this with gay humor."]

229.
TO CZERNY.

DEAR CZERNY,--

I beg you will say nothing *on that particular subject* at Giannatasio's, who dined with us on the day you were so good as to call on me; he requested this himself. *I will tell you the reason* when we meet. I hope to be able to prove my gratitude for your patience with my nephew, that I may not always remain your debtor. In haste,

Your friend,
BEETHOVEN.

230.
TO CZERNY.

DEAR CZERNY,--

Can you in any way assist the man I now send to you (a pianoforte maker and tuner from Baden) in selling his instruments? Though small in size, their manufacture is solid. In haste,

Your friend,
BEETHOVEN.

231.
TO ZMESKALL.

Wednesday, July 3, 1817.

DEAR ZMESKALL,--

I have changed my mind. It might hurt the feelings of Carl's mother to see her child in the house of a stranger, which would be more harsh than I like; so I shall allow her to come to my house to-morrow; a certain tutor at Puthon, of the name of Bihler, will also be present. I should be *extremely* glad if you could be with me about six o'clock, but not later. Indeed, I earnestly beg you to come, as I am desirous to show the Court that you are present, for there is no doubt that a *Court Secretary* will be held in higher estimation by them than a man *without an official character, whatever his moral character may be!*

Now, jesting apart, independent of my real affection for you, your coming will be of great service to me. I shall therefore expect you without fail. I beg you will not take my *badinage* amiss. I am, with sincere esteem,

Your friend,
BEETHOVEN

232.
TO G. DEL RIO.

Your friend has no doubt told you of my intention to send for Carl early to-morrow. I wish to place his mother in a more creditable position with the neighborhood; so I have agreed to pay her the compliment of taking her son to see her in the company of a third person. This is to be done once a month.

As to all that is past, I beg you will never allude to it again, either in speaking or writing, but forget it all--as I do.

233.
TO FRAU VON STREICHER.

I have been occupied in arranging my papers; an immense amount of patience is required for such an affair as putting them in order, but having once summoned it to our aid we must persevere, or the matter would never be completed. My papers, both musical and unmusical, are nearly arranged at last; it was like one of the seven labors of Hercules![1]

[Footnote 1: Ries (in Wegeler's *Notizen*) relates: "Beethoven placed very little value on the MSS. of his pieces written out by himself; when once engraved they were usually scattered about the anteroom, or on the floor in the middle of his apartment, together with other music. I often arranged his music for him, but the moment Beethoven began to search for any piece, it was all strewed about again."]

234.
TO FRAU VON STREICHER.

You see what servants are! [He had gone out and taken the key with him.] Such is housekeeping! So long as I am ill, I would fain be on a different footing with those around me; for dearly as I usually love solitude, it is painful to me now, finding it scarcely possible, while taking baths and medicine, to employ myself as usual,--to which is added the grievous prospect that I may perhaps never get better. I place no confidence in my present physician, who at length pronounces my malady to be *disease of the lungs*. I will consider about engaging a housekeeper. If I could only have the faintest hope, in this corrupt Austrian State, of finding an honest person, the arrangement would be easily made; but-- but!! [He wishes to hire a piano and pay for it in advance; the tone to be as loud as possible, to suit his defective hearing.]

Perhaps you do not know, though I have not always had one of your pianos, that since 1809 I have invariably preferred yours.

It is peculiarly hard on me to be a burden on any one, being accustomed rather to serve others than to be served by them.

235.
TO FRAU VON STREICHER.

I can only say that I am better; I thought much of death during the past night, but such thoughts are familiar to me by day also.

236.
TO F. RIES,--LONDON.

Vienna, July 9, 1817.

MY DEAR FRIEND,--

The proposals in your esteemed letter of the 9th of June are very flattering, and my reply will show you how much I value them. Were it not for my unhappy infirmities, which entail both attendance and expense, particularly on a journey to a foreign country, I would *unconditionally* accept the offer of the Philharmonic Society. But place yourself in my position, and consider how many more obstacles I have to contend with than any other artist, and then judge whether my demands (which I now annex) are unreasonable. I beg you will convey my conditions to the Directors of the above Society, namely:--

1. I shall be in London early in January.

2. The two grand new symphonies shall be ready by that time; to become the exclusive property of the Society.

3. The Society to give me in return 300 guineas, and 100 for my travelling expenses, which will, however, amount to much more, as I am obliged to bring a companion.

4. As I am now beginning to work at these grand symphonies for the Society, I shall expect that (on receiving my consent) they will remit me here the sum of 150 guineas, so that I may provide a carriage, and make my other preparations at once for the journey.

5. The conditions as to my non-appearance in any other public orchestra, my not directing, and the preference always to be given to the Society on the offer of equal terms by them, are accepted by me; indeed, they would at all events have been dictated by my own sense of honor.

6. I shall expect the aid of the Society in arranging one, or more, benefit concerts in my behalf, as the case may be. The very friendly feeling of some of the Directors in your valuable body, and the kind reception of my works by all the artists, is a sufficient guaranty on this point, and will be a still further inducement to me to endeavor not to disappoint their expectations.

7. I request that I may receive the assent to and confirmation of these terms, signed by three Directors in the name of the Society. You may easily imagine how much I rejoice at the thoughts of becoming acquainted with the worthy Sir George Smart [Music Director], and seeing you and Mr. Neate again; would that I could fly to you myself instead of this letter!

Your sincere well wisher and friend,

LUDWIG VAN BEETHOVEN.

[P.S. ON A SEPARATE SHEET OF PAPER.]

DEAR RIES,--

I cordially embrace you! I have purposely employed another hand in my answer to the Society, that you might read it more easily, and present it to them. I place the most implicit reliance on your kindly feelings toward me. I hope that the Philharmonic Society may accept my proposals, and they may rest assured that I shall employ all my energies to fulfil in the most satisfactory manner the flattering commission of so eminent a society of artists. What is the strength of your orchestra? How many violins, &c.? Have you *one or two sets of wind instruments*? Is the concert room large and sonorous?

237.
TO ZMESKALL.

NUSSDORF, July 23, 1817.

MY DEAR GOOD ZMESKALL,--

I shall soon see you again in town. What is the proper price for fronting a pair of boots? I have to pay my servant for this, who is always running about.

I am really in despair at being condemned by my defective hearing to pass the greater part of my life with this most odious class of people, and to be in some degree dependent on them. To-morrow, early, my servant will call on you, and bring me back a *sealed answer*.

238.
TO ZMESKALL.

August 12, 1817.

MY DEAR GOOD Z.,--

I heard of your indisposition with great regret. As for myself, I am often in despair, and almost tempted to put an end to my life, for all these remedies seem to have no end. May God have compassion on me, for I look upon myself to be as good as lost! I have a great deal to say to you. That this servant is a *thief*, I cannot doubt--he must be sent away; my health requires living *at home* and greater comfort. I shall be glad to have your opinion on this point. If my condition is not altered, instead of being in London I shall probably be in my grave. I thank God that the thread of my life will soon be spun out.

In haste, your
BEETHOVEN.

N.B. I wish you to buy me a quarter of a yard of green wax-cloth, green on both sides. It seems incredible that I have not been able to get anything of the kind from these *green* people here. It is far.... [illegible].

[X. brought the Trio in C minor (Op. 1, No. 3) to show to Beethoven, having arranged it as a quintet for stringed instruments (published by Artaria as Op. 104). Beethoven evidently discovered a good many faults in the work; still, the undertaking had sufficient attractions to induce him to correct it himself, and to make many changes in it. A very different score was thus of course produced from that of X., on the cover of whose work the genial master, in a fit of good humor, inscribed with his own hand the following title:--

A Terzet arranged as a Quintet,
by *Mr. Well-meaning*,

translated from the semblance into the reality of five parts, and exalted from the depths of wretchedness to a certain degree of excellence,

by *Mr. Goodwill*.
Vienna, Aug. 14, 1817.

N.B. The original three-part score of the Quintet has been sacrificed as a solemn burnt-offering to the subterranean gods.][1]

[Footnote 1: This Quintet appeared as Op. 104 at Artaria's in Vienna.]

239.
TO FRAU VON STREICHER.

When we next meet, you will be surprised to hear what I have in the mean time learned. My poor Carl was only misled for the moment; but there are men who are brutes, and of this number is the priest here, who deserves to be well cudgelled.

240.
TO G. DEL RIO.

August 19, 1817.

I unluckily received your letter yesterday too late, for she had already been here; otherwise I would have shown her to the door, as she richly deserved. I sincerely thank Fraulein N. for the trouble she took in writing down the gossip of this woman. Though an enemy to all tattling and gossip, still this is of importance to us; so I shall write to her, and also give her letter to me to Herr A.S. [Advocate Schönauer?] I may possibly have let fall some words in her presence in reference to the recent occurrence, and the irregularity on your part, but I cannot in the slightest degree recall ever having written to her about you.

It was only an attempt on her side to exasperate you against me; and thus to influence you and obtain more from you, in the same way that she formerly reported to me all sorts of things that you had said about me; but I took no heed of her talk. On this recent occasion I wished to try whether she might not be improved by a more patient and conciliatory mode of conduct: I imparted my intention to Herr A.S., but it has utterly failed; and on Sunday I made up my mind to adhere to the former necessary severity, as even during the glimpse she had of Carl, she contrived to inoculate him with some of her venom. In short, we must be guided by the zodiac, and only allow her to see Carl twelve times a year, and then barricade her so effectually that she cannot smuggle in even a pin, whether he is with you or me, or with a third person. I really thought that by entirely complying with her wishes, it might have been an incitement to her to improve, and to acknowledge my complete unselfishness.

Perhaps I may see you to-morrow. Frau S. can order the shoes and stockings and all that Carl requires, and I will remit her the money at once. I beg that you will always order and buy anything Carl ought to have, without any reference to me, merely informing me of the amount, which I will forthwith discharge, without waiting for the end of the quarter. I will take care that Carl has a new coat for the next examination.

One thing more. The mother affects to receive her information from a person in your house. If you cannot arrange with Czerny to bring Carl home, he must not go at all; "*trau, schau, wem!*" [trust not till you try.] The only impression that his mother ought to make on Carl is what I have already told him,--namely, to respect her as *his mother*, but *not to follow her example in any respect*; he must be strongly warned against this.

Yours truly,
L. V. BEETHOVEN.

241.
TO ZMESKALL.

Sept. 11, 1817.

DEAR Z.,--

The answer from London arrived yesterday [see No. 236], but in English. Do you know any one who could translate it verbally for us? In haste,

Your

BEETHOVEN.

242.
TO ZMESKALL.

Oct. 20, 1817.

DEAR Z.,--

The devil himself cannot persuade your *Famulus* to take away the wine. Pray forgive my behavior yesterday; I intended to have asked your pardon this very afternoon. *In my present condition* I require *indulgence* from every one, for I am a poor unfortunate creature!

In haste, as ever, yours.

243.
TO ZMESKALL.

DEAR Z.,--

I give up the journey; at least I will not pledge myself on this point. The matter must be more maturely considered. In the mean time the work is already sent off to the Prince Regent. *If they want me they can have me*, and I am still at *liberty* to say *yes*! or *no*! Liberty!!!! what more can any one desire!!!

244.
TO ZMESKALL.

DEAR Z.,--

Don't be angry about my note. Are you not aware of my present condition, which is like that of Hercules with Queen Omphale??? I asked you to buy me a looking-glass like yours, which I now return, but if you do not require it, I wish you would send yours back to me to-day, for mine is broken. Farewell, and do not write in such high-flown terms about me, for never have I felt so strongly as now the strength and the weakness of human nature.

Continue your regard for me.

245.
TO FRAU VON STREICHER.

The Autumn of 1817.

I have had an interview with your husband, whose sympathy did me both good and harm, for Streicher almost upset my resignation. God alone knows the result! but as I have always assisted my fellow-men when I had the power to do so, I also rely on his mercy to me.

Educate your daughter carefully, that she may make a good wife.

To-day happens to be Sunday; so I will quote you something out of the Bible,--"Love one another." I conclude with best regards to your best of daughters, and with the wish that all your wounds may be healed.

When you visit the ancient ruins [Frau Streicher was in Baden], do not forget that Beethoven has often lingered there; when you stray through the silent pine forests, do not forget that Beethoven often wrote poetry there, or, as it is termed, *composed*.

246.
TO FRAU VON STREICHER.

How deeply am I indebted to you, my excellent friend, and I have become such a poor creature that I have no means of repaying you. I am very grateful to Streicher for all the trouble he has taken on my behalf [about a house in the Gärtner Strasse], and beg he will continue his inquiries. God will, I hope, one day enable me to return benefit for benefit, but this being at present impossible, grieves me most of all....

Now Heaven be praised! [he thus winds up a long letter about a bad servant,] I have contrived to collect all these particulars for you with no little toil and trouble, and God grant that I may never, never more be obliged to speak, or write, or think again on such a subject, for mud and mire are not more pernicious to artistic soil, than such devilry to any man!!!

247.
TO FRAU VON STREICHER.

As to Frau von Stein [stone], I beg she will not allow Herr von Steiner to turn into stone, that he may still be of service to me; nor must Frau von Stein become too stony towards Herr von Steiner, &c.

My good Frau von Streicher, do not play any trick [Streiche] to your worthy little husband, but rather be to all others Frau von Stein [stone]!!!!

Where are the coverlets for the beds?

Where? where?

248.
TO FRAU VON STREICHER.

... It is now very evident from all this that if *you* do not kindly superintend things for me, I, with my *infirmities*, must meet with the *same fate* as usual at the hands of these people.

Their *ingratitude* towards you is what chiefly degrades both of them in my eyes. But I don't understand your allusion about gossip? on one occasion alone can I remember having forgotten myself for the moment, but *with very different people*. This is all I can say on the subject. For my part I neither encourage nor listen to the gossip of the lower orders. I have often given you hints on the subject, without telling you a word of what I had heard. Away! away! away! with such things!

249.
TO THE ARCHDUKE RUDOLPH.

Nussdorf, Sept. 1, 1817.

I hope to be able to join you in Baden; but my invalid condition still continues, and though in some respects improved, my malady is far from being entirely cured. I have had, and still have, recourse to remedies of every kind and shape; I must now give up the long-cherished hope of ever being wholly restored. I hear that Y.R.H. looks wonderfully well, and though many false inferences may be drawn from this as to good health, still every one tells me that Y.R.H. is much better, and in this I feel sincerely interested. I also trust that when Y.R.H. again comes to town, I may assist you in those works dedicated to the Muses. My confidence is placed on Providence, who will vouchsafe to hear my prayer, and one day set me free from all my troubles, for I have served Him faithfully from my childhood, and done good whenever it has been in my power; so my trust is in Him alone, and I feel that the Almighty will not allow me to be utterly crushed by all my manifold trials. I wish Y.R.H. all possible good and prosperity, and shall wait on you the moment you return to town.

[K.]

250.
TO G. DEL RIO

Vienna, Nov. 12, 1817.

My altered circumstances render it possible that I may not be able to leave Carl under your care beyond the end of this quarter; so, as in duty bound, I give you this *warning* a quarter in advance. Though it is painful to admit it, my straitened circumstances leave me no choice in the matter; had it been otherwise, how gladly would I have presented you with an additional quarter's payment when I removed Carl, as a slight tribute of my gratitude. I do hope you will believe that such are my *genuine and sincere* wishes on the subject. If on the other hand I leave Carl with you for the ensuing quarter, commencing in February, I will apprise you of it early in January, 1818. I trust you will grant me this *favor*, and that I shall not solicit it in vain. If I ever enjoy better health, so that I can *earn more money*, I shall not fail to evince my gratitude, knowing well how much more you have done for Carl than I had any right to expect; and I can with truth say that to be obliged to confess my inability to requite your services at this moment, distresses me much.

I am, with sincere esteem, your friend,
L. V. BEETHOVEN.

251.
TO G. DEL RIO.

MY DEAR FRIEND,--

I have been hitherto unable to answer your friendly letter, having been much occupied and still far from well.

As to your proposal, it merits both gratitude and consideration. I must say that the same idea formerly occurred to me about Carl; at this moment, however, I am in the most unsettled state. This was why I made the stipulation to which I begged you to agree, namely, to let you know in the last month of the present quarter whether Carl was to continue with you. In this way our plans would neither be hurried nor demolished. I am, besides, well aware that it can be no advantage to you to have Carl either on his present terms, or according to your last proposal, and on that very account I wished to point out to you in my letter how gladly, besides the usual remuneration, I would have testified my gratitude in some additional manner.

When I spoke of my *inability*, I knew that his education would cost me even more elsewhere than with you; but what I intended to convey was that every father has a particular object in the education of his child, and it is thus with me and Carl. No doubt we shall soon discover what is best for him;

whether to have a tutor here, or to go on as formerly. I do not wish to tie myself down for the moment, but to remain free to act as his interests may dictate.

Carl daily costs me great sacrifices, but I only allude to them on his own account. I know too well the influence his mother contrives to acquire over him, for she seems resolved to show herself well worthy of the name of "Queen of the Night." Besides, she everywhere spreads a report that I do nothing whatever for Carl, whereas she pays everything!! As we have touched on this point, I must thank you for your most considerate letter, which in any event will be of great use to me. Pray ask Herr L.S. to be so kind as to make my excuses to his brother for not having yet called on him. Partly owing to business and also to indisposition, it has been nearly impossible for me to do so. When I think of this oft-discussed affair, I should prefer going to see him on any other subject. She has not applied to me; so it is not my business to promote a meeting between her and her son.

With regard to the other matter, I am told that in *this* case we must have recourse to compulsion, which will cost me more money, for which I have chiefly to thank Herr Adlersburg [his advocate]. As Carl's education, however, must be carried on so far as possible independent of his mother, for the future as well as the present we must act as I have arranged.

I am, with esteem, your attached friend,
L. V. BEETHOVEN.

252.
TO THE ARCHDUKE RUDOLPH.

Last day of December, 1817.

The old year has nearly passed away, and a new one draws near. May it bring Y.R.H. no sorrow, but rather may it bestow on you every imaginable felicity! These are my wishes, all concentrated in the one I have just expressed. If it be allowable to speak of myself, I may say that my health is very variable and uncertain. I am unhappily obliged to live at a great distance from Y.R.H., which shall not, however, prevent my having the extreme gratification of waiting on you at the first opportunity. I commend myself to your gracious consideration, though I may not appear to deserve it. May Heaven, for the benefit of so many whom you befriend, enrich each day of your life with an especial blessing! I am always, &c., &c.

[K.]

253.
TO G. DEL RIO.

Jan. 6, 1818.

To prevent any mistake I take the liberty to inform you that it is finally settled my nephew Carl should leave your excellent institution the end of this month. My hands are also tied with regard to your other proposal, as if I accepted it, my further projects for Carl's benefit would be entirely frustrated; but I sincerely thank you for your kind intentions.

Circumstances may cause me to remove Carl even before the end of the month, and as I may not be here myself, I will appoint some one to fetch him. I mention this to you now, that it may not appear strange when the time comes; and let me add, that my nephew and I shall feel grateful to you through life. I observe that Carl already feels thus, which is to me a proof that although thoughtless, his disposition is not evil; far less has he a bad heart. I am the more disposed to augur well of him from his having been for two years under your admirable guidance.

I am, with esteem, your friend,
L. V. BEETHOVEN.

254.
TO G. DEL RIO.

Vienna, Jan. 24, 1818.

I do not come to you myself, as it would be a kind of leave-taking, and this I have all my life avoided. Pray accept my heartfelt thanks for the zeal, rectitude, and integrity with which you have conducted the education of my nephew. As soon as I am at all settled, we mean to pay you a visit; but on account of the mother, I am anxious that the fact of my nephew being with me should not be too much known.

I send you my very best wishes, and I beg especially to thank Frau A.Z. for her truly maternal care of Carl.

I am, with sincere esteem, yours,
L. V. BEETHOVEN.

255.
TO CZERNY.

MY DEAR GOOD KIND CZERNY,--[1]

I have this moment heard that you are in a position I really never suspected; you might certainly place confidence in me, and point out how matters could be made better for you (without any pretensions to patronage on my part). As soon as I have a moment to myself, I must speak to you. Rest assured that I highly value you, and am prepared to prove this at any moment by deeds.

Yours, with sincere esteem,
L. VAN BEETHOVEN.

[Footnote 1: Zellner, in his *Blätter für Musik*, relates what follows on Czerny's own authority:--In 1818 Czerny was requested by Beethoven in a letter (which he presented some years ago to Cocks, the London music publisher) to play at one of his last concerts in the large *Redoutensaal*, his E flat major Concerto, Op. 73. Czerny answered, in accordance with the truth, that having gained his livelihood entirely for many years past by giving lessons on the piano, for more than twelve hours daily, he had so completely laid aside his pianoforte playing, that he could not venture to attempt playing the concerto properly within the course of a few days (which Beethoven desired). On which he received, in the above letter, a touching proof of Beethoven's sympathy. He also learned subsequently that Beethoven had exerted himself to procure him a permanent situation.]

256.
TO F. RIES,--LONDON.

Vienna, March 5, 1818.

MY DEAR RIES,--

In spite of my wishes it was impossible for me to go to London this year [see No. 236]. I beg you will apprise the Philharmonic Society that my feeble health prevented my coming; I trust, however, I shall be entirely restored this spring, so that in the autumn I may avail myself of their offers and fulfil all their conditions.

Pray request Neate, in my name, to make no public use of the various works of mine that he has in his hands, at least not until I come. Whatever he may have to say for himself, I have cause to complain of him.

Potter[1] called on me several times; he seems to be a worthy man, and to have a talent for composition. My wish and hope for you is that your circumstances may daily improve. I cannot, alas! say that such is the case with my own.... I cannot bear to see others want, I must give; you may therefore believe what a loser I am by this affair. I do beg that you will write to me soon. If possible I shall try to get away from this earlier, in the hope of escaping utter ruin, in which case I shall arrive in London by the winter at latest. I know that you will assist an unfortunate friend. If it had only been in my power, and had I not been chained to this place, as I always have been, by circumstances, I certainly would have done far more for you.

Farewell; remember me to Neate, Smart, and Cramer. Although I hear that the latter is a *counter subject* both to you and to myself, still I rather understand how to manage people of that kind; so notwithstanding all this we shall yet succeed in producing an agreeable harmony in London. I embrace you from my heart. Your friend,

L. VAN BEETHOVEN.

Many handsome compliments to your charming, (and as I hear) handsome wife.

[Footnote 1: Schindler, in his *Biography* (Vol. II. 254), states that Cipriani Potter came to Vienna in 1817.]

257.
TO THE RECHNUNGSRATH, VINCENZ HAUSCHKA.[1]

1818.

First and foremost member of our society, and grand cross of the violon--cello! You wish for an *heroic* subject, whereas I have none but a *spiritual* one! I am contented; still, I think an infusion of the spiritual would be quite appropriate in such a mass. I have no objections to H. v. Bernard, but you must pay him; I do not speak of myself. As you call yourselves "Friends of Music," it is only natural that you should expect a great deal to be done on the score of friendship.

Now farewell, my good Hauschka! As for myself, I wander about here with music paper, among the hills and dales and valleys, and scribble a great deal to get my daily bread; for I have brought things to such a pass in this mighty and ignominious *land of the Goths and Vandals*, that in order to gain time for a great composition, I must always previously *scrawl away* a good deal for the sake of money, to enable me to complete an important work.

However, my health is much improved, and if the matter is urgent, I can do as you wish now.

In haste, your friend,
BEETHOVEN.

[Footnote 1: Hauschka was at that time on the committee, and agent for the "Friends to Music" who commissioned Beethoven to write an Oratorio in 1815. Schindler is of opinion that the repeated performance of the Abbé Stadler's heroic Oratorio, *Die Befreiung von Jerusalem*, was the cause of the Society in 1818 bespeaking, through Hauschka, "An oratorio of the heroic order."]

258.
TO THE ARCHDUKE RUDOLPH.

1819.

I have the honor to send the masterly variations[1] of Y.R.H. by the copyist Schlemmer, and to-morrow I shall come in person to wait upon Y.R.H., and much rejoice at being able to serve as a companion to my illustrious pupil on the path of fame.

[K.]

[Footnote 1: The letters 258 and 259, allude to the pianoforte variations composed by the Archduke Rudolph and dedicated to his instructor.]

259.
TO THE ARCHDUKE RUDOLPH.

Jan. 1, 1819.

All that can be comprehended in one wish, or individually named,--health, happiness, and prosperity,--all are included in the prayer I offer up for Y.R.H. on this day. May the wish that I also form for myself be graciously accepted by Y.R.H., namely, that I may continue to enjoy the favor of Y.R.H. A dreadful occurrence[1] has lately taken place in my family, which for a long time stunned my senses, and to this must be ascribed my not having waited on Y.R.H., nor taken any notice of the masterly variations of my much-honored and illustrious pupil, and favorite of the Muses. The gratitude I feel for the surprise and the honor you have done me, I dare not venture to express either verbally or in writing, for I am *too far beneath you*, even if I *could* or wished ever so ardently *to return like for like*. May Heaven accept and listen with peculiar favor to my prayers for Y.R.H.'s health. In the course of a few days I trust I shall myself hear the masterpiece Y.R.H. has sent to me, and nothing will rejoice me more than to assist Y.R.H. as early as possible, in taking the place already prepared for you on Parnassus.

[K.]

[Footnote 1: The "dreadful occurrence" which took place in the end of 1818 in Beethoven's family cannot be discovered.]

260.
TO RIES.

Vienna, April [March?] 30, 1819.

DEAR RIES,--

I am only now able to answer your letter of December 18th. Your sympathy does me good. It is impossible for me to go to London at present, being involved here in various ways; but God will, I trust, aid me, and enable me to visit London next winter, when I shall bring the new symphonies with me.

I every day expect the text for a new *oratorio*, which I am to write for our Musical Society here, and no doubt it will be of use to us in London also. Do what you can on my behalf, for I greatly need it. I should have been glad to receive any commission from the Philharmonic, but Neate's report of the all but failure of the three overtures vexed me much. Each in its own style not only pleased here, but those in E flat major and C major made a profound impression, so that the fate of those works at the Philharmonic is quite incomprehensible to me.

You have no doubt received the arrangement of the Quintet [Op. 104, see No. 238] and the Sonata [Op. 106]. See that both, especially the Quintet, be engraved without loss of time. There is no such hurry about the Sonata, though I should like it to appear within two or three months. Never having received the previous letter to which you allude, I had no scruple in disposing of both works here; but for Germany only. It will be at any rate three months before the Sonata appears here, but you must make haste with the Quintet. As soon as you forward me a check for the money, I will send an authority to the publisher, securing him the exclusive right to these works for England, Scotland, Ireland, France, &c., &c.

You shall receive by the next post the *Tempi* of the Sonata marked in accordance with Maelzel's metronome. Prince Paul Esterhazy's courier, De Smidt, took the Quintet and the Sonata with him. You shall also have my portrait by the next opportunity, as I understand that you really wish for it.

Farewell! Continue your regard for me,

Your friend,
BEETHOVEN.

All sorts of pretty compliments to your pretty wife!!! From me!!!!

261.
TO RIES.

Vienna, April 16, 1819.

DEAR RIES,--
Here are the *Tempi* of the Sonata.

1st Allegro, Allegro (alone), erase the *assai*. Maelzel's metronome ♩ = 138.

2d movement, Scherzoso. Maelzel's metronome ♩ = 80.

3d movement, Maelzel's metronome ♪ = 92.
Observe that a previous bar is to be inserted here, namely:--

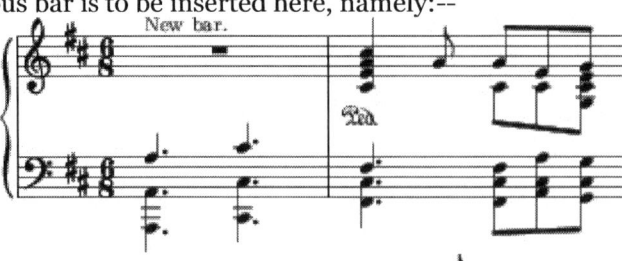

4th movement, Introduzione--largo. Maelzel's metronome ♪ = 76.

5th and last movement, 3/4 time. Maelzel's metronome ♩ = 144.

Pray forgive the confused way in which this is written. It would not surprise you if you knew my situation; you would rather marvel that I accomplish so much in spite of it. The Quintet can no longer be delayed, and must shortly appear; but not the Sonata, until I get an answer from you and the check, which I long to see. The name of the courier is De Smidt, by whom you will receive both the Quintet and Sonata. I beg you will give me an immediate answer. I will write more fully next time.

In haste, your
BEETHOVEN.

262.
TO RIES.

April 19, 1819.

MY DEAR FRIEND,--

I ask your forgiveness a thousand times for the trouble I cause you. I cannot understand how it is that there are so many mistakes in the copying of the Sonata. This incorrectness no doubt proceeds from my no longer being able to keep a copyist of my own; circumstances have brought this about. May God send me more prosperity, till ---- is in a better position! This will not be for a whole year to come. It is really dreadful the turn affairs have taken, and the reduction of my salary, while no man can tell what the issue is to be till the aforesaid year has elapsed.

If the Sonata be not suitable for London, I could send another, or you might omit the *Largo*, and begin at once with the *Fugue* in the last movement, or the first movement, *Adagio*, and the third the *Scherzo*, the *Largo*, and the *Allegro risoluto*. I leave it to you to settle as you think best. This Sonata was written at a time of great pressure. It is hard to write for the sake of daily bread; and yet I have actually come to this!

We can correspond again about my visit to London. To be rescued from this wretched and miserable condition is my only hope of deliverance, for as it is I can neither enjoy health, nor accomplish what I could do under more favorable auspices.

263.
TO THE PHILHARMONIC SOCIETY IN LAIBACH.[1]

Vienna, May 4, 1819.

I fully appreciate the high compliment paid to me by the respected members of the Philharmonic Society, in acknowledgment of my poor musical deserts, by electing me honorary member of their Society, and sending me the diploma through Herr von Tuscher; and as a proof of my sense of this honor, I intend in due course to forward to the Society an unpublished work of mine.[2] Moreover, at any time when I can be of use to the Society, I shall be prepared to forward their wishes.

I remain,
the humble servant and honorary member
of the Philharmonic Society,
LUDWIG VAN BEETHOVEN.

[Footnote 1: In Dr. Fr. Keesbacher's pamphlet, "*The Philharmonic Society in Laibach, from 1702 to 1862*," he says:--"The Philharmonic Society, always anxious to add to its lustre by attracting honorary members, resolved to appoint the great master of harmony as one of these. This idea had previously occurred to them in 1808. At that time they asked Dr. Anton Schmidt whether he thought that the election of Beethoven, and also Hummel's son, would contribute to the advancement of the Society. On that occasion the Society appear to have had recourse to Haydn for the composition of a Canon; whether they applied to him for a new one or an already existing one is not known. Schmidt replied, 'I, for my part, with such an object in view, would prefer giving my vote for the latter, (Hummel's son, who is second Kapellmeister, Haydn being the first, to the reigning Prince Niklas Esterhazy.) *Beethoven is as full of caprice as he is devoid of complaisance.* I have not seen Father Haydn for a long time, his residence being so distant. He is now in failing health and scarcely ever writes; I will, however, shortly call on him and make the attempt to get a Canon from him.' This discouraging picture of Beethoven, who had indeed too often a repulsive manner, might well deprive the Society of all courage to think any more of him as one of their honorary members. On the 15th of March, 1819, however, the Society prepared the diploma for Beethoven, the usually stereotyped form being exceptionally varied in his honor, and running thus:--'The Philharmonic Society here, whose aim it is to promote refinement of feeling and cultivation of taste in the science of music, and who strive by their incessant efforts to impart to the Society both inwardly and outwardly, by the judicious selection of new members, greater value, solidity, and distinction, are universally animated with the desire to see their list adorned by the name of Beethoven. The organ of this society, the undersigned directors, fulfil the general wish in thus performing *their most agreeable duty*, and giving you, sir, the strongest proof of their profound admiration, by appointing you one of their honorary members.--Laibach, March 15, 1819.'" A fac-simile of Beethoven's handwriting is hung up in a frame under glass in the hall of the Society and affixed to Dr. Keesbacher's pamphlet.]

[Footnote 2: We are told, "One work alone of Beethoven's in the collection of the Society bears visible marks of coming from his own hand, and that is the *Pastoral Symphony*." The above-mentioned copy is a MS. score (though not in his writing); on the cover is written by himself in red pencil, now almost illegible, "Sinfonie Pastorale;" and underneath are inscribed the following words in ink by another hand: "Beethoven's writing in red pencil." This score contains various corrections in pencil. Two of these appear to be by Beethoven, but unluckily the pencil marks are so much effaced that it is difficult to decide as to the writing. In the scene "By the Rivulet," where the 12/8 time begins (in B flat major), these words are written, "Violoncelli tutti con Basso." The B especially recalls his mode of writing. Moreover the *tempo* at the beginning of "The Shepherd's Song," (in F, 6/8 time,) *allegretto*, is qualified by the same hand in pencil thus, *Quasi allegro*. No direct proof exists of this being sent by him.]

264.
TO F. RIES,--LONDON.

Vienna, May 25, 1819.

... I was at the time burdened with cares beyond all I had ever in my life known,[1] caused solely by my too lavish benefits to others. Do compose industriously! My dear pupil the Archduke Rudolph and I frequently play your works, and he says that my quondam pupil does honor to his master. Now farewell! as I hear that your wife is so handsome, I venture to embrace her in imagination only, though I hope to have that pleasure in person next winter.

Do not forget the Quintet, and the Sonata, and the money, I mean the *Honoraire, avec ou sans honneur*. I hope soon to hear good news from you, not in *allegro* time, but *veloce prestissimo*.

This letter will be given to you by an intelligent Englishman; they are generally very able fellows, with whom I should like to pass some time in their own country.

Prestissimo--Responsio
De suo amico e Maestro,

BEETHOVEN.

[Footnote 1: In Schindler's *Beethoven's Nachlass* there is a large calendar of the years 1819 used by Beethoven, in which he has marked, "Arrived at Mödling May 12!!!--*miser sum pauper*." Carl too was again ill at that time. Beethoven took him to Blöchlinger's Institution, June 22.]

265.
TO THE ARCHDUKE RUDOLPH.

1819.

I learned with deep sorrow of your being again unwell; I trust it will only be a passing indisposition. No doubt our very variable spring is the cause of this. I intended to have brought the variations [see No. 259] yesterday; they may well boldly face the light of day, and no doubt Y.R.H. will receive an application for your consent on this point. I very much regret being only able to express a *pia desideria* for Y.R.H's. health. I earnestly hope the skill of your Aesculapius may at length gain the victory and procure permanent health for Y.R.H.

[K.]

266.
TO THE ARCHDUKE RUDOLPH.

Mödling, July 15, 1819.

I have been very ill since my last visit to Y.R.H. in town; I hope however to be much better by next week, in which case I will instantly join Y.R.H. at Baden. Meanwhile I went several times to town to consult my physician. My continued distress about my nephew, whose moral character has been almost totally ruined, has been the main cause of my illness. At the beginning of this week I was obliged to resume my guardianship, the other guardian having resigned, and much has taken place for which he has asked my forgiveness. The solicitor has also given up his office, because, having interested himself in the good cause, he has been loudly accused of partiality. Thus these endless perplexities go on, and no help, no consolation! The whole fabric that I had reared now blown away as if by the wind! A pupil of Pestalozzi, at present an inmate of the Institute where I have placed my nephew, seems to think that it will be a difficult matter for him and for my poor Carl to attain any desirable goal. But he is also of opinion that the most advisable step is the removal of my nephew to a foreign country! I hope that the health of Y.R.H., always so interesting to me, leaves nothing to be desired, and I look forward with pleasure to soon being with Y.R.H., that I may be enabled to prove my anxiety to serve you.

[K.]

267.
TO THE ARCHDUKE RUDOLPH.

1819.

May I beg the favor of Y.R.H. to inform H.R.H. Archduke Ludwig of the following circumstances. Y.R.H. no doubt remembers my mentioning the necessary removal of my nephew from here, on account of his mother. My intention was to present a petition to H.R.H. Archduke Ludwig on the subject; no difficulties however have hitherto arisen on the subject, as all the authorities concerned are in my favor. Among the chief of these are the College of Privy Councillors, the Court of Guardians, and the guardian himself, who all entirely agree with me in thinking that nothing can be more conducive to the welfare of my nephew than being kept at the greatest possible distance from his mother; moreover, all is admirably arranged for the education of my nephew in Landshut, as the estimable and renowned Professor Sailer is to superintend everything connected with the studies of the youth, and I have also some relations there, so no doubt the most desirable results may be thus attained for my nephew. Having, as I already said, as yet encountered no obstacles, I had no wish whatever to trouble H.R.H. the Archduke Ludwig, but I now understand that the mother of my nephew intends to demand an audience from H.R.H. in order to *oppose* my scheme. She will not scruple to utter all sorts of *calumnies against me*, but I trust these can be easily refuted by my well known and acknowledged moral character, and I can fearlessly appeal to Y.R.H. for a testimony on this point for the satisfaction of H.R.H. Archduke Ludwig. As for the conduct of the mother of my nephew, it is easily to be inferred from the fact of her having been declared by the Court wholly incapable of undertaking the guardianship of her son. All that she *plotted* in order to ruin her poor child can only be credited from her own depravity, and thence arises the *unanimous agreement* about this affair, and the boy being entirely withdrawn from her influence. Such is the natural and unnatural state of the case. I therefore beg Y.R.H. to intercede with H.R.H. Archduke Ludwig, and to warn him against listening to the slanders of the mother, who would plunge her child into an abyss whence he could never be rescued. That sense of justice which guides every party in our just Austrian land, does not entirely exclude her either; at the same time, this *very same sense of justice* must render all her remonstrances unavailing. A religious view of the Fourth Commandment is what chiefly decides the Court to send away the son as far as possible. The difficulty those must have who conduct the boy's education in not offending against this commandment, and the necessity that the son should never be tempted to fail in this duty or to repudiate it, ought certainly to be taken into consideration. Every effort has been made by forbearance and generosity to amend this unnatural mother, but all has been in vain. If necessary I will supply H.R.H. Archduke Ludwig with a statement on the subject, and, favored by the advocacy of my gracious master Y.R.H. the Archduke Rudolph, I shall certainly obtain justice.

[K.]

268.
TO THE ARCHDUKE RUDOLPH.

1819.

I regret to say that, owing to a judicial meeting about the affairs of my nephew (being unable to alter the hour fixed), I must give up the pleasure of waiting on Y.R.H. this evening, but shall not fail to do so to-morrow at half-past four o'clock. As for the affair itself, I know that I shall be treated with indulgence. May Heaven at length bring it to a close! for my mind suffers keenly from such a painful turmoil.

[K.]

269.
TO THE ARCHDUKE RUDOLPH.

Mödling, July 29, 1819.

I heard with deep regret of Y.R.H.'s recent indisposition, and having received no further reliable information on the subject, I am extremely uneasy. I went to Vienna to search in Y.R.H.'s library for what was most suitable to me. The chief object must be to *hit off our idea at once*, and *in accordance with a high class of art*, unless the object in view should require different and more *practical* treatment. On this point the ancient composers offer the best examples, as most of these possess real artistic value (though among them the *German Handel* and Sebastian Bach can alone lay claim to *genius*); but *freedom* and *progress* are our true aim in the world of art, just as in the great creation at large; and if we moderns are not so far advanced as our *forefathers* in *solidity*, still the refinement of our ideas has contributed in many ways to their enlargement. My illustrious musical pupil, himself a competitor for the laurels of fame, must not incur the reproach of *onesidedness, et iterum venturus judicare vivos et mortuos*. I send you three poems, from which Y.R.H. might select one to set to music. The Austrians have now learned that the *spirit of Apollo* wakes afresh in the Imperial House; I receive from all sides requests for something of yours. The editor of the "Mode Zeitung" is to write to Y.R.H. on the subject. I only hope that I shall not be accused of being *bribed*--to be *at court and yet no courtier*! After that, what is not credible??!!!

I met with some opposition from His Excellency the Obersthofmeister[1] *in selecting the music.* It is not worth while to trouble Y.R.H. on the subject in writing; but this I will say, that such conduct might have the effect of repelling many talented, good, and noble-minded men, who had not enjoyed the good fortune to learn from personal intercourse with Y.R.H. all the admirable qualities of your mind and heart. I wish Y.R.H. a speedy, speedy recovery, and, *for my own peace of mind*, that I may hear some good tidings of Y.R.H.

[K.]

[Footnote 1: Probably the Obersthofmeister, Count Laurencin, by no means approved of the manner in which Beethoven searched for music, which accounts for this outbreak on the part of the irritable *maestro*.]

270.
TO THE ARCHDUKE RUDOLPH.

1819.

I have unhappily only myself to blame! I went out yesterday for the first time, feeling pretty well, but I forgot, or rather paid no attention to the fact, that, being an invalid only just recovering, I ought to have gone home early; I have consequently brought on another attack. I think, however, that by staying at home to-day, all will be right by to-morrow, when I hope to be able to wait on my esteemed and illustrious pupil without fail. I beg Y.R.H. not to forget about Handel's works, as they certainly offer to your mature musical genius the highest nourishment, and their study will always be productive of admiration of this great man.

[K.]

271.
TO THE ARCHDUKE RUDOLPH.

Mödling, Aug. 31, 1819.

I yesterday received the intelligence *of a fresh recognition and homage*[1] *offered to the admirable qualities of your head and heart*. I beg that Y.R.H. will graciously accept my congratulations. They spring from the heart, and do not require to be suggested! I hope things will soon go better with me also. So much annoyance has had a most prejudicial effect on my health, and I am thus far from well; so for some time past I have been obliged to undergo a course of medicine which has only permitted me to devote myself for a few hours in the day to the most cherished boon of Heaven, my art and the Muses. I hope, however, to be able to finish the Mass[2] so that it can be performed on the 19th--if that day is still fixed. I should really be in despair[3] were I prevented by bad health from being ready by that time. I trust, however, that my sincere wishes for the accomplishment of this task may be fulfilled. As to that *chef-d'oeuvre*, the variations of Y.R.H., I think they should be published under the following title:--

Theme or Subject
composed by L. van Beethoven,
forty times varied,
and dedicated to his Instructor,
by the Illustrious Author.

The inquiries about this work are numerous, and yet, after all, this excellent composition may be ushered into the world in mutilated copies, for Y.R.H. yourself cannot possibly resist giving it first to one person and then to another; so, in Heaven's name, together with the great homage Y.R.H. now publicly receives, let the homage to Apollo (or the Christian Cecilia) also be made public. Perhaps Y.R.H. may accuse me of *vanity*; but I do assure you that precious as this dedication is to my heart, and truly proud of it as I am, this is certainly not my chief object. Three publishers have offered to take the work,--Artaria, Steiner, and a third whose name does not at this moment occur to me. So of the two I have named, which is to have the variations? I await the commands of Y.R.H. on this point. They are to be engraved at the cost of either of those publishers, according to their own offer. The question now is whether Y.R.H. *is satisfied with the title*. My idea is that Y.R.H. should entirely close your eyes to the fact of the publication; when it does appear, Y.R.H. may deem it a misfortune, *but the world will consider it the reverse*. May Providence protect Y.R.H., and shower down the richest blessings of His grace on Y.R.H.'s sacred head, and preserve for me your gracious regard! [On the cover] My indisposition must be my excuse with Y.R.H. for this confused letter.

[K.]

[Footnote 1: The Emperor Francis had sent the new Archbishop of Olmütz, Archduke Rudolph, the Grand Cross of the Order of St. Stephen.]

[Footnote 2: The Mass for the solemnities of the Archduke Rudolph's enthronization in Olmütz (March 20, 1820) was not completed by Beethoven till 1822.]

[Footnote 3: Beethoven had, however, no cause for despair on the subject. The kind-hearted Archduke showed the utmost indulgence to him on this occasion as well as on many others, and even at a later period accepted the dedication of this long delayed composition.]

272.[1]
TO THE ARCHDUKE RUDOLPH.

1819.

I perceive that Baron Schweiger has not informed Y.R.H. of the attack I had yesterday. I was suddenly seized with such sharp fever that I entirely lost consciousness; a bruised foot may have contributed to bring this on. It is therefore impossible for me to leave the house to-day. I hope, however, to be quite recovered by to-morrow, and I request Y.R.H. to appoint the orchestra to come to-morrow afternoon at a quarter to three o'clock, that the musicians may appear a little earlier, and leave sufficient time to try over the two Overtures. If Y.R.H. wishes to hear these, I shall require four horns; the Symphonies, however, require only two. For the proper performance of the Symphonies we must have at least four violins, four second, four first, two double basses, two violoncellos. I beg you will be so good as to let me know what you decide on. No pleasure can ever be greater to me than hearing my works performed before my illustrious pupil. May God speedily restore your health, which often causes me anxiety!

[K.]

[Footnote 1: The letters 272, 273, 274, relate to arrangements for musical meetings at which Beethoven caused his new works to be played for the Archduke.]

273.
TO THE ARCHDUKE RUDOLPH.

1819.

I beg you will be so kind as to let Herr von Wranitzky[1] know your commands about the music, and whether to bespeak two or four horns. I have already spoken with him, and suggested his only selecting musicians who can accomplish a performance, rather than a mere rehearsal.

[K.]

[Footnote 1: Anton Wranitzky (born 1760, died 1819), director of Prince Lobkowitz's opera and band. His brother Paul (born 1756, died 1808) was from 1785 to 1808 Kapellmeister at the Royal Opera in Vienna.]

274.
TO THE ARCHDUKE RUDOLPH.

1819.

It is impossible to double the parts by eleven o'clock to-morrow, most of the copyists having so much to write this week. I think therefore you will perhaps appoint next Saturday for our *resurrection day*, and by that time I expect to be entirely recovered, and better able to conduct, which would have been rather an arduous task for me to-morrow, in spite of my good-will. On Friday I do hope to be able to go out and inquire for Y.R.H.

[K.]

275.
TO THE ARCHDUKE RUDOLPH.

1819.

(*A Fragment.*)
The day when a High Mass of mine is performed in honor of the solemnities for Y.R.H. will be the most delightful of my life, and God will enlighten me so that my poor abilities may contribute to the splendors of that solemn occasion. I send you the Sonata with heartfelt gratitude; I think the violoncello part is wanting,--at least I could not lay my hand on it at the moment. As the work is beautifully engraved, I have taken the liberty to add a published copy, and also a violin quintet. In addition to the two pieces written in my hand on Y.R.H.'s name-day, there are two more; the last a grand *Fugato*, so that it forms one great sonata,[1] which is now shortly to appear, and has been long *in my heart* dedicated to Y.R.H. *The recent occurrence connected with Y.R.H.*[2] *is not in the slightest degree the cause of this.* I beg you will forgive my bad writing. I implore the Lord to bestow His richest blessings on Y.R.H., whose love of humanity is so comprehensive,--one of the choicest of all qualities; and in this respect Y.R.H. will always, either in a *worldly* or *spiritual* point of view, be one of our brightest examples.

[K.]

[Footnote 1: The Grand Sonata with two movements, and two additional ones, of which the last is a grand fugued one, can scarcely be any other than the pianoforte Sonata (Op. 106) composed in 1818, dedicated to the Archduke Rudolph, and published in September, 1819.]

[Footnote 2: The "recent occurrence" to which Beethoven alludes is no doubt his being appointed Archbishop.]

276.
TO HERR BLÖCHLINGER.

Mödling, Sept. 14, 1819.

85 florins enclosed.

DEAR SIR,--

I have the honor to send you payment for the ensuing month, which begins on the 22d Sept., and I add 10 florins in order to provide for any unforeseen expenses, which you will please account for to me on the 12th October. The following persons alone are to have free access to my nephew: Herr von Bernard, Herr von Oliva, Herr von Piuss.

If any persons, exclusive of those I have named, wish to see my nephew, I will give them a letter to you, when you will be so obliging as to admit them; for the distance to your house is considerable, and those who go there can only do so to oblige me, as, for example, the bandage-maker, &c., &c.

My nephew must never leave your house without a written permission from me. From this you will at once plainly perceive your line of conduct towards Carl's mother. I must impress on you the necessity of these rules (proceeding from the magistrates and myself) being strictly enforced. You, dear sir, are too little experienced in these circumstances, however obvious your other merits are to me, to act on your own judgment in the matter, as you have hitherto done. Credulity can in the present instance only lead to embarrassment, the result of which might prove injurious to you rather than beneficial, and this I wish to avoid for the sake of your own credit.

I hear that my nephew requires, or at all events wishes to have, a variety of things from me; he has only to apply to myself. Be so good as to forward all his letters through Herr Steiner & Co., Pater Noster Gässel, auf'm Graben.

Your obedient
BEETHOVEN,
Sole guardian of my nephew Carl Van Beethoven.

N.B. Any outlay will be at once repaid.

277.

Vienna, Sept. 21, 1819.

In honor of the visit of Herr Schlesinger of Berlin.

L. V. BEETHOVEN.

278.
TO HERR ARTARIA,--VIENNA.

Oct. 1, 1819.

MOST EXCELLENT AND MOST VIRTUOUS OF VIRTUOSI, AND NO HUMBUG!

While informing you of all sorts of things from which we hope you will draw the best conclusions, we request you to send us six (say 6) copies of the Sonata in B flat major, and also six copies of the variations on the Scotch songs, as the author's right. We beg you to forward them to Steiner, in Pater Noster Gässel, whence they will be sent to us with some other things.

In the hope that you are conducting yourself with all due propriety and decorum, we are your, &c.,

B----.

279.
A SKETCH WRITTEN BY BEETHOVEN,--

Corrected by Artaria's Bookkeeper, Wuister.

1819.

Having heard from Herr B. that Y.R. Highness [the Archduke Rudolph] has written a most masterly work, we wish to be the first to have the great honor of publishing Y.R. Highness's composition, that the world may become acquainted with the admirable talents of so illustrious a Prince. We trust Y. Royal Highness will comply with our respectful solicitation.

FALSTAFF--[1]
Ragged Rascal!

[Footnote 1: The name Beethoven gave to Artaria's partner, Bolderini.]

280.
TO ARTARIA.

Mödling, Oct. 12, 1819.

Pray forgive me, dear A. (?), for plaguing you as follows:--

We are coming to town the day after to-morrow, and expect to arrive at four o'clock. The two days' festival compels us to return the same day, as Carl must prepare with his master here for the second examination, these very holidays enabling the tutor to devote more time to him; but I must soon return to town on account of the certificate of Carl's birth, which costs more time and money than I like. I at all times dislike travelling by the *diligence*, and this one has moreover one peculiarity, that you may wish to go on what day you please, but it always turns out to be a Friday on which it sets off; and though a good Christian, still one Friday in the year is sufficient for me. I beg you will request the leader of the choir (the devil alone knows what the office is!) to be so good as to give us Carl's *certificate of birth* on the afternoon of the same day if possible. He might do so at seven o'clock in the morning, at the time we arrive; but he ought to be punctual, for Carl is to appear at the examination at half-past seven o'clock. So it must be *either to-morrow at* seven, or *at all events in the afternoon*. We shall call on you to-morrow before seven o'clock to inquire about this, with the proviso of a visit later in the day. In haste, and asking your pardon,

Your
L. VAN BEETHOVEN.

281.
PETITION TO THE MAGISTRACY.[1]

Oct. 30, 1819.

GENTLEMEN,--

My brother, Carl van Beethoven, died on November 5, 1815, leaving a boy twelve years old,--his son Carl. In his will, by clause 5, he bequeathed to me the guardianship of the boy, and in the codicil B he expressed a wish that his widow, Johanna, should have a share in this duty, adding that, for the sake of his child, he recommended her to submit to my guidance. This explicit declaration of the father, added to my legal claim, I being the nearest relative (clause 198), entitles me clearly to the guardianship of my nephew, Carl van Beethoven; and the Court of Justice, by their Decree E, committed to me, under existing circumstances, the guardianship, to the exclusion moreover of Beethoven's widow. A journey on business having compelled me to be for some time absent, I did not object to an official guardian supplying my place for the time, which was effected by the nomination of the Town Sequestrator, Herr Nussböck.

Being now, however, finally settled here, and the welfare of the boy very precious to me, both love and duty demand that I should resume my rights; especially as this talented lad is coming to an age when greater care and expense must be bestowed on his education, on which his whole future prospects depend. This duty ought not to be confided to any woman, far less to his mother, who possesses neither the will nor the power to adopt those measures indispensable to a manly and suitable education.

I am the more anxious to reclaim my guardianship of Carl, as I understand that, in consequence of want of means to defray the expenses of the school where I placed him, he is to be removed, and his mother wishes him to live with her, in order herself to spend his trifling provision, and thus save the one half of her pension, which, according to the decree, she is bound to apply to his use.

I have hitherto taken a paternal charge of my nephew, and I intend to do the same in future at my own expense, being resolved that the hopes of his deceased father, and the expectations I have formed for this clever boy, shall be fulfilled by his becoming an able man and a good citizen.

With this view I accordingly request that the highly respected magistrates whom I now address will be pleased to annul the Town Sequestrator Nussböck's interim office, and forthwith transfer to me the sole guardianship of my nephew Carl van Beethoven.[2]

LUDWIG VAN BEETHOVEN.

[Footnote 1: Evidently drawn up by his advocate, Dr. Bach, from Beethoven's notes.]
[Footnote 2: The magisterial decree of Nov. 4, 1819, was adverse to Beethoven.]

282.
TO F. RIES,--LONDON.

Vienna, Nov. 10, 1819.

DEAR RIES,--

I write to let you know that the Sonata is already out, though only a fortnight ago, and it is nearly six months since I sent you both the Quintet and the Sonata. In the course of a few days I will send them both to you engraved, and from them you can correct the two works.

Having received no letter from you on the subject, I thought the thing was at an end. I have indeed made shipwreck already with Neate this year! I only wish you could contrive to get me the fifty ducats which I have yet to receive, as I calculated on them, and really am in great want of money. I shall say no more to-day, but must inform you that I have nearly completed a *new Grand Mass*. Write to me whether you could do anything with this in London; but soon, very soon, and send the money soon also for both works. I will write more fully next time. In haste,

Your true and faithful friend,
BEETHOVEN.

283.
TO THE ARCHDUKE RUDOLPH.

Dec. 14, 1819.

Immediately on last leaving Y.R.H. I was taken ill, of which I apprised Y.R.H., but owing to a change in my household, neither the letter in question nor another to Y.R.H. was ever sent. In it I begged Y.R.H.'s indulgence, having some works on hand that I was obliged to dispatch with all speed, owing to which I was, alas! compelled to lay aside the Mass also.[1] I hope Y.R.H. will ascribe the delay solely to the pressure of circumstances. This is not the time to enter fully into the subject, but I must do so as soon as the right moment arrives, that Y.R.H. may not form too severe or undeserved a judgment of me. My heart is always with Y.R.H., and I trust at length circumstances may in so far change, that I may be able to contribute more than I have hitherto done, to perfecting your great talent. I think, however, Y.R.H. is already aware of my good-will in this respect, and is fully convinced that insurmountable obstacles alone can ever detain me from the most excellent of all princes, so revered by me, and so entwined with every feeling of my heart. I did not till yesterday hear of the mistake about the two letters, and I now intend to bring them myself, for I have no one in my service on whom I can depend. I will present myself at your house this afternoon at half-past four o'clock. My warmest thanks for Y.R.H.'s kind letter to me. When Y.R.H. thus vouchsafes to declare your esteem for me, it only heightens and increases my impulse to all that is good.

[Footnote 1: Another allusion to the Grand Mass in D, which seemed likely never to be completed.]

284.
MEMORANDUM.

1822.

The Mass[1] will soon be all in Y.R.H.'s hands; it ought to have been, and would have been so long ago, but--but--but--when Y.R.H. becomes acquainted with my circumstances, you will be surprised that I have even now been able to finish it.

[K.]

[Footnote 1: The circumstances which prevented the completion of this work were undoubtedly his perpetual state of strife with his nephew and his sister-in-law.]

285.
TO THE ARCHDUKE RUDOLPH.

I heard with heartfelt sorrow of Y.R.H.'s indisposition, but hope soon to hear of your recovery. Why am I also ill? for I might possibly discover the best mode of restoring Y.R.H. I will call again to inquire after Y.R.H., and hope to hear good news.

[K.]

286.
TO THE ARCHDUKE RUDOLPH.

I have been rather an invalid all this time, though I try to think myself tolerably well. I deeply regret to hear of Y.R.H.'s attack, especially as I knew nothing of it, or I certainly should have hastened to inquire whether it was in my power in any way to alleviate your sufferings. To-morrow, in compliance with Y.R.H.'s wish, I shall certainly enjoy the pleasure of seeing my own most dear and illustrious master.

[K.]

287.
TO THE ROYAL AND IMPERIAL HIGH COURT OF APPEAL.

Jan. 7, 1820.

GENTLEMEN,--

On the plea of the Decree A, I sought to have transferred to myself the guardianship of my nephew, Carl v. Beethoven, but was referred by the magistracy to the previous decision. On my consequent remonstrance the same result ensued.

I find myself the more aggrieved by this, inasmuch as not only are my own rights set at naught, but even the welfare of my nephew is thus utterly disregarded. I am therefore compelled to have recourse to the highest Court of Appeal to lay before them my well-founded claim, and rightfully to demand that the guardianship of my nephew should be restored to me.

My reasons are the following:--

1st. I am entitled to the guardianship of my nephew, not only by his father's will, but by law, and this the Court of Justice confirmed to the exclusion of the mother. When business called me away from Vienna, I conceded that Herr Nussböck should act for me *ad interim*. Having now, however, taken up my residence here, the welfare of my nephew demands that I should again undertake the office of his guardian.

2d. My nephew has arrived at an age when he requires to be trained to a higher degree of cultivation. Neither his mother nor his present guardian are calculated to guide the boy in the pursuit of his studies. The former, in the first place, because she is a woman; and as to her conduct, it has been legally proved that, to say the least of it, she has no creditable testimonials to bring forward,[1] on which account she was expressly prohibited from acting by the Court of Justice. How the Honorable Magistracy could nevertheless again appoint her is quite incomprehensible. The latter is unfit; because, on the one hand, his office as sequestrator and administrator of houses and lands, occupies his time too much to enable him properly to undertake the duties of guardian to the boy; and, on the other, because his previous occupation as a paper manufacturer, does not inspire me with any confidence that he possesses the intelligence or judgment indispensable to conduct a scientific education.

3d. The welfare of my nephew is dearer to my heart than it can be to any one else. I am myself childless, and have no relations except this boy, who is full of talent, and I have good grounds to hope the best for him, if properly trained. Now I am compelled to hear that he has been delayed a whole year by remaining in his previous class, from want of means to defray the expense, and that his mother intends to remove him from his present school, and wishes him to live with her. What a misfortune to the boy, were he to become a victim to the mismanagement of his mother, who would fain squander on herself that portion of her pension which she is obliged to devote to the education of her son!

I have therefore declared in due form to the Honorable Magistracy that I am myself willing to undertake the expenses of his present school, and also to provide the various masters required. Being rather deaf, which is an impediment to conversation, I have requested the aid of a colleague, and suggested for this purpose Herr Peters, Councillor of Prince Lobkowitz, in order that a person may forthwith be appointed to superintend the education and progress of my nephew, that his moral character may one day command esteem, and whose acquirements may be a sure guaranty to all those who feel an interest in the youth's welfare, that he will undoubtedly receive the education and culture necessary to develop his abilities.

My efforts and wishes have no other aim than to give the boy the best possible education,--his abilities justifying the brightest hopes,--and to fulfil the trust placed in my brotherly love by his father. The shoot is still flexible; but if longer neglected it will become crooked, and outgrow the gardener's training hand, and upright bearing, intellect, and character, be destroyed forever.

I know no duty more sacred than the education and training of a child. The chief duties of a guardian consist in knowing how to appreciate what is good, and in adopting a right course; then alone has proper attention been devoted to the welfare of his ward, whereas in opposing what is good he neglects his duty.

Indeed, keeping in view what is most for the benefit of the boy, I do not object to the mother in so far sharing in the duties of a guardian that she may visit her son, and see him, and be apprised of all the measures adopted for his education; but to intrust her with the sole guardianship of the boy without a strict guardian by her side, would cause the irrevocable ruin of her son.

On these cogent grounds I reiterate my well-founded solicitation, and feel the more confident of a favorable answer, as the welfare of my nephew alone guides my steps in this affair.[2]

LUDWIG VAN BEETHOVEN.

[Footnote 1: Schindler states that during these law proceedings the widow of Beethoven's brother had another child.]

[Footnote 2: The Court excluded Carl's mother from all share in his education, and from all direct influence over her son, and again restored to Beethoven the full authority of a guardian.]

288.
TO HIS HIGHNESS THE ARCHDUKE RUDOLPH.

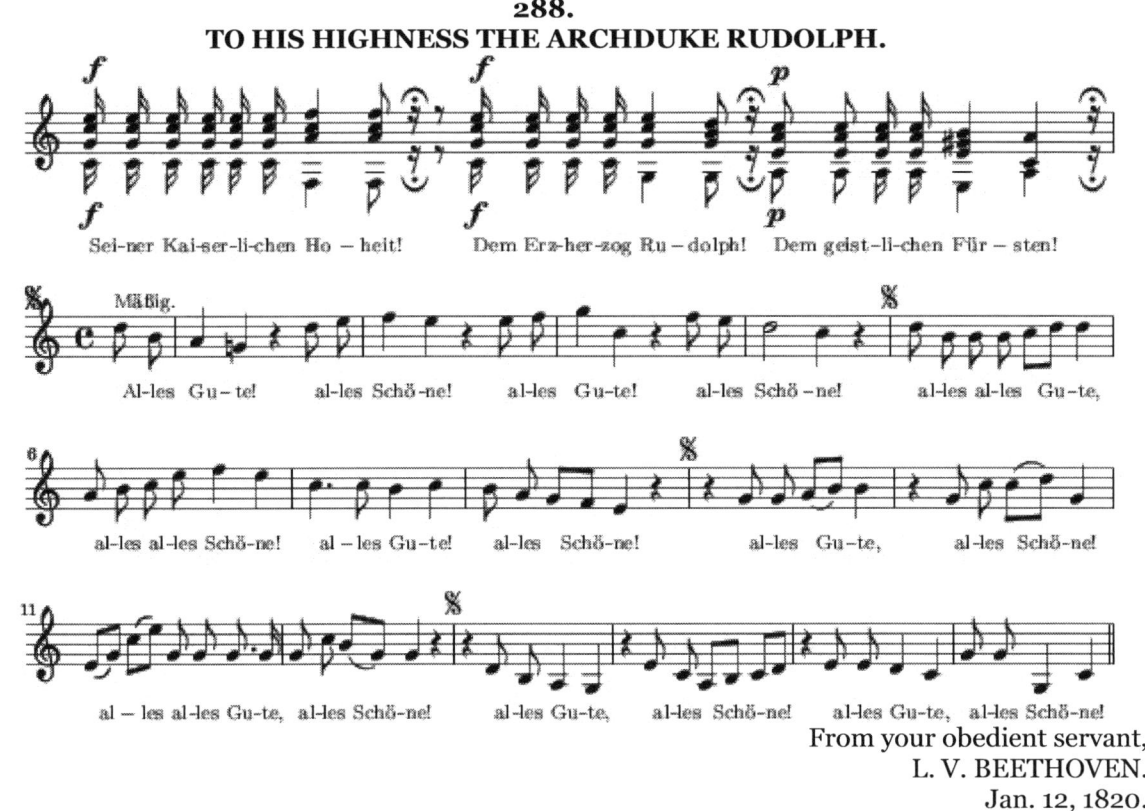

From your obedient servant,
L. V. BEETHOVEN.
Jan. 12, 1820.

289.
TESTIMONIAL IN FAVOR OF HERR V. KANDELER.

It is certainly the duty of every musical composer to become acquainted with all the earlier as well as more modern poets, in order to select what is most suitable to his purpose for songs. Such, however, not being invariably the case, this present collection of Herr v. Kandeler's cannot fail to be useful and commendable to many who wish to write songs, and also tend to induce more able poets to contribute something in the same direction.

LUDWIG V. BEETHOVEN.--M.P.

I entirely agree with Herr v. Beethoven.

JOS. WEIGEL.

290.
TO THEODORE AMADEUS HOFFMANN.[1]

Vienna, March 23, 1820.

I seize the opportunity through Herr N. of approaching a man so gifted as yourself. You have also written of my humble self, and Herr N.N. showed me some lines of yours about me in his album; I have, therefore, every reason to believe that you feel some interest in me. Permit me to say that, on the part of so talented a man as yourself, this is truly gratifying to me. I wish you all possible good and happiness, and remain,

Sir, with esteem, your obedient
BEETHOVEN.

[Footnote 1: It is well known that Hoffmann, in the years 1809 to 1812, wrote the first really important articles on Beethoven's works for the *Leipzig A.M. Zeitung* on his instrumental music, his trios, and masses, &c., &c.]

291.
TO HERR HASLINGER,--ADJUTANTERL.

I request the Adjutant to lend me the score of the Overture in E flat, which I will return as soon as the performance is over. I also beg he will be so good as to send me Kirnberger's work to supply the place of mine, as I am at this moment giving lessons in counterpoint, and have been unable to find my own manuscript amid my confused mass of papers. Yours,

MI CONTRA FA.

292.
TO TOBIAS,--ADJUTANT.

MOST WORTHY ADJUTANT,--

I have made a bet of ten florins, W.W., against the truth of your having been obliged to pay a compensation of 2000 florins to Artaria for the new edition of Mozart's works, which have been again and again engraved and sold everywhere. I really wish to know the truth on this subject, for I cannot possibly believe what is said. If it be the fact that you have been so unhandsomely treated, then *Ah, dolce contento* must pay the ten florins. Send me a true report. Farewell; be a good Christian. Your

BEETHOVEN.

293.
TO THE ARCHDUKE RUDOLPH.

Vienna, April 3, 1820.

YOUR ROYAL HIGHNESS,--

So far as I can recollect, when I was about to wait on you, I was told that Y.R.H. was indisposed; I called on Sunday evening to inquire, having been assured that Y.R.H. did not intend to set off on Monday. In accordance with my usual custom, not to remain long in an anteroom, I hurried away after receiving this information, though I observed that the gentleman in waiting wished to say something to me. Unhappily I did not hear till Monday afternoon that Y.R.H. had really gone to Olmütz. I must confess that this caused me a very painful feeling, but my consciousness of never having neglected my duty in any respect, induced me to suppose that the same may have been the case on this occasion, as it often is in human life,--for I can easily conceive that Y.R.H., immersed in ceremonies and novel impressions, had very little time to spare in Olmütz for other things. I should otherwise certainly have anticipated Y.R.H. in writing. May I ask you graciously to inform me what length of stay you intend to make in Olmütz? It was reported that Y.R.H. intended to return here towards the end of May; but a few days ago I heard that you were to remain a year and a half in Olmütz; owing to this I may perhaps have adopted wrong measures, not with regard to Y.R.H., but myself. As soon as I receive information from you on the subject, I will enter into further explanations. May I also beg that in the mean time Y.R.H. will not listen to certain reports about me? I have heard a great deal of what may be termed gossip here, which people seem to think may be acceptable to Y.R.H. As Y.R.H. is pleased to say that I am one of those whom you esteem, I can confidently declare that Y.R.H. is the person whom I value most in the universe. Although no courtier, I believe that Y.R.H. knows me too thoroughly to believe that mere selfish interest has ever attached or attracted me towards Y.R.H., but, on the contrary, true and heartfelt affection alone. I can with truth say that a second Blondel has long since set forth on his pilgrimage, and if no Richard can be found in this world for me, God shall be my Sovereign!

It seems to me that my idea of giving a quartet is the best; even though some works have been already performed on a grand scale at Olmütz, still something might thus be introduced into Moravia to attract the attention of the musical world, and for the benefit of Art.

If, according to the above reports, Y.R.H. should return here in May, I advise Y.R.H. to reserve your *spiritual children* for me [see No. 279] till then, because it would be better that I should hear them performed by yourself. But if your stay in Olmütz is really to be of such long duration, I will receive them now with the greatest pleasure, and strive to accompany Y.R.H. to the summit of Parnassus. May God preserve Y.R.H. in health for the good of humanity, and also for that of all your warm admirers. I beg you will be graciously pleased soon to write to me. Y.R.H. cannot fail to be convinced of my readiness at all times to fulfil your wishes.

I am Y.R.H.'s humble and faithful servant,

LUDWIG V. BEETHOVEN

294.
TO THE ARCHDUKE RUDOLPH.

Mödling, Aug. 3, 1820.

I have this moment received the letter in which Y.R.H. informs me yourself of your journey hither, and I sincerely thank Y.R.H. for such a mark of attention. I intended to have hastened to town to-morrow to wait on Y.R.H., but no carriage is to be had; I expect however to get one before next Saturday, when I shall lose no time, and set off at an early hour to inquire for Y.R.H. With regard to the sacrifice Y.R.H. intends to offer up to the Muses, I will make a proposal verbally on the subject. I heartily rejoice in knowing that Y.R.H. is once more so near me. May I in all respects be enabled to assist in fulfilling your wishes! May Heaven bless Y.R.H., and mature all your plans!

[K.]

295.
TO HERR ARTARIA, FALSTAFF, & CO.

Vienna, Oct. 26, 1820.

I politely request that you will hand over to Herr Oliva the sum of 300 florins, which has no doubt already been received by you in full. Having been entirely occupied by removing to my new lodgings, I could not do myself the honor of expressing my thanks to you and Sir John Falstaff in person.

Your obedient servant,
LUDWIG V. BEETHOVEN.

296.
TO BOLDERINI.

MY VERY WORTHY FALSTAFF!--

I request, with all due civility, that you will send me a copy of each of the two works for pianoforte and flute, with variations. As for the receipt, you shall have it to-morrow; and I also beg you will forward it forthwith. Give my compliments to Herr Artaria, and thank him from me for his kind offer of an advance, but as I have received from abroad the money due to me, I do not require to avail myself of his aid. Farewell, Knight Falstaff; do not be too dissipated, read the Gospel, and be converted!

We remain, your well-affected
BEETHOVEN.

To Sir John Falstaff, Knight.
To the care of Herr Artaria & Co.

297.
TO THE ARCHDUKE RUDOLPH.

Mödling, Sept. 1820.

Since last Tuesday evening I have been far from well, but hoped by Friday, certainly, to have had the happiness of waiting on Y.R.H. This proved a delusion, and it is only to-day that I am able to say confidently that I expect to present myself before Y.R.H. next Monday or Tuesday at an early hour. I ascribe my illness to having taken an open *calèche*, in order not to miss my appointment with Y.R.H. The day was very wet and positively *cold* here towards the evening. Nature seems almost to have been offended by the liberty I took, and by my audacity, and to have punished me in consequence. May Heaven bestow on Y.R.H. all that is good and holy, as well as every charm and blessing, and on *me* your favor, *but only in so far as justice sanctions*!

[K.]

298.
TO HERR ARTARIA & CO.

Vienna, Dec. 17, 1820.

I thank you warmly for the advance of 150 florins, for which I have made out the receipt in the name of his Imperial Highness the Cardinal, and I beg, as I am in danger of losing one of my bank shares, that you will advance me another 150 florins, which I pledge myself to repay within three months at latest from this date. As a proof of my gratitude, I engage in this letter to make over to you, as your exclusive property, one of my compositions, consisting of two or more movements, without claiming payment for it hereafter.

Your ever-complaisant
BEETHOVEN.
[L.S.]

299.
TO TOBIAS V. HASLINGER.

Baden, Sept. 10, 1821.

MY VERY DEAR FRIEND,--

On my way to Vienna yesterday, sleep overtook me in my carriage, which was by no means strange, for having been obliged to rise so early every morning, I never had a good night's sleep. While thus slumbering I dreamt that I had gone on a far journey, to no less a place than to Syria, on to Judea, and back, and then all the way to Arabia, when at length I actually arrived at Jerusalem. The Holy City gave rise to thoughts of the Holy Books. No wonder then if the man Tobias occurred to me, which also naturally led me to think of our own little Tobias and our great Tobias. Now during my dream-journey, the following Canon came into my head:--

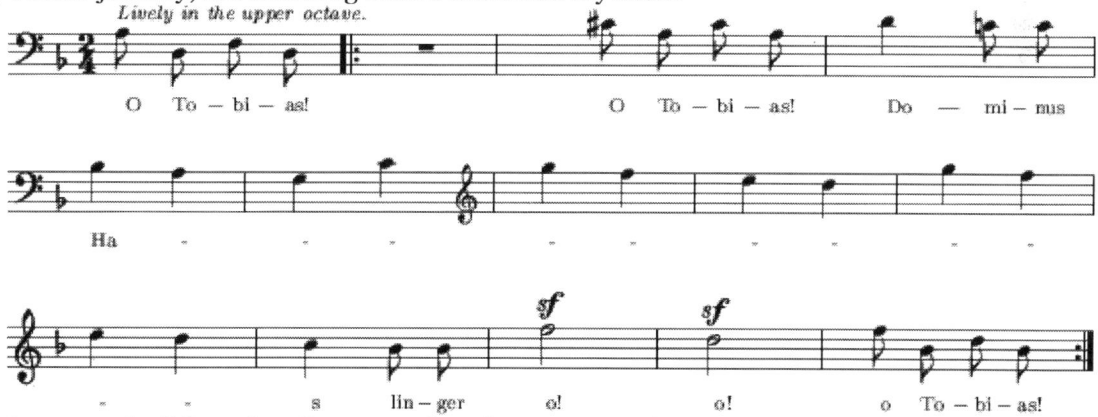

But scarcely did I wake when away flew the Canon, and I could not recall any part of it. On returning here however, next day, in the same carriage, (that of a poor Austrian musician,) I resumed my dream-journey, being, however, on this occasion wide awake, when lo and behold! in accordance with the laws of the association of ideas the same Canon again flashed across me; so being now awake I held it as fast as Menelaus did Proteus, only permitting it to be changed into three parts.

Farewell! I intend to send next something composed on Steiner's name, to show that his is no heart of stone [Stein]. Adieu, my good friend; it is my most heartfelt wish that you may prosper as a publisher; may all credit be given to you, and yet may you never require credit. Sing daily the Epistles of St. Paul, and daily visit Father Werner, who can show you in his little book how to go straight to heaven. See, how anxious I am about the welfare of your soul!

I remain always, with infinite pleasure, henceforth and forever,

Your faithful debtor,
BEETHOVEN.

300.
TO THE ARCHDUKE RUDOLPH.

Unterdöbling, July 18, 1821.

I yesterday heard of Y.R.H.'s arrival here; joyful tidings for me, but saddened by knowing that it must be some time before I can have the good fortune to wait on Y.R.H.; having been long very ill, at last *jaundice* declared itself, which I consider a most loathsome malady. I trust, however, I shall be so far recovered as to see Y.R.H. before you leave this. Last winter, too, I had some very severe rheumatic attacks. Much of this proceeds from the melancholy state of my family affairs; I have hitherto hoped, by every possible exertion on my part, at last to remedy these. That Providence, who searches my inmost heart, and knows that as a man I have striven sacredly to fulfil all the duties imposed on me by humanity, God, and Nature, will no doubt one day extricate me from all these troubles. The Mass [in D] will be delivered to Y.R.H. here. I hope Y.R.H. will excuse my entering into the various causes of the delay. The details could not be otherwise than painful to Y.R.H. I would often gladly have written to Y.R.H. from here, but you told me to wait till I first heard from you. What, then, was I to do? Y.R.H. might have been displeased had I not attended to your injunction, and I know that there are people who are glad to calumniate me to Y.R.H., which pains me exceedingly. I therefore often think that my sole recourse is to keep quiet till Y.R.H. expresses a wish either to see or to hear of me. I was told that Y.R.H. had been indisposed, but I hope it was nothing serious. May Heaven shower down its most precious blessings on Y.R.H.! I trust it may not be very long before I shall be so fortunate as to assure Y.R.H. how entirely I am, &c., &c.

[K.]

301.
TO THE ARCHDUKE RUDOLPH.

Unterdöbling, July 18, 1821.

I have written a long and minute letter to Y.R.H., which my copyist Schlemmer will deliver. I wrote it on hearing the day before yesterday of the arrival of Y.R.H. How much I grieve that the attack of jaundice with which I am affected prevents my at once hastening to Y.R.H. to express in person my joy at your arrival. May the Lord of all things, for the sake of so many others, take Y.R.H. under His protection!

[K.]

302.
TO THE MOST CELEBRATED MUSIC FIRM IN EUROPE, MESSRS. STEINER & CO., PATERNOSTER-(MISERERE) GÄSSEL.

I request Geh'-bauer[1] to send me two tickets, as some of my friends wish to attend your hole-and-corner music. You probably have some of these worthless admission tickets; so let me have one or two.

The part I send belongs to the Chorus, of which Bauer has the other portions. Your *amicus*

BEETHOVEN.

[Footnote 1: Gebauer established the "Concerts Spirituels" in 1819, and died in 1822.]

303.
ADDRESS UNKNOWN.

Baden, Sept. 27, 1821.

I hope, sir, that you will forgive the liberty I take in thus intruding on you. The bearer of this, H. v.----, has been commissioned by me to exchange or sell a bank-note. Being ignorant of everything connected with these matters, I beg you will be so good as to communicate your views and advice to the bearer. The two illnesses I had last winter and summer rather deranged all my calculations. I have been here since the 7th of September, and must remain till the end of October. All this costs a great deal of money, and prevents my earning it as usual. I indeed expect shortly to receive money from abroad, but as bank-notes stand so high at present, I consider this the easiest resource, and intend subsequently to purchase a new bank-note in its place.

Immediate--in haste.

Your friend,
BEETHOVEN.

[This unsealed letter was enclosed in an envelope on which was written:]

You will at once see what kind of commercial genius I am. After writing the enclosed, I for the first time consulted a friend about the note, who pointed out to me that all I had to do was to cut off a *coupon*, and the affair was completed. I rejoice, therefore, not to be obliged to plague you further on the subject.

Yours,
BEETHOVEN.

304.
TO THE ARCHDUKE RUDOLPH.

Feb. 27, 1822.

I went to-day early to the Palace, not, indeed, with the intention of meeting Y.R.H., (not being yet dressed), but only to beg Zips to mention that I had called, and was sincerely rejoiced at your arrival here; but I could no longer discover Y.R.H.'s apartments, and wherever I knocked in the hope of finding Y.R.H., my dress seemed to be so closely scrutinized that I hurried away, and write to-day to recommend myself to Y.R.H. To-morrow I intend to pay my respects to Y.R.H., when I hope also to hear whether the usual *musical and intellectual meetings* are to continue, and when they are to take place. My not having written all this time to Y.R.H. has indeed a very bad appearance, but I delayed from day to day, hoping always to send the Mass, the mistakes in which were really quite dreadful; so much so that I was obliged to revise *every part*, and thus the delay occurred. Other pressing occupations and various circumstances tended to impede me, which is often the case when a man least expects it. That Y.R.H., however, was ever present with me is shown by the following copies of some novelties,[1] which have been lying finished by me for some time for Y.R.H., but I resolved not to forward them till I could at the same time send the Mass. The latter now only requires binding, when it shall be respectfully delivered to Y.R.H. by myself. Sincerely rejoiced at the hope of soon personally waiting on Y.R.H., I remain, with devoted homage, yours till death.

[K.]

[Footnote 1: The *novelties* which Beethoven sends to the Archduke are:--
Six *bagatelles* for the pianoforte,   Op. 126 (composed in 1821).
Sonata for pianoforte in E major   " 109 (" " ?1821).
   "   "   "   A flat major   " 110 ("   " 1821).
]

305.
TO F. RIES,--LONDON.

Vienna, April 6, 1822.

MY DEAREST AND BEST RIES,--

Having been again in bad health during the last ten months, I have hitherto been unable to answer your letter. I duly received the 26l. sterling, and thank you sincerely; I have not, however, yet got the sonata you dedicated to me. My greatest work is a *Grand Mass* that I have recently written. As time presses, I can only say what is most urgent. What would the Philharmonic give me for a symphony?

I still cherish the hope of going to London next spring, if my health admits of it! You will find in me one who can thoroughly appreciate my dear pupil, now become a great master, and who can tell what benefit art might derive from our conjunction! I am, as ever, wholly devoted to my Muse, who constitutes the sole happiness of my life, and I toil and act for others as I best can. You have two children; I only one (my brother's son); but you are married, so both yours will not cost you so much as my one costs me.

Now farewell! kiss your handsome wife for me until I can perform this solemn act in person.
Your attached

BEETHOVEN.

Pray send me your dedication, that I may strive to return the compliment, which I mean to do as soon as I receive your work.

306.
TO HERREN PETERS & CO., MUSIC PUBLISHERS,--LEIPZIG.

Vienna, June 5, 1822.

GENTLEMEN,--

You did me the honor to address a letter to me at a time when I was much occupied, and I have also been extremely unwell for the last five months. I now only reply to the principal points. Although I met Steiner by chance a few days ago, and asked him jestingly what he had brought me from Leipzig, he did not make *the smallest* allusion to *your commission or to yourself.* He urged me, however, in the very strongest manner, to *pledge myself to give him the exclusive right of publishing all my works, both present and future*,--and indeed to *sign a contract to that effect*,--which I declined. This *trait* sufficiently proves to you why I often give the preference to other publishers both home and foreign. I love uprightness and integrity, and am of opinion that no one should drive a hard bargain with artists, for, alas! however brilliant the exterior of Fame may appear, an artist does not enjoy the privilege of being the daily guest of Jupiter on Olympus; unhappily commonplace humanity only too often unpleasantly drags him down from these pure ethereal heights.

The *greatest* work I have hitherto written is a *Grand Mass* with Choruses, and four *obbligati* voice parts, and full orchestra. Several persons have applied to me for this work, and I have been offered 100 Louis d'or, hard cash, for it; but I demand at least 1000 florins C.M. [20 florins to the mark], for which sum I will also furnish a pianoforte arrangement. Variations on a waltz [Diabelli's] for the piano (they are numerous), 30 ducats in gold,--N.B. Vienna ducats. With regard to songs, I have several rather important descriptive ones: as, for example, a comic Aria, with full orchestra, on Goethe's text, "Mit Mädeln sich vertragen;" and another Aria, in the same style, 16 ducats each (furnishing also a pianoforte arrangement if required); also several descriptive songs, with pianoforte accompaniment, 12 ducats each; among these is a little Italian Cantata, with Recitative; there is also a Song with recitative among the German ones. A Song with pianoforte accompaniment, 8 ducats. An Elegy, four voices, with the accompaniment of *two violins, viola, and violoncello*, 24 ducats. A Dervise Chorus, with full orchestra, 20 ducats.

Also the following instrumental music: a Grand March for full orchestra, with pianoforte accompaniment, 12 ducats, written for the tragedy of "Tarpeia." Romance for the violin (a solo with full orchestra), 15 ducats. Grand Terzet for two oboes, and one English horn (which might be arranged for other instruments), 30 ducats. Four military Marches with Turkish music; when applied for, I will name the sum. *Bagatelles*, or minor pianoforte solos, the price to be fixed when required. The above works are all completed. Solo pianoforte Sonata, 40 ducats (which could soon be delivered); Quartet for *two violins, tenor, and violoncello*, 50 ducats (this will also soon be ready). I am by no means so anxious about these, however, as about *a full and complete edition of my works*, being desirous to edit them during my lifetime. I have indeed received many proposals on this subject, but accompanied by stipulations to which I could scarcely agree, and which I neither could nor would fulfil. I am willing to undertake, in the course of two years, or possibly a year, or a year and a half, with proper assistance, to edit and superintend a complete edition of my works, and to furnish a new composition in each style; namely, a new work in the style of variations, one in the sonata style, and so on in every separate class of work that I have ever composed, and for the whole combined I ask 10,000 florins C.M.

I am no man of business, and only wish I were; as it is, I am guided by the offers made to me by different competitors for my works, and such a competition is rather strong just now. I request you to say nothing on the subject, because, as you may perceive from the proceedings of these gentlemen, I am exposed to a great deal of annoyance. When once my works appear published by you, I shall no longer be plagued. I shall be very glad if a connection be established between us, having heard you so well spoken of. You will then also find that I infinitely prefer dealing with *one* person of your description than with a variety of people of the ordinary stamp.

Pray, let me have an immediate answer, as I am now on the verge of deciding on the publication of various works. If you consider it worth while, be so good as to send me a duplicate of the list with which you furnished Herr Steiner. In the expectation of a speedy reply, I remain, with esteem,

Your obedient
LUDWIG VAN BEETHOVEN.

307.
TO HERREN PETERS & CO.

Vienna, July 26, 1822.

I write merely to say that I agree to give you the Mass and pianoforte arrangement of it for 1000 florins C.M. You shall receive the above, written out in score, by the end of July, perhaps a few days sooner or later. As I am always very much occupied, and have been indisposed for the last five months, and works to be sent to a distance requiring the most careful supervision, I must proceed rather more slowly than usual. At all events, Steiner shall get nothing further from me, as he has just played me a most Jewish trick; so he is not one of those who might have had the Mass. The competition for my works is at present very great, for which I thank the Almighty, as I have hitherto been such a loser. I am the foster-father of my brother's destitute child, a boy who shows so much aptitude for scientific pursuits that not only does his study of these, and his maintenance, cost a great deal of money, but I must also strive to make some future provision for him; being neither Indians nor Iroquois, who, as we know, leave everything to Providence, whereas we consider a pauper's existence to be a very sad one.

I assure you on my honor, which, next to God, is what I prize most, that I authorized no one to accept commissions for me. My fixed principle has always been never to make any offer to publishers; not from pride, but simply from a wish to ascertain how far the empire of my small talents extended.

I must conclude for to-day, and wishing you every success, I am, with esteem,

Your obedient
BEETHOVEN.

308.[1]
TO HERR PETERS.

Vienna, August 3, 1822.

I already wrote to you that my health was still far from being quite restored. I am obliged to have recourse to baths and mineral waters as well as to medicine; all this makes me rather unpunctual, especially as I must go on writing; corrections, too, run away with a great deal of time.

As to the songs and marches and other trifles, my choice is still undecided, but by the 15th of this month everything shall be ready to be sent off. I await your orders on the subject, and in the mean time shall make no use of your bill of exchange. As soon as I know that the money for the Mass and the other works has arrived here, all shall be ready for delivery by the 15th; and after that date I must set off to some mineral waters near this, when it will be most desirable for me to avoid all business for a time. More as to other matters when less occupied. Pray, do not suspect me of any ignoble motives. It pains me when I am obliged to bargain.

In haste. With esteem, yours,
BEETHOVEN.

[Footnote 1: Schindler states that the advance of 360 florins C.M. was made to Beethoven in August, 1822. The receipt is dated Nov. 30, 1825.]

309.
TO HERR ARTARIA.

August 22, 1822.

Being overwhelmed with work, I can only briefly say that I will always do what I can to repay your obliging kindness to me. With regard to the Mass, I have been offered 1000 florins (C.M.) for it. My circumstances do not permit me to accept a less sum from you; all that I can do is to give you the preference. Rest assured that I do not ask you one farthing more than others have offered me, which I can prove to you by written documents. You can consider about this, but I must request you to send me an answer on the subject to-morrow, it being a post-day, and my decision expected elsewhere. With regard to the 150 florins for which I am your debtor, I intend to make you a proposal, as I stand in great need of the 1000 florins.

I beg you will observe strict secrecy as to the Mass. Now, as ever,

Your grateful friend,
BEETHOVEN.

310.
TO HERR PETERS,--LEIPZIG

Vienna, November 22, 1822.

I now reply to your letter of the 9th November, in which I expected to find just reproaches for my apparent negligence, you having sent me the money and as yet received nothing in return. Unfair as this may appear, I know you would be mollified towards me in a few minutes were we to meet.

Everything is now ready for you, except selecting the songs, but at all events you shall receive one more than our agreement. I can send you more *bagatelles* than I promised, as I have got ten others beside; if you write to me immediately, I will send you these, or as many as you wish for, along with the rest.

My health, indeed, is not entirely reestablished by the baths, yet on the whole I think I have improved. I had another annoyance here, owing to a person having engaged an unsuitable lodging for me, which is hard on me, as I cannot yet accustom myself to it, and my occupations are thus sadly deranged.

The case with regard to the Mass stands thus: I finished one long ago, and another is in progress. There is always a certain degree of gossip about people of our class, which has, no doubt, misled you. I don't yet know which you are to get. Besieged on all sides, I am almost forced to testify the reverse of the *dictum* that "the spirit cannot be weighed." I send you my best wishes, and trust that time will foster a beneficial and honorable connection between us.

BEETHOVEN.

311.
TO THE ARCHDUKE RUDOLPH.

I was extremely unwell both yesterday and the day before; unfortunately there was no one whom I could send to apprise Y.R.H. of the fact. As I felt better towards evening, I went into the town to make Schlemmer correct the Sonata.[1] He was not at home, so I requested him to come here to-day. I send the Sonata by him, and will come in to-day before four o'clock to wait on Y.R.H.

[K.]

[Footnote 1: The C minor pianoforte Sonata, Op. 111?]

312.
TO HERR PETERS.

Vienna, December 20, 1822.

I take advantage of a moment's leisure to-day to answer your letter. Not one of all the works that are your property is unfinished, but time is too precious to particularize all the details that prevent the copying and sending off the music to you. I recollect in a former letter having offered you some more *bagatelles*, but I by no means press you to take them. If you wish only to have the four, so be it; but in that case I must make a different selection. Herr ---- has not as yet got anything from me. Herr ---- begged me to make him a present of the songs for the "Journal de la Mode," which, in fact, I did not write for money; indeed, I find it quite impossible to act in every case according to so much *per cent*. It is painful for me to calculate in this manner oftener than is absolutely necessary. My position is far from being so brilliant as you think, &c., &c. It is not possible to listen to all these proposals at once, being far too numerous, but many cannot be refused. A commission is not always quite in accordance with the inclinations of an author. If my salary were not so far reduced as to be no salary at all,[1] I would write nothing but symphonies for a full orchestra, and church music, or at most quartets.

Of my minor works, you can still have Variations for two oboes and one English horn, on the theme from "Don Giovanni," "*La ci darem la mano*," and a Gratulation Minuet for a full orchestra. I should be glad, likewise, to have your opinion about the full edition of my works.

In the most desperate haste, your obedient

BEETHOVEN.

[Footnote 1: It was reduced from 4000 gulden to 800.]

313.
TO F. RIES,--LONDON

Vienna, December 20, 1822.

MY DEAR RIES,--

I have been so overburdened with work that I am only now able to reply to your letter of November 15. I accept with pleasure the proposal to write a new symphony for the Philharmonic Society. Although the prices given by the English cannot be compared with those paid by other nations, still I would gladly write even gratis for those whom I consider the first artists in Europe-- were I not still, as ever, the poor Beethoven.

If I were only in London, what would I not write for the Philharmonic! For Beethoven, thank God! can write--if he can do nothing in the world besides! If Providence only vouchsafes to restore my health, which is at least improving, I shall then be able to respond to the many proposals from all parts of Europe, and even North America, and may thus perhaps be some day in clover.

314.
TO IGNAZ RITTER VON SEYFRIED.

1822.

MY DEAR AND WORTHY BROTHER IN APOLLO,--

I heartily thank you for the trouble you have taken in aiding my *charitable work*.[1] I rejoice that its success is universally admitted, and hope you will never fail to let me know when it is in my power to serve you by my poor talents. The worthy municipal corporation is, no doubt, thoroughly convinced of my good-will; in order to give fresh proofs of it, we ought to have a friendly interview as to the mode in which I can best serve the corporation. When such a master as yourself takes an interest in us, our pinions ought never to droop.

I am, with the warmest esteem,
Your friend,
BEETHOVEN.

[Footnote 1: Seyfried, at a concert for the benefit of the Burgher Hospital, performed Beethoven's grand fugue *Fest Ouverture* (in C major, in Op. 124), 1822, in celebration of the opening of the new Josephstadt Theatre. The written parts were returned to him with the grateful thanks of the committee.]

THIRD PART

LIFE'S TROUBLES AND CLOSE.
1823 TO 1827.

315.
TO ZELTER.[1]

Vienna, Feb. 8, 1823.

MY BRAVE COLLEAGUE IN ART,--

I write, having a favor to ask of you, for we are now so distant from each other that we can no longer converse together, and, indeed, unhappily, we can seldom write either. I have written a grand mass, which might also be given as an oratorio (for the benefit of the poor, a good established custom here). I do not wish to publish it in the usual way, but to dispose of it to some of the leading courts alone. I ask fifty ducats for it. No copies are to be sold except those subscribed for, so that the mass will be, as it were, in manuscript; but there must be a fair number of subscribers, if any profit is to accrue to the author. I have made an application to the Prussian embassy here, to know if the King of Prussia would vouchsafe to take a copy, and I have also written to Prince Radziwill, to ask him to interest himself in the affair. I beg you likewise to do what you can for me. It is a work that might likewise be useful to the Academy of Singing, for there is scarcely any portion of it that could not be almost entirely executed by voices. The more these are increased and multiplied in combination with instruments, the more effective would be the result. It ought to be appropriate also as an oratorio, for such societies as those for the benefit of the poor require marks of this kind. Having been an invalid for some years past, and consequently my position anything but brilliant, I have had recourse to this scheme. I have written much; but as to profits, they are nearly *nil*! The more do I look upwards; but both for his own sake, and that of others, man is obliged to turn his eyes earthwards; for this, too, is part of the destiny of humanity. I embrace you, my dear fellow-artist, and am, with sincere esteem,

Your friend,
BEETHOVEN.

[Footnote 1: Zelter was in Vienna in 1819.]

316.
TO F. RIES,--LONDON.

... Manage this as soon as you can for your poor friend. I also expect my travelling route from you. Things have become quite too bad here, and I am fleeced worse than ever. If I do not go at all, lo! and behold a *crimen laesae*!... As it seems that you wish soon to have a dedication from me, I gladly comply with your request, much more so than with that of any great man; though, *entre nous*, the devil alone can tell how soon one may fall into their hands! The dedication to you will be written on the new symphony; and I hope I shall at length receive yours to me.

B. is to open the letter he took charge of for the King [George IV.], in which he will see what I have written to His Majesty on the subject of the "Battle of Vittoria." The tenor of the enclosed is the same; but not a word as to the mass.[1] Our amiable friend B. must try to get me at least a battle-axe or a turtle for it! The engraved copy of the score of "The Battle" must also be presented to the King. This letter will cost you a good deal [seventeen shillings]; but I beg you will deduct it from your remittance to me. How much I regret being so troublesome! May God prosper you!

Say all that is amiable to your wife till I come myself. Beware! you think me old; but I am a young veteran!

Yours, as ever,
B.

[Footnote 1: On February 24, 1823, Beethoven wrote to the King of England that, so far back as 1813, he had sent him "Wellington's Victory," but never had received any communication on the subject; he, therefore, now sent an engraved copy of the work, which had been intended for him since 1815. He closed the letter by saying: "Convinced of the discrimination and kindness which your Majesty has always evinced in protecting and encouraging art and artists, the undersigned ventures to hope that your Majesty will graciously take the matter into consideration, and vouchsafe to comply with his respectful solicitation."]

317.
TO SCHINDLER.

MY VERY BEST OPTIMUS OPTIME,--

Pray try to hunt out a philanthropist who will advance me some money on a bank-share, that I may not put the generosity of my friends too much to the test, nor myself be placed in difficulty by the delay of this money, for which I have to thank the fine plans and arrangements of my precious brother.

You must not let it appear that this money is really wanted.

318.
TO SCHINDLER.

DEAR SCHINDLER,--

Don't forget the bank-share. It is greatly needed; it would be very annoying to be brought into court; indeed, I would not be so for the whole world. My brother's conduct is quite worthy of him. The tailor is appointed to come to-day, still I hope to be able to get rid of him for the present by a few polite phrases.

319.
TO HERR KIND.

DEAR KIND,--

I intend to call on you at latest on Wednesday afternoon at four o'clock, when I will settle everything.

Your obedient
BEETHOVEN.

320.
TO CHERUBINI.[1]

March 15, 1823.

HIGHLY ESTEEMED SIR,--

I joyfully take advantage of this opportunity to address you. I have done so frequently in spirit, as I prize your theatrical works beyond others. The artistic world has only to lament that, in Germany at least, no new dramatic piece of yours has appeared. Highly as all your works are valued by true connoisseurs, still it is a great loss to art not to possess any fresh production of your great genius for the theatre.

True art is imperishable, and the true artist feels heartfelt pleasure in grand works of genius, and that is what enchants me when I hear a new composition of yours; in fact, I take greater interest in it than in my own; in short, I love and honor you. Were it not that my continued bad health prevents my going to see you in Paris, with what exceeding delight would I discuss questions of art with you! Do not think that this is merely intended to serve as an introduction to the favor I am about to ask of you. I hope and feel convinced that you do not for a moment suspect me of such base sentiments.

I recently completed a grand solemn mass, and have resolved to offer it to the various European courts, as it is not my intention to publish it at present. I have therefore solicited the King of France, through the French embassy here, to subscribe to this work, and I feel certain that his Majesty would, at your recommendation, agree to do so. *Ma situation critique demande que je ne fixe pas seulement, comme ordinaire, mes voeux au ciel; au contraire, il faut les fixer aussi* ["aussi" in Beethoven's hand] *en bas pour les nécessités de la vie.* Whatever may be the fate of my request to you, I shall forever continue to love and esteem you, *et vous resterez toujours celui de mes contemporains que je l'estime le plus. Si vous me voulez faire un extrême plaisir, c'était si vous m'écrivez quelques lignes, ce que me soulagera bien. L'art unit tout le monde,* how much more, then, true artists, *et peut-être vous me dignez aussi* to include me in that number. *Avec le plus haut estime,*

Votre ami et serviteur,
BEETHOVEN.

[Footnote 1: Cherubini declared that he never received this letter.]

321.
TO SCHINDLER.[1]

DEAR SCHINDLER,--

I am not sure whether the other copy was corrected or not, so I send you this one instead. As to N. in S----, I beg you not to say a word; Bl. is already very uneasy on the subject. In haste, your friend,

BEETHOVEN.

[Footnote 1: We cannot understand what induced Beethoven, who lived in the same house with Schindler, to write to him; but he often did so to persons with whom he could easily have spoken, partly in order to get rid of the matter while it was in his thoughts, and also because he was a great deal from home; that is, going backwards and forwards from one lodging to another, having often several at the same time.]

322.
TO HERR PETERS,--LEIPZIG.

Vienna, March 20, 1823.

The other three marches are only to be sent off to-day, as I missed the post last week. Irregular as I have been on this occasion in our transactions, you would not think me so culpable if you were here, and aware of my position, a description of which would be too tedious both for you and me.

I have now an observation to make with regard to what I have sent off to you.

Several sets of wind instruments may combine in the performance of the Grand March, and if this cannot be done, and a regimental band is not strong enough for its present arrangement, any bandmaster can easily adapt it by omitting some of the parts.

You can, no doubt, find some one in Leipzig to show you how this can be managed with a smaller number, although I should regret if it were not to appear engraved exactly as it is written.

You must forgive the numerous corrections in the works I send; my old copyist no longer sees distinctly, and the younger one has yet to be trained, but at all events there are no errors left.

It is impossible for me to comply at once with your request for a stringed and a pianoforte quartet, but if you will write to me fixing the time you wish to have both works, I will do what I can to complete them. I must, however, apprise you that I cannot accept less than 50 ducats for a stringed quartet, and 70 for a pianoforte one, without incurring loss; indeed, I have repeatedly been offered more than 50 ducats for a violin quartet. I am, however, always unwilling to ask more than necessary, so I adhere to the sum of 50 ducats, which is, in fact, nowadays the usual price.

The other commission is indeed an uncommon one, and I, of course, accept it, only I must beg you to let me know soon when it is required; otherwise, willing as I am to give you the preference, I might find it almost impossible to do so. You know I wrote to you formerly that quartets were precisely what had risen most in value, which makes me feel positively ashamed when I have to ask a price for a *really great work*. Still, such is my position that it obliges me to secure every possible advantage. It is very different, however, with the work itself; when I never, thank God, think of *profit*, but solely of *how I write it*. It so happens that two others besides yourself wish to have a mass of mine, and I am quite disposed to write at least three. The first has long been finished, the second not yet so, and the third not even begun. But in reference to yourself, I must have a certainty, that I may in any event be secure.

More of this next time I write; do not remit the money, at any rate till you hear from me that the work is ready to be sent off.

I must now conclude. I hope your distress is, by this time, in some degree alleviated.

Your friend,
BEETHOVEN.

323.
TO ZELTER.

Vienna, March 25, 1823.

SIR,--

I avail myself of the present opportunity to send you my best wishes. The bearer of this asked me to recommend her to you; her name is Cornega; she has a fine *mezzo soprano*, and is a very artistic singer, and has, moreover, been favorably received in several operas.

I have also specially considered your proposals about your Academy for Singing. If the Mass is ever published, I will send you a copy free of all charge. There is no doubt that it might be almost entirely executed *à la capella*; in which case, however, the work would have to be arranged accordingly; perhaps you have patience to do this. Besides, there is already a movement in the work quite *à la capella*, and that style may be specially termed the true church style. Thanks for your wish to be of service to me, but never would I accept anything whatever from so highly esteemed an artist as yourself. I honor you, and only wish I could have an opportunity to prove this by my actions.

I am, with high consideration,
Your friend and servant,
BEETHOVEN.

324.
TO HIS IMPERIAL HIGHNESS THE ARCHDUKE RUDOLPH.

The Spring of 1823.

YOUR IMPERIAL HIGHNESS,--

It must still be some days before I can wait on you again, as I am in the greatest hurry to send off the works that I named to your R.H. yesterday, for if they are not punctually dispatched, I might lose all profit. Your R.H. can easily understand how much time is occupied in getting copies made, and looking through every part; indeed, it would not be easy to find a more troublesome task. Your R.H. will, I am sure, gladly dispense with my detailing all the toil caused by this kind of thing, but I am compelled to allude to it candidly, though only in so far as is absolutely necessary to prevent your R.H. being misled with regard to me, knowing, alas! only too well what efforts are made to *prejudice your R.H. against* me. But time will prove that I have been in all respects most faithful and attached to your R.H., and if my position were only as great as my zeal to serve your R.H., no happier man than myself would exist.

I am your R.H.'s faithful and obedient servant,

BEETHOVEN.

325.
TO SCHINDLER.

Imprimis.--Papageno, not a word of what I said about Prussia. No reliance is to be placed on it; Martin Luther's table-talk alone can be compared to it. I earnestly beg my brother also not to remove the padlock from his lips, and not to allow anything to transpire beyond the Selchwurst-Gasse.[1]

Finis.--Inquire of that arch-churl Diabelli when the French copy of the Sonata in C minor [Op. 111] is to be published. I stipulated to have five copies for myself, one of which is to be on fine paper, for the Cardinal [the Archduke Rudolph]. If he attempts any of his usual impertinence on this subject, I will sing him in person a bass aria in his warehouse which shall cause it and all the street (Graben) to ring![2]

[Footnote 1: Schindler relates: "The royal decision (to subscribe for a copy of the mass) was brought to Beethoven by the Chancellor of the Embassy, Hofrath Wernhard. Whether Prince Hatzfeld [the Ambassador] made the following offer from his own impulse, or in consequence of a commission from Berlin, is not known. At all events, the Hofrath put this question in the name of the prince to the great composer, 'Whether he would be disposed to prefer a royal order to the fifty ducats' [the sum demanded for the mass]. Beethoven replied at once, 'The fifty ducats.' Scarcely had the Chancellor left the room when Beethoven, in considerable excitement, indulged in all kinds of sarcastic remarks on the manner in which many of his contemporaries hunted after orders and decorations, these being in his estimation generally gained at the cost of the sanctity of art."]

[Footnote 2: Schindler relates that Diabelli had refused to let Beethoven again have the MS. of the Sonata, which he had repeatedly sent for when in the hands of the engraver, in order to correct and improve it. Diabelli therefore coolly submitted to all this abuse of the enraged composer, and wrote to him that he would note down the threatened bass aria, and publish it, but would give him the usual gratuity for it, and that Beethoven had better come to see him. On this Beethoven said no more. This Sonata is dedicated to the Archduke Rudolph, and is also published by Schlesinger.]

326.
TO F. RIES,--LONDON.

Vienna, April 25, 1823.

DEAR RIES,--

The Cardinal's stay here of a month robbed me of a great deal of time, being obliged to give him daily lessons of two or three hours each; and after such lessons I was scarcely able next day to think, far less to write. My continued melancholy situation compels me, however, to write immediately what will bring me in sufficient money for present use. What a sad revelation is this! I am, besides, far from well, owing to my many troubles,--weak eyes among others.

But do not be uneasy, you shall shortly receive the Symphony; really and truly, my distressing condition is alone to blame for the delay. In the course of a few weeks you shall have thirty-three new variations on a theme [Valse, Op. 120] dedicated to your wife.

Bauer [First Secretary to the Austrian Embassy] has the score of the "Battle of Vittoria," which was dedicated to the then Prince Regent, and for which I have still to receive the costs of copying. I do beg you, my dear friend, to remit me as soon as possible anything you can get for it. With regard to your tender conjugal discussion, you will always find an opponent in me,--that is, not so much an opponent of yours as a partisan of your wife's. I remain, as ever, your friend,

BEETHOVEN.

327.
TO HERR LISSNER,--PETERSBURG.

Vienna, May 7, 1823.

SIR,--

Herr v. Schuppanzigh assured me, when he was here, that you were anxious to acquire some of my productions for your house. Perhaps the following works might suit your purpose, namely: six *bagatelles* for pianoforte, 20 gold ducats; thirty-five variations on a favorite theme for pianoforte, forming one entire work, 30 gold ducats; two grand airs with chorus, the poetry by Goethe and Matthisson, which can be sung either with instrumental or pianoforte accompaniment, 12 gold ducats.

I request an answer as soon as possible, for others also wish to have my works.

I am, sir, your obedient
LUDWIG VAN BEETHOVEN.

328. [1]
TO SCHINDLER.

Hetzendorf, 1823.

SAMOTHRACIAN VAGABOND!--[2]

You must hunt out from Schlemmer [the copyist] what is still wanting in the "Kyrie;" show him the postscript, and so, *satis*, no more of such a wretch! Farewell! arrange everything; I am to bind up my eyes at night, and to spare them as much as possible; otherwise, says Smetana, I shall write little more music in the time to come.

[Footnote 1: "We arrived at Hetzendorf on May 17" is written by Carl in Beethoven's note-book of 1823; and on this note is written, in the "scamp's" hand, Hetzendorf, 1823.]

[Footnote 2: "By the word 'Samothracian,' Beethoven alludes to the Samothracian Mysteries, partly grounded on music. Their mutual participation in the Beethoven Mysteries is intended to be thus indicated. Among the initiated were also Brunswick, Lichnowsky, and Zmeskall." [From a note of Schindler's on the subject.]]

329.
TO SCHINDLER.

Hetzendorf, 1823 (?).

Pray, forward the packet to-day, and inquire this afternoon, if possible, about the housekeeper in the Glockengasse, No. 318, 3d Étage. She is a widow, understands cookery, and is willing to serve merely for board and lodging, to which, of course, I cannot consent, or only under certain conditions. My present one is too shameful. I cannot invite you here, but be assured of my gratitude.

330.
TO SCHINDLER.[1]

Hetzendorf, 1823.

I enclose the letter to Herr v. Obreskow [Chargé d'Affaires of the Russian Legation]; as soon as I receive the money, I will immediately send you 50 florins for your trouble. Not a word more than what is absolutely necessary!

I have advertised your house. You can mention, merely as a casual remark at the right moment, that France also remitted the money to you.

Never forget that such persons represent Majesty itself.

[Footnote 1: Louis VIII. sent a gold medal for his subscription copy of the Mass on February 20, 1824.]

331.
TO SCHINDLER.

I beg you will kindly write out the enclosed invitation neatly for me on the paper I send you, for Carl has too much to do. I wish to dispatch it early on Wednesday. I want to know where Grillparzer lives; perhaps I may pay him a visit myself.[1] You must have a little patience about the 50 florins; as yet it is impossible for me to send them, for which you are as much to blame as I am.

[Footnote 1: It is well known that in the winter of 1822-23 Beethoven was engaged in the composition of an opera for the Royal Theatre; for which purpose Grillparzer had given him his *Melusina*.]

332.
TO SCHINDLER.

I send K.'s [Kanne's] book [libretto]. Except the first act, which is rather insipid, it is written in such a masterly style that it does not by any means require a first-rate composer. I will not say that on this very account it would be the more suitable for me; still, if I can get rid of previous engagements, who knows what may or will happen! Please acknowledge the receipt of this.

333.
TO SCHINDLER.

I wish to know about Esterhazy, and also about the post. A letter-carrier from the Mauer [a place near Hetzendorf] was here; I only hope the message has been properly delivered. Nothing as yet from Dresden [see No. 330]. I mean to ask you to dine with me a few days hence, for I still suffer from my weak eyes; to-day, however, for the first time, they seem to improve, but I scarcely dare make any use of them as yet.

Your friend,
BEETHOVEN.

P.S. As for the Tokay,[1] it is better adapted for *summer* than for *autumn*, and also for some fiddler who could *respond* to its noble fire, and yet *stand firm as a rock*.

[Footnote 1: A musical friend had sent the *maestro* six bottles of genuine Tokay, expressing his wish that it might tend to restore his strength. Schindler, he says, wrote to Beethoven at Hetzendorf, to tell him of this, and received the above answer, and the order through "Frau Schnaps" to do as he pleased with the wine. He sent one bottle of it to Hetzendorf, but Beethoven at that time had inflamed eyes.]

334.
TO SCHINDLER.

I cannot at present accept these tempting invitations [from Sonntag and Unger]; so far as my weak eyes permit, I am very busy, and when it is fine, I go out. I will myself thank these two fair ladies for their amiability. No tidings from Dresden. I shall wait till the end of this month, and then apply to a lawyer in Dresden. I will write about Schoberlechner to-morrow.

335.
TO SCHINDLER.

June 18, 1823.

You ought to have perfectly well known that I would have nothing to do with the affair in question. With regard to my being "liberal," I think I have shown you that I am so on principle; indeed, I suspect you must have observed that I even have gone *beyond* these principles. *Sapienti sat.*[1]

[Footnote 1: Franz Schoberlechner, pianist in Vienna, wrote to Beethoven on June 25, 1823, to ask him for letters of introduction to Leipzig, Dresden, Berlin, and Russia, etc. The *maestro*, however, wrote across the letter, "An active fellow requires no other recommendation than from one respectable family to another," and gave it back to Schindler, who showed it to Schoberlechner, and no doubt at his desire urged Beethoven to comply with his request. Beethoven, however, did not know Schoberlechner, and had no very high opinion of him, as he played chiefly *bravura* pieces, and, besides, on the bills of his concerts, he pompously paraded all his titles, decorations, and as member of various societies, which gave ample subject for many a sarcastic remark on the part of Beethoven.]

336.
TO THE ARCHDUKE RUDOLPH.

Vienna, June 1, 1823.

I have been always ailing since Y.R.H. left this, and latterly afflicted by severe inflammation of the eyes, which has now in so far subsided that for the last eight days I have been able once more to use my sight, though very sparingly. Y.R.H. will perceive from the enclosed receipt of June 27, the dispatch of some music. As Y.R.H. seemed to take pleasure in the C minor Sonata,[1] I thought I did not take too much on myself by surprising Y.R.H. with the dedication. The Variations[2] have been written out for at least five or six weeks past, but the state of my eyes did not permit me to revise them thoroughly myself. My hope of being entirely restored proved vain. At last I made Schlemmer look them over, so, though they may not look very neat, still they are correct. The C minor Sonata was engraved in Paris in a very faulty manner, and being engraved here from that copy, I tried to make it as correct as possible. I intend shortly to send you a beautifully engraved copy of the Variations. With regard to the Mass[3] that Y.R.H. wished should be more generally known, my continued bad health for some years past, causing me to incur heavy debts, and compelling me to give up my intention of going to England, induced me to ponder on some mode of improving my condition. This Mass seemed well adapted to my purpose. I was advised to offer it to different courts. Painful as this was to me, I felt that I should have cause for self-reproach if I neglected doing so. I therefore applied to various courts to subscribe to the Mass, fixing the price at fifty ducats; the general opinion being that this was not too much, and if there were a good many subscribers, the scheme would not be unprofitable. Hitherto the subscription is indeed flattering to me, as their Majesties of France and Prussia have each taken a copy. I also received a letter from my friend Prince Nicolaus Gallizin a few days ago, from Petersburg, in which this most amiable Prince mentions that H.M. the Emperor of Russia had become a subscriber, and that I should soon hear further on the subject from the Imperial Russian Embassy. Notwithstanding all this (and though there are some other subscribers), I have not yet realized as much as the sum a publisher offered me for it; the only advantage being that the work remains *mine*. The costs of copying are also great, and further increased by three new pieces being added, which, as soon as they are completed, I will send to Y.R.H. Perhaps you would not think it too much trouble to apply to H.R.H. the Grand Duke of Tuscany to take a copy of this Mass. The application was indeed made some time ago to the Grand Duke of Tuscany through the agent here, V. Odelga, who faithfully assured me that the proposal would be graciously accepted. I place no great faith, however, in this, as some months have elapsed, and no notice has been again taken of the application. As the affair is now set agoing, it is but natural that I should do all I can to attain my desired object. The undertaking was from the first disagreeable to me, and still more so to mention it to Y.R.H., or to allude to it at all, but "*necessity has no law.*" I only feel grateful to Him who dwells above the stars that I now begin once more to be able to use my eyes. I am at present writing a new symphony for England,[4] bespoken by the Philharmonic Society, and hope it will be quite finished fourteen days hence. I cannot strain my eyes as yet long at a time; I beg therefore Y.R.H.'s indulgence with regard to your Variations,[5] which appear to me very charming, but still require closer revision on my part. Y.R.H. has only to persevere, especially to accustom yourself to write down your ideas at once at the piano, quickly and briefly. For this purpose a small table ought to be placed close beside the piano. By this means not only is the imagination strengthened; but you learn instantly to hold fast the most fugitive ideas. It is equally necessary to be able to write without any piano; and sometimes a simple choral melody, to be carried out in simple or varied phrases, in counterpoint, or in a free manner, will certainly entail no headache on Y.R.H., but rather, in finding yourself thus right amid the centre of art, cause you very great pleasure. The faculty of representing precisely what we wish and feel comes by degrees; an essential *desideratum* for a noble-minded man. My eyes warn me to conclude. With every kind and good wish for Y.R.H., I remain, &c., &c.

[K.]

POSTSCRIPT.

If Y.R.H. should confer the happiness of a letter on me, I beg you will address to me at Vienna, for I shall receive all my letters here safely forwarded by the post from there. If agreeable to Y.R.H., I would beg you to recommend the Mass to Prince Anton in Dresden,[6] so that the King of Saxony may subscribe to it, which he will, no doubt, do if Y.R.H. shows any interest in the matter. As soon as I know that you have actually done me this favor, I will forthwith apply to the General-Director there[7] of the Royal Theatre and of Music, whose office it is to arrange these things, and send him a request to procure a subscription from the King of Saxony, which I am reluctant to do without a recommendation from Y.R.H.

My opera, "Fidelio," was performed with much applause in Dresden at the festivities there in honor of the visit of the King of Bavaria, when their Majesties were all present. I received this intelligence from the above-named director-general, who asked me for the score through Weber, and afterwards sent me really a very handsome present in return. I hope Y.R.H. will excuse my intruding such a request on you, but Y.R.H. knows that I am not usually importunate. Should, however, the slightest obstacle arise to render my request disagreeable to you, I shall not be the less convinced of your generosity and kindness. Neither avarice, nor the love of speculation, which I have always avoided, prompted this scheme; but necessity compels me to use every effort to rescue my self from my present condition. Candor is best, for it will prevent my being too hardly judged. Owing to constant ill health, which has prevented my writing as usual, I have incurred a debt of 200 to 300 florins C.M.,[8] which can only be discharged by vigorous exertions on my part. If my subscription succeeds better than it has hitherto done, it will be an effectual help, and if my health improves, of which there is every hope, I shall be able once more to resume my compositions with fresh energy. In the mean time I trust Y.R.H. will not be offended by my candor. Had it not been the fear of being accused of not sufficiently *bestirring* myself, I would have persevered in my usual silence. As to the recommendation, I am at all events convinced that Y.R.H. is always glad to effect good results for others when *possible*, and that you are not likely to make any exception in my case.

[Footnote 1: This Sonata, Op. 111, dedicated to the Archduke Rudolph, was composed in 1822, and published by Schlesinger in the beginning of 1823.]

[Footnote 2: These *Variations* are, no doubt, the 33 C major Variations for pianoforte, Op. 120, on a waltz of Diabelli's, dedicated to Madame Brentano, composed in 1823, and published in the June of the same year.]

[Footnote 3: The Grand Mass in D.]

[Footnote 4: The symphony which Beethoven declared he had completed in fourteen days was the 9th in D minor, composed in 1822 or 1823, first performed on the 7th May, and published in 1826.]

[Footnote 5: The Archduke's Variations alluded to by Beethoven are not published or now known.]

[Footnote 6: In a letter from the Archduke Rudolph of July 31, 1823, he says, "My brother-in-law, Prince Anton, has written to me that the King of Saxony is expecting your beautiful Mass."]

[Footnote 7: The director-general of the musical Court band and opera in Dresden (1823) was Von Könneritz.]

[Footnote 8: This debt of 200 to 300 florins had only been incurred by Beethoven in order not to sell out his shares in the Austrian Loan; he was in no need.]

337.
TO SCHINDLER.

Hetzendorf, July 1, 1823.

I am myself writing to Wocher [cabinet courier to Prince Esterhazy? No. 333], and for more speed I send by Carl, who chances to be driving in, the application to Prince E. Be so good as to inquire the result; I doubt its being favorable, not expecting much kindly feeling on his part towards me, judging from former days.[1] I believe that female influence alone ensures success with him in such matters;

at all events, I now know, by your obliging inquiries, how I can safely write to this Scholz. The bad weather, and more especially the bad atmosphere, prevented my paying her [Countess Schafgotsch] a visit about this affair.[2]

Your *amicus*,
BEETHOVEN.

P.S. Nothing yet from Dresden! Schlemmer [the copyist] has just been here asking again for money. I have now advanced him 70 Gulden. Speculations are for commercial men, and not for poor devils like myself. Hitherto the sole fruit of this unlucky speculation [a subscription for his Mass] are only more debts. You have, no doubt, seen that the "Gloria" is completed. If my eyes were only strong again, so that I could resume my writing, I should do well enough. [Written on the cover:] Are the Variations [Op. 120] sent off yet to London? N.B.--So far as I can remember, it was not mentioned in the application to Prince Esterhazy that the Mass was to be delivered in manuscript only. What mischief may ensue from this! I suspect that such was the intention of Herr Artaria in proposing to present the Mass *gratis* to the Prince, as it would give Artaria an opportunity for the third time to steal one of my works. Wocher's attention must be called to this.

Of course, there is nothing obligatory on Papageno in the matter.

[Footnote 1: Beethoven wrote the Mass in C for him in the year 1807, which was by no means satisfactory to the prince when performed at Eisenstadt in the year following, and conducted by Beethoven himself.]

[Footnote 2: Scholz, music director at Warmbrunn in Silesia, had written a German text for the Mass in C. Beethoven also wished to have from him a German translation from the Latin words adapted to the music of the Grand Mass. Schindler says, that the words "prevented my visiting her" refer to Countess Schafgotsch, whom Beethoven wished to see on account of Scholz, who unhappily died in the ensuing year. His text, however, is given in the *Cecilia*, 23-54.]

338.
TO PILAT, EDITOR OF THE "AUSTRIAN OBSERVER."

SIR,--

I shall feel highly honored if you will be so good as to mention in your esteemed journal my nomination as an honorary member of the Royal Swedish Musical Academy. Although neither vain nor ambitious, still I consider it advisable not wholly to pass over such an occurrence, as in practical life we must live and work for others, who may often eventually benefit by it. Forgive my intrusion, and let me know if I can in any way serve you in return, which it would give me much pleasure to do.

I am, sir, with high consideration,
Your obedient
BEETHOVEN.

339.
TO SCHINDLER.

Hetzendorf, July, 1823.

MOST WORTHY RAGAMUFFIN OF EPIRUS AND BRUNDUSIUM!--

Give this letter to the editor of the "Observer," but write the address on it first; ask him at the same time whether his daughter makes great progress on the piano, and if I can be of any use to her by sending her a copy of one of my compositions. I wrote that I was an "*honorary* member;" I don't know, however, whether this is correct; perhaps I ought to have said, "a corresponding member;" neither knowing nor caring much about such things. You had also better say something on the subject to *Bernardum non sanctum* (editor of the "Vienna Zeitschrift"). Make inquiries, too, from Bernard about that knave Ruprecht; tell him of this queer business, and find out from him how he can punish the villain. Ask both these philosophical newspaper scribes whether this may be considered an honorable or dishonorable nomination.

340.
TO SCHINDLER.

Master flash in the pan, and wide of the mark! full of reasons, yet devoid of reason!--Everything was ready yesterday for Gläser (the copyist). As for you, I shall expect you in Hetzendorf to dinner at half-past two o'clock. If you come later, dinner shall be kept for you.

341.
TO SCHINDLER.

Hetzendorf, July 2, 1823.

WORTHY HERR V. SCHINDLER,--

The incessant insolence of my landlord from the hour I entered his house up to the present moment compels me to apply for aid to the police; so I beg you will do so for me at once. As to the double winter windows, the housekeeper was desired to see about them, and especially to state if they were not necessary after such a violent storm, in case of the rain having penetrated into the room; but her report was that the rain had not come in, and, moreover, that it could not possibly do so. In accordance with her statement, I locked the door to prevent this rude man entering my room during my absence (which he had threatened). Say also further what his conduct to you was, and that he put up a placard of the lodgings being to let, without giving me notice, which, besides, he has no right to do till St. James's Day. He is equally unfair in refusing to give up the receipt from St. George's Day till St. James's, as the enclosure shows; I am charged, too, for lighting, of which I know nothing. This detestable lodging,[1] without any open stove, and the principal flue truly abominable, has cost me (for extra outlay, exclusive of the rent) 259 florins, in order merely to keep me alive while I was there during the winter. It was a deliberate fraud, as I never was allowed to see the rooms on the first floor, but only those on the second, that I might not become aware of their many disagreeable drawbacks. I cannot understand how a flue *so destructive to health can be tolerated by the Government.* You remember the appearance of the walls of your room owing to smoke, and the large sum it cost even to lessen in any degree this discomfort, although to do away with it wholly was impossible. My chief anxiety at present is that he may be ordered to take down his placard, and to give me a receipt for the house-rent I have paid; but nothing will induce me to pay for the abominable lighting, without which it cost me enough actually to preserve my life in such a lodging. My eyes do not yet suffer me to encounter the town atmosphere, or I would myself apply in person to the police.

Your attached
BEETHOVEN.

[Footnote 1: The Pfarrgasse, in the Laimgrube, where Schindler lived with him.]

342.
TO SCHINDLER.

I must have an attested copy of all the writings; I send you 45 kreutzers. How could you possibly accept such a proposal from our churlish landlord when accompanied by a threat? Where was your good sense? Where it always is.

To-morrow early I shall send for the Variations, copy and originals. It is not certain whether the Pr. comes or not; so be so good as to stay at home till eight o'clock. You can come to dinner either to-day or to-morrow; but you must settle which you mean to do, as it is not easy *for me* to provide provisions. Not later than half-past two o'clock. The housekeeper will tell you about a lodging in the Landstrasse. It is high time, truly! As soon as you hear of anything to be had on the Bastei or the Landstrasse, you must at once give me notice. We must find out what room the landlord uses on account of the well.--*Vale!*

343.
TO SCHINDLER.[1]

Hetzendorf, 1823.

SAMOTHRACIAN VAGABOND!--

You were dispatched yesterday to the South Pole, whereas we went off to the North Pole, a slight difference now equalized by Captain Parry. There were, however, no mashed potatoes there.

Bach [his lawyer], to whom I beg my best regards, is requested to say what the lodging in Baden is to cost; we must also try to arrange that Carl should come to me once every fortnight there (but cheaply; good heavens! poverty and economy!). I intrust this matter to you, as you have your friends and admirers among the drivers and liverymen. If you get this in time, you had better go to Bach to-day, so that I may receive his answer to-morrow forenoon. It is almost too late now.

You might also take that rascal of a copyist by surprise; I don't expect much good from him. He has now had the Variations for eight days.

Your ["friend" stroked out] amicus,
BEETHOVEN.

[Footnote 1: He no doubt alludes to Captain Parry, the celebrated traveller, who wrote an article in the *A.M. Zeitung* on the music of the Esquimaux.]

344.
TO SCHINDLER.[1]

June, 1823.

SAMOTHRACIAN!--

Don't trouble yourself to come here till you receive a *Hati Scherif*. I must say you do not deserve the *golden* cord. My fast-sailing frigate, the worthy and well-born Frau Schnaps, will call every three or four days to inquire after your health.

Farewell! Bring *no one whatever* with you: farewell!

[Footnote 1: Schindler says in his *Biography*: "These *Variations* [Op. 120] were completed in June, 1823, and delivered to the publisher, Diabelli, without the usual amount of time bestowed on giving them the finishing touches; and now he set to work at once at the ninth Symphony, some jottings of which were already written down. Forthwith all the gay humor that had made him more sociable, and in every respect more accessible, at once disappeared. All visits were declined," &c.]

345.
TO THE ARCHDUKE RUDOLPH.

Hetzendorf, July 15, 1823.

I trust that you are in the best possible health. As for my eyes, they are improving, though slowly, and in six or seven days at most I hope to have the good fortune to wait on Y.R.H. If I were not obliged to use spectacles, I should get better sooner. It is a most distressing occurrence, and has thrown me back in everything. What soothes my feelings, however, is Y.R.H. being fully aware that I am always to be of service to you. I have another favor to ask of Y.R.H., which I hope you will graciously accede. Will Y.R.H. be so kind as to grant me a testimonial to the following effect: "That I wrote the Grand Mass expressly for Y.R.H.; that it has been for some time in your possession; and that you have been pleased to permit me to circulate it." This ought to have been the case, and being no untruth, I hope I may claim this favor. Such a testimonial will be of great service to me; for how could I have believed that my slight talents would have exposed me to so much envy, persecution, and calumny. It has always been my intention to ask Y.R.H.'s permission to circulate the Mass, but the pressure of circumstances, and above all my inexperience in worldly matters, as well as my feeble health, has caused this confusion.

If the Mass is engraved hereafter, I hope to dedicate it to Y.R.H. when published,[1] and not till then will the limited list of royal subscribers appear. I shall ever consider Y.R.H. as my most illustrious patron, and make this known to the world whenever it is in my power. In conclusion, I entreat you again not to refuse my request about the testimonial. It will only cost Y.R.H. a few lines, and ensure the best results for me.

I will bring the Variations[2] of Y.R.H. with me. They require little alteration, and cannot fail to become a very pretty pleasing work for all lovers of music. I must indeed appear a most importunate suitor. I beg you will kindly send me the testimonial as soon as possible, for I require it.

[K.]

[Footnote 1: The Grand Mass (*Op.* 123) was published in 1827.]

[Footnote 2: The *Variations* composed by the Archduke Rudolph, mentioned in the letters 345 and 351, are not the same as the published ones, and are unknown.]

346.
TO F. RIES.

Hetzendorf, July 16, 1823.

MY DEAR RIES,--

I received your letter with much pleasure the day before yesterday. The Variations have, no doubt, arrived by this time. I could not write the dedication to your wife, not knowing her name; so I beg you will write it yourself on the part of your wife's friend and your own; let it be a surprise to her, for the fair sex like that.--*Entre nous*, surprise is always the greatest charm of the beautiful! As for the *Allegri di Bravura*, I must make allowance for yours. To tell you the truth, I am no great friend to that kind of thing, as it is apt to entail too much mere mechanism; at least, such is the case with those I know. I have not yet looked at yours, but I shall ask ---- about them. I recommend you to be cautious in your intercourse with him. Could I not be of use to you in many ways here? These printers, or rather *misprinters*, as they ought to be called to deserve their names, pirate your works, and give you nothing in return; this, surely, might be differently managed. I mean to send you some choruses shortly, even if obliged to compose some new ones, for this is my favorite style.

Thanks for the proceeds of the *bagatelles*, with which I am quite satisfied. Give nothing to the King of England. Pray accept anything you can get for the Variations. I shall be perfectly contented. I only must stipulate to take no other reward for the dedication to your wife than the kiss which I am to receive in London.

You name *guineas*, whereas I only get *pounds sterling*, and I hear there is a difference between these. Do not be angry with *un pauvre musicien autrichien*, who is still at a very low ebb. I am now writing a new violin quartet. Might not this be offered to the musical or unmusical London Jews?--*en vrai Juif*.

I am, with cordial regard,
Your old friend,
BEETHOVEN.

347.
TO HERR GEHEIMRATH VON KÖNNERITZ,--DRESDEN,[1] DIRECTOR OF THE ROYAL ORCHESTRA AND THEATRE IN SAXONY.

Hetzendorf, July 17, 1823.

SIR,--

I have too long deferred sending you a signed receipt and thanks, but I feel sure you will pardon the delay from my great pressure of business, owing to my health having improved, and God knows how long this may continue. The description given by my dear friend Maria Weber[2] of your generous and noble disposition encourages me to apply to you on another subject, namely, about a Grand Mass which I am now issuing in manuscript. Though I have met with a previous refusal on this matter [337], still, as my esteemed Cardinal, H.R. Highness the Archduke Rudolph, has written to H.R.H. Prince Anton, requesting him to recommend the Mass to his Majesty the King of Saxony, I think this fresh application might at all events be made, as I should consider it a great honor to number among my distinguished subscribers (such as the King of Prussia, the Emperor of Russia, the King of France, &c.) so great a connoisseur in music as the King of Saxony.

I leave it to you, sir, to decide from this statement how and when you can best effect my purpose. I am unable to send you to-day the application for a subscription to my Mass to H.M. the King of Saxony, but I will do so by the next post. In any event I feel assured that you will not think I am one of those who compose for the sake of paltry gain; but how often do events occur which constrain a man to act contrary to his inclinations and his principles? My Cardinal is a benevolent Prince, but means are wanting! I hope to receive your forgiveness for my apparent importunity. If my poor abilities can in any way be employed in your service, what extreme pleasure it would give me.

I am, sir, with esteem,
Your expectant
BEETHOVEN.

[Footnote 1: The director-general of the Dresden theatre at that time was Von Könneritz, who sent Beethoven forty ducats (requesting a receipt) for his opera of *Fidelio*, performed with great applause April 29, 1823, and conducted by C.M. von Weber. Madame Schröder-Devrient made her *début* in the character of Leonore.]

[Footnote 2: In Weber's *Biography* it is stated (Vol. II. p. 465) that Beethoven and Weber exchanged several letters about the performance of *Fidelio*, and in fact Weber did receive letters from Beethoven on February 16, April 10, and June 9. Unhappily, no part of this correspondence has yet been discovered, except a fragment of the sketch of a letter written by Weber of January 28, 1823, which sufficiently proves that Beethoven was right in calling him his *friend*. It is as follows:--"This mighty work, teeming with German grandeur and depth of feeling, having been given under my direction at Prague, had enabled me to acquire the most enthusiastic and instructive knowledge of its inner essence, by means of which I hope to produce it before the public here with full effect, provided as I am with all possible accessories for the purpose. Each performance will be a festival to me, permitting me to pay that homage to your mighty spirit which dwells in the inmost recesses of my heart, where love and admiration strive for the mastery." On October 5 of this year, Weber visited Beethoven in Baden, with Haslinger and Benedict.]

348.
TO HERR V. KÖNNERITZ,--DRESDEN.

Vienna, July 25, 1823.

SIR,--

Forgive my importunity in sending to your care the enclosed letter from me to his R.H. Prince Anton of Saxony; it contains an application to his Majesty the King of Saxony to subscribe to a mass of mine. I recently mentioned to you that the Cardinal Archduke Rudolph had written to his M. the King of Saxony about this Mass; I entreat you to use all your influence in this matter, and I leave it entirely to your own judgment and knowledge of local matters to act as you think best. Although I do not doubt that the recommendation of my Cardinal will have considerable weight, still the decision of his Majesty cannot fail to be much influenced by the advice of the Administrator of objects connected with the fine arts. Hitherto, in spite of apparent brilliant success, I have scarcely realized as much as a publisher would have given me for the work, the expenses of copying being so very great. It was the idea of my friends to circulate this Mass, for, thank God! I am a mere novice in all speculations. In the mean time, there is not a single *employé* of our Government who has not been, like myself, a loser. Had it not been for my continued bad health for many years past, a foreign country would at least have enabled me to live free from all cares except those for art. Judge me kindly, and not harshly; I live only for my art, and my sole wish is to fulfil my duties as a man; but this, alas! cannot always be accomplished without the influence of the *subterranean powers*. While commending my cause to you, I also venture to hope that your love of art, and above all your philanthropy, will induce you to be so good as to write me a few lines, informing me of the result as soon as you are acquainted with it.

I am, sir, with high consideration,

Your obedient
BEETHOVEN.

349.
TO SCHINDLER.

August, 1823.

YOU SAMOTHRACIAN VILLAIN!--

Make haste and come, for the weather is just right. Better early than late--*presto, prestissimo*! We are to drive from here.[1]

[Footnote 1: Beethoven had apartments in a summer residence of Baron Pronay's on his beautiful property at Hetzendorf. Suddenly, however, the *maestro*, deeply immersed in the *Ninth Symphony*, was no longer satisfied with this abode, because "the Baron would persist in making him profound bows every time that he met him." So, with the help of Schindler and Frau Schnaps, he removed to Baden in August, 1823.]

350.
TO HIS NEPHEW.

Baden, August 16, 1823.

MY DEAR BOY,--

I did not wish to say anything to you till I found my health improving here, which, however, is scarcely even yet the case. I came here with a cold and catarrh, which were very trying to me, my constitution being naturally rheumatic, which will, I fear, soon cut the thread of my life, or, still worse, gradually wear it away. The miserable state of my digestive organs, too, can only be restored by medicines and diet, and for this I have to thank my *faithful* servants! You will learn how constantly I am in the open air when I tell you that to-day for the first time I properly (or improperly, though it was involuntary) resumed my suit to my Muse. I *must* work, but do not wish it to be known. Nothing can be more tempting (to me at least) than the enjoyment of beautiful Nature at these baths, but *nous sommes trop pauvres, et il faut écrire ou de n'avoir pas de quoi*. Get on, and make every preparation for your examination, and be unassuming, so that you may prove yourself higher and better than people expect. Send your linen here at once; your gray trousers must still be wearable, at all events at home; for, my dear son, you are indeed very *dear* to me! My address is, "At the coppersmith's," &c. Write instantly to say that you have got this letter. I will send a few lines to that contemptible creature, Schindler, though I am most unwilling to have anything to do with such a wretch. If we could write as quickly as we think and feel, I could say a great deal not a little remarkable; but for to-day I can only add that I wish a certain Carl may prove worthy of all my love and unwearied care, and learn fully to appreciate it.

Though not certainly exacting, as you know, still there are many ways in which we can show those who are better and nobler than ourselves that we acknowledge their superiority.

I embrace you from my heart.

Your faithful and true
FATHER.

351.
TO THE ARCHDUKE RUDOLPH.

August, 1823.

I am really very ill, and not suffering from my eyes alone. I intend to drag myself to-morrow to Baden, to look out for a lodging, and to go there altogether in the course of a few days. The air in town has a very bad effect on my whole organization, and has really injured my health, having gone twice to town to consult my physicians. It will be easier for me to repair to Y.R.H. in Baden. I am quite inconsolable, both on account of Y.R.H. and myself, that my usefulness is thus limited. I have marked some things in the Variations, but I can explain these better verbally.

[K.]

352.
TO THE ARCHDUKE RUDOLPH.

Baden, August 22, 1823.

Your gracious letter led me to believe that Y.R.H. intended to return to Baden, where I arrived on the 13th, very ill; but I am now better. I had recently another inflammatory cold, having just recovered from one. My digestion, too, was miserable, and my eyes very bad; in short, my whole system seemed impaired. I was obliged to make the effort to come here, without even being able to see Y.R.H. Thank God, my eyes are so much better that I can again venture to make tolerable use of them by daylight. My other maladies, too, are improving, and I cannot expect more in so short a period. How I wish that Y.R.H. were only here, when in a few days we could entirely make up for lost time. Perhaps I may still be so fortunate as to see Y.R.H. here, and be able to show my zeal to serve Y.R.H. How deeply does this cause me to lament my unhappy state of health. Much as I wish for its entire restoration, still I greatly fear that this will never be the case, and on this account I hope for Y.R.H.'s indulgence. As I can now at length prove how gladly I place myself at Y.R.H.'s disposal, my most anxious desire is that you would be pleased to make use of me.

[K.]

353.
TO THE ARCHDUKE RUDOLPH.

1823.

I have just been enjoying a short walk and composing a Canon, "Grossen Dank, ÷ ÷ ÷," when, on returning home, with the intention of writing it out for Y.R.H., I find a petitioner who is under the delusion that his request will be better received if made through me. What can I do? A good action cannot be too soon performed, and even a whim must be sometimes humored. The bearer of this is Kapellmeister Drechsler, of the Josephstadt and Baden Theatre; he wishes to obtain the situation of second Court organist. He has a good knowledge of thorough bass, and is also a good organist, besides being favorably known as a composer,--all qualities that recommend him for this situation. He *rightly* thinks that the best recommendation to secure him the appointment is that of Y.R.H., who, being yourself so great a connoisseur and performer, know better than any one how to appreciate true merit; and assuredly H.I. Majesty would prefer such testimony to every other. I therefore add my entreaties, though with some hesitation, to those of Herr D., relying on the indulgence and kindness of Y.R.H., and in the hope that the illustrious patron and protector of all that is good will do what lies in his power to be of use on this occasion.

My Canon shall be sent to-morrow,[1] together with the confession of my sins, intentional and unintentional, for which I beg your gracious absolution. My eyes, alas! prevent me from saying to-day as I could wish my hopes and desires that all good may attend you.

P.S. I ought also to mention that Herr Drechsler is the unsalaried professor of thorough bass at St. Anna's, and has been so for the last ten years.

[K.]

[Footnote 1: The Canon, *Grossen Dank*, ÷ ÷ ÷, is not to be found in either Breitkopf & Härtel's or Thayer's catalogue, nor anywhere else.]

354.
TO F. RIES.

Baden, September 5, 1823.

MY DEAR FRIEND,--

You advise me to engage some one to look after my affairs; now I did so as to the Variations; that is, my brother and Schindler took charge of them, but how?

The Variations were not to have appeared here till after being published in London; but everything went wrong. The dedication to Brentano [Antonie v. Brentano, *née* Edlen von Birkenstock] was to be confined to Germany, I being under great obligations to her, and having nothing else to spare at the moment; indeed, Diabelli, the publisher, alone got it from me. But everything went through Schindler's hands. No man on earth was ever more contemptible,--an arch villain; but I soon sent him packing! I will dedicate some other work to your wife in the place of this one. You, no doubt, received my last letter [No. 346]. I think thirty ducats would be enough for one of the *Allegri di Bravura*, but I should like to publish them here at the same time, which might easily be arranged. Why should I give up so much profit to these rogues here? It will not be published here till I am told that it has arrived in London; moreover, you may yourself fix the price, as you best know London customs.

The copyist to-day at last finished the score of the Symphony; so Kirchhoffer and I are only waiting for a favorable opportunity to send it off. I am still here, being very ill when I arrived, and my health still continues in a most precarious condition, and, good heavens! instead of amusing myself like others at these baths, my necessities compel me to write every day. I am also obliged to drink the mineral waters besides bathing. The copy will shortly be sent off; I am only waiting till I hear of an opportunity from Kirchhoffer, for it is too bulky to forward by post.

My last letter must have given you an insight into everything. I will send you some choruses; let me have any commissions for oratorios as soon as you can, that I may fix the time at once. I am sorry about the Variations on account of ----, as I wrote them more for London than here. This is not my fault. Answer me very soon, both as to particulars and time. Kind regards to your family.

355.
TO F. RIES,--LONDON.

Baden, September 5, 1823.

MY DEAR KIND RIES,--

I have still no tidings of the Symphony, but you may depend on its soon being in London. Were I not so poor as to be obliged to live by my pen, I would accept nothing from the Philharmonic Society; but as it is, I must wait till the money for the Symphony is made payable here; though as a proof of my interest and confidence in that Society, I have already sent off the new Overture, and I leave it to them to settle the payment as they please.

My brother, who keeps his carriage, wished also to profit by me; so without asking my permission, he offered this Overture to Boosey, a London publisher. Pray, tell him that my brother was mistaken with regard to the Overture. I see now that he bought it from me in order to practise usury with it. *O Frater!!*

I have never yet received the Symphony you dedicated to me. If I did not regard this dedication as a kind of challenge to which I am bound to respond, I would ere this have dedicated some work to you. I always, however, wished first to see yours, and how joyfully would I then testify my gratitude to you in one way or another.

I am, indeed deeply your debtor for your kind services and many proofs of attachment. Should my health improve by my intended course of baths, I hope to kiss your wife in London in 1824.

Yours, ever,
BEETHOVEN.

356.
TO THE ARCHDUKE RUDOLPH.

1823.

I have just heard that Y.R.H. is expected here to-morrow. If I am still unable to follow the impulse of my heart, I hope you will ascribe it to the state of my eyes. I am better, but for some days to come I dare not breathe the town air, so prejudicial to my eyes. I only wish that the next time Y.R.H. returns from Baden, you would be so good as to let me know, and also name the hour at which I am to present myself, and once more have the good fortune to see my gracious master. But as it is probable Y.R.H. will not long remain here, it is the more incumbent on us to take advantage of the short time at our disposal to carry out our artistic discussions and practice. I will myself bring "Grossen Dank, ÷ ÷ ÷," as it must be sent to Baden. Herr Drechsler thanked me to-day for the *liberty* I had taken in recommending him to Y.R.H., who received him so graciously that I beg to express my warmest gratitude for your kindness. I trust that Y.R.H. will continue firm, for it is said that Abbé Stadler is endeavoring to procure the situation in question for some one else. It would also be very beneficial to Drechsler if Y.R.H. would vouchsafe to speak to Count Dietrichstein[1] on the subject. I once more request the favor of being told the date of your return from Baden, when I will instantly hasten into town to wait on the best master I have in this world. Y.R.H.'s health seems to be good; Heaven be praised that it is so, for the sake of so many who wish it, and among this number I may certainly be included.

[K.]

[Footnote 1: Count Moritz Dietrichstein was in 1823 Court director of the royal band.]

357.
TO THE ARCHDUKE RUDOLPH.

I was very much affected on receiving your gracious letter yesterday. To flourish under the shade of a stately verdant fruit-tree is refreshing to any one capable of elevated thought and feeling, and thus it is with me under the aegis of Y.R.H. My physician assured me yesterday that my malady was disappearing, but I am still obliged to swallow a whole bottle of some mixture every day, which weakens me exceedingly, and compels me, as Y.R.H. will see from the enclosed instructions of the physician, to take a great deal of exercise. I have every hope, however, that soon, even if not entirely recovered, I shall be able to be a great deal with Y.R.H. during your stay here. This hope will tend to recruit my health sooner than usual. May Heaven bestow its blessings on me through Y.R.H., and may the Lord ever guard and watch over you! Nothing can be more sublime than to draw nearer to the Godhead than other men, and to diffuse here on earth these godlike rays among mortals. Deeply impressed by the gracious consideration of Y.R.H. towards me, I hope very soon to be able to wait on you.

[K.]

358.
TO SCHINDLER.

Baden, September, 1823.

SIGNORE PAPAGENO,--

That your scandalous reports may no longer distress the poor Dresdener, I must tell you that the money reached me to-day, accompanied by every possible mark of respect to myself.

Though I should have been happy to offer you a *substantial* acknowledgment for the [illegible, effaced by Schindler] you have shown me, I cannot yet accomplish to the full extent what I have so much at heart. I hope to be more fortunate some weeks hence. [See No. 329.]

Per il Signore Nobile, Papageno Schindler.

359.
TO SCHINDLER.

1823.

The occurrence that took place yesterday, which you will see in the police reports, is only too likely to attract the notice of the established police to this affair. The testimony of a person whose name is not given entirely coincides with yours. In such a case private individuals cannot act; the authorities alone are empowered to do so.[1]

Yours,
BEETHOVEN.

[Footnote 1: Schindler says, "Brother Johann, the apothecary, was ill in the summer of 1823, and during that time his disreputable wife visited her lover, an officer, in the barracks, and was often seen walking with him in the most frequented places, besides receiving him in her own house. Her husband, though confined to bed, could see her adorning herself to go in search of amusement with her admirer. Beethoven, who was informed of this scandal from various quarters, appealed vigorously to his brother, in the hope of persuading him to separate from his ill-conducted wife, but failed in his attempt, owing to the indolence of this ill-regulated man." It was Schindler, too, who prevented Beethoven making any further application to the police. The following note probably refers to this. In his note-book of November, 1823, is a Canon written by Beethoven on his brother Johann and his family, on these words, "Fettlümerl Bankert haben triumphirt," no doubt an allusion to the disgraceful incident we have mentioned. Brother Johann's wife had a very lovely daughter before she married him.]

360.
TO SCHINDLER.

WISEACRE! I kiss the hem of your garment!

361.
TO HERR GRILLPARZER, COURT COMPOSER.

ESTEEMED SIR,--

The directors wish to know your terms with regard to "Melusina." [See No. 331.] In so far she has asserted herself, which is certainly better than being obliged to importune others on such matters. My household has been in great disorder for some time past, otherwise I should have called on you, and requested you to visit me in return.[1] Pray, write your conditions at once, either to the directors or to myself, in which case I will undertake to deliver them. I have been so busy that I could not call on you, nor can I do so now, but hope to see you before long. My number is 323.

In the afternoons you will find me in the coffee-house opposite the "Goldene Birne." If you do come, I beg that you may be *alone*. That obtrusive appendage, Schindler, has long been most obnoxious to me, as you must have perceived when at Hetzendorf,[2] *otium est vitium*. I embrace and esteem you from my heart.

Yours,
BEETHOVEN.

[Footnote 1: In the note-book of 1823 is written, in Beethoven's hand:
8th or 9th November, bad humor.
Another bad day.
Another bad day.
And underneath, in Schindler's hand:
Devil take such a life!]

[Footnote 2: The *Elegante Zeitung* of 1858, No. 73, relates the following anecdote about this visit:--"During the composition of the Opera many conferences took place between the two artistic colleagues, when the new work was zealously discussed on both sides. On one occasion the poet drove out to visit the composer in the country. Beethoven's writing-desk was placed somewhat like a sentry-box opposite a cupboard for provisions, the contents of which compelled the housekeeper to be perpetually coming and going, attracting thereby many an admonitory look askance in the midst of his conversation from the deaf *maestro*. At last the clock struck the dinner-hour. Beethoven went down to his cellar, and soon after returned carrying four bottles of wine, two of which he placed beside the poet, while the other two were allotted to the composer himself and a third guest. After dinner Beethoven slipped out of the room, and held a short parley with the coachman hired for the occasion, who was still waiting at the door. When the time arrived for returning to town, Beethoven proposed driving part of the way with his guests, and did not get out of the carriage till close to the Burgthor. Scarcely was he gone when the companions he had just quitted found some papers lying on the seat he had vacated, which proved to be six *gulden*, the amount of the carriage-hire. They instantly stopped the carriage, and shouted to their friend (who was making off as quick as he could) that he had forgotten some money; but Beethoven did not stand still till he was at a safe distance, when he waved his hat, rejoicing with the glee of a child at the success of his trick. There was no possibility of refusing his *naïf* generosity, and they had sufficient delicacy of feeling not to poison his enjoyment by any untimely remonstrances."]

362.
TO PROBST, MUSIC PUBLISHER,--LEIPZIG.

Vienna, March 10, 1824.

... These are all I can at present give you for publication. I must, alas! now speak of myself, and say that this, the greatest work I have ever written, is well worth 1000 florins C.M. It is a new grand symphony, with a finale and voice parts introduced, solo and choruses, the words being those of Schiller's immortal "Ode to Joy," in the style of my pianoforte Choral Fantasia, only of much greater breadth. The price is 600 florins C.M. One condition is, indeed, attached to this Symphony, that it is not to appear till next year, July, 1825; but to compensate for this long delay, I will give you a pianoforte arrangement of the work gratis, and in more important engagements you shall always find me ready to oblige you.

363.
TO SCHINDLER.

1824.

Frau S. [Schnaps] will provide what is required, so come to dinner to-day at two o'clock. I have good news to tell you,[1] but this is quite *entre nous*, for the *braineater* [his brother Johann] must know nothing about it.

[Footnote 1: This no doubt refers to a letter from Prince Gallizin, March 11, 1824:--"I beg you will be so good as to let me know when I may expect the Quartet, which I await with the utmost impatience. If you require money, I request you will draw on Messrs. Stieglitz & Co., in St. Petersburg, for the sum you wish to have, and it will be paid to your order."]

364.
TO HERR V. RZEHATSCHEK.

1824.

MY WORTHY HERR V. RZEHATSCHEK,--

Schuppanzigh assures me that you intend to be so kind as to lend me the instruments required for my concert;[1] thus encouraged, I venture to ask you to do so, and hope not to meet with a refusal when thus earnestly soliciting you to comply with my request.

Your obedient servant,
BEETHOVEN.

[Footnote 1: It seems highly probable that this concert is the celebrated one in the spring of 1824, when the Ninth Symphony and a portion of the Grand Mass were performed.]

365.
TO THE HIGH CHAMBERLAIN PRINCE TRAUTMANNSDORF.[1]

I am deeply indebted to your Highness for your invariable politeness, which I prize probably the more from Y.H. being by no means devoid of sympathy for my art. I hope one day to have the opportunity of proving my esteem for your H.

[Footnote 1: Enclosed in a note to Schindler, who was to apply for the great *Redoutensaal* for the concert on April 8, 1824.]

366.
TO COUNT MORITZ LICHNOWSKY.[1]

Insincerity I despise; visit me no more; my concert is not to take place.

BEETHOVEN.

[Footnote 1: The originals of these three well-known notes were found by Schindler on the piano, where Beethoven usually left things of the kind, which he intended his amanuensis to take charge of. Lichnowsky, Schuppanzigh, and Schindler had all met at Beethoven's, as if by chance, in order to discuss with him some difficulties which stood in the way of the concert. The suspicious *maestro* saw only collusion and treachery in this, and wrote these notes, which Schindler did not allow to be sent.]

367.
TO HERR SCHUPPANZIGH.

Come no more to see me. I give no concert.

BEETHOVEN.

368.
TO HERR SCHINDLER.

Do not come to me till I summon you. No concert.

BEETHOVEN.

369.
TO HERR V. SARTORIUS, ROYAL CENSOR.

SIR,--

As I hear that obstacles are likely to arise on the part of the royal censorship to a portion of sacred music being given at an evening concert in the Theatre "an der Wien," I must inform you that I have been particularly requested to give these pieces, that the copies for this purpose have already caused serious expense, and the intervening time is too short to produce other new works. Besides, only three sacred compositions are to be given, and these under the title of hymns. I do earnestly entreat you, sir, to interest yourself in this matter, as there are always so many difficulties to contend with on similar occasions. Should this permission not be granted, I do assure you that it will be impossible to give a concert at all, and the whole outlay expended on the copying be thrown away. I hope you have not quite forgotten me.

I am, sir, with high consideration, yours,
BEETHOVEN.

370.
TO SCHINDLER.

1824.

If you have any information to give me, pray write it down; but seal the note, for which purpose you will find wax and a seal on my table. Let me know where Duport[1] lives, when he is usually to be met with, and whether I could see him alone, or if it is probable that people will be there, and who?

I feel far from well. *Portez-vous bien.* I am still hesitating whether to speak to Duport or to write to him, which I cannot do without bitterness.

Do not wait dinner for me; I hope you will enjoy it. I do not intend to come, being ill from our bad fare of yesterday. A flask of wine is ready for you.

[Footnote 1: Schindler says that on April 24, 1824, he applied to Duport, at that time administrator of the Kärnthnerthor Theatre, in Beethoven's name, to sanction his giving a grand concert there, allowing him to have the use of the house for the sum of 400 florins C.M. Further, that the conducting of the concert should be intrusted to Umlauf and Schuppanzigh, and the solos to Mesdames Unger and Sonntag, and to the bass singer Preisinger.]

371. [1]
TO SCHINDLER.

TO SCHINDLER.

I beg you will come to see me to-morrow, as I have a tale to tell you as sour as vinegar. Duport said yesterday that he had written to me, though I have not yet got his letter, but he expressed his satisfaction, which is best of all. The chief feat however is not yet performed, that which is to be acted in front of the *Proscenium*!

[In Beethoven's writing:] Yours, *from C# below to high F,*

BEETHOVEN.

[Footnote 1: Written by his nephew.]

372.
TO SCHINDLER.

After six weeks of discussion, here, there, and everywhere, I am fairly boiled, stewed, and roasted. What will be the result of this much-talked-of concert if the prices are not raised? What shall I get in return for all my outlay, as the copying alone costs so much?

373.
TO SCHINDLER.

At twelve o'clock to-day "in die Birne" [an inn on the Landstrasse]--thirsty and hungry--then to the coffee-house, back again here, and straight to Penzing, or I shall lose the lodging.

374.
TO SCHINDLER.

When you write to me, write exactly as I do to you, without any formal address or signature--*vita brevis, ars longa*. No necessity for details; only the needful!

375.
TO HERR STEINER & CO.

Baden, May 27, 1824.

P.N.G. [PATERNOSTERGÄSSEL],--

Have the goodness to give me a proof of your great complaisance, by using your hand-rostrum (ruler) (not *Rostrum Victoriatum*) to rule 202 lines of music for me, somewhat in the style I now send, and also on equally fine paper, which you must include in your account. Send it, if possible, to-morrow evening by Carl, for I require it.

Perhaps plenary indulgence may then be granted.

376.
POUR M. DE HASLINGER, GÉNÉRAL MUSICIEN ET GÉNÉRAL-LIEUTENANT.

MY DEAR FRIEND,--

You would really do me great injustice were you to suppose that negligence prevented my sending you the tickets; I assure you that it was my intention to do so, but I forgot it like many other things. I hope that some other opportunity may occur to enable me to prove my sentiments with regard to you. I am, I assure you, entirely innocent of all that Duport has done, in the same way that it was *he* who thought fit to represent the Terzet [Op. 116] as new, *not I*. You know too well my love of truth; but it is better to be silent now on the subject, as it is not every one who is aware of the true state of the case, and I, though innocent, might incur blame. I do not at all care for the other proposals Duport makes, as by this concert I have lost both time and money. In haste, your friend,

BEETHOVEN.

377.
TO STEINER & CO.

MY KIND FRIEND,--

Be so good as to read the enclosed, and kindly forward it at once to the authorities.

Your servant and *amicus*,
BEETHOVEN.

378.
TO HERR TOBIAS PETER PHILIP HASLINGER.

The horn part and the score are shortly to follow. We are immensely indebted to you. Observe the laws. Sing often my Canon in silence,--*per resurrectionem*, &c. Farewell!

Your friend,
BEETHOVEN.

379.
TO HASLINGER.

Have the goodness to send me my shoes and my sword. You can have the loan of the "Eglantine" for six days, for which, however, you must give an acknowledgment. Farewell!

Yours,
BEETHOVEN.

380.
TO HASLINGER.

Baden, June 12.

MY GOOD FRIEND,--

Something worth having has been put in your way; so make the most of it. You will no doubt come off with a handsome fee, and all expenses paid. As for the March with Chorus [in the "Ruins of Athens," Op. 114], you have yet to send me the sheets for final revision, also the Overture in E flat ["To King Stephen," Op. 117]; the Terzet [Op. 116]; the Elegy [Op. 118]; the Cantata ["*Meeresstille und glückliche Fahrt*," Op. 112]; and the Opera. Out with them all! or I shall be on very little ceremony, your right having already expired. My liberality alone confers on you a larger sum than you do on me. I want the score of the Cantata for a few days, as I wish to write a kind of recitative for it; mine is so torn that I cannot put it together, so I must have it written out from the parts. Has the Leipzig musical paper yet retracted its lies about the medal I got from the late King of France?

I no longer receive the paper, which is a shabby proceeding. If the editor does not rectify the statement, I shall cause him and his consumptive chief to be *harpooned* in the northern waters among the whales.

Even this barbarous Baden is becoming enlightened, and now instead of *gutten Brunn*, people write *guten Brun*. But tell me what are they about in Paternoster Street?

I am, with all esteem for yourself, but with none for the barbarian Paternoster-Gässel,

Your devoted, *incomparativo*,
B----N.

Paternoster-Gässel *primus* will no doubt, like Mephistopheles, emit fiery flames from his jaws.

381.
TO M. DIABELLI.

SIR,--

Pray forgive my asking you to send me the score of my Mass,[1] being in urgent need of it; but I repeat that no public use is to be made of it until I can let you know *how* and *when*. It will be at first performed under my direction, with the addition of several new pieces composed expressly for it, which I will with pleasure send to you afterwards. There are certain conventionalities which must be observed, especially as I am so dependent on foreign connections, for Austria does not furnish me with the means of existence, and gives me nothing but vexation. I will soon appoint a day for you to visit Carl.

I remain, sir, with the highest esteem, yours,

BEETHOVEN.

[Footnote 1: This letter seems to be addressed to Diabelli, who in the summer of 1824 begged the loan of the Mass in D for a few days, but neglected to return it.]

382.
TO PROBST,--LEIPZIG.

Vienna, July 3, 1824

SIR,--

Overwhelmed with work and concerts, it is only now in my power to inform you that the works you wished to have are finished and transcribed, and can be delivered at any time to Herr Glöggl [music publisher in Vienna]. I therefore request you will transmit the 100 Viennese ducats to Herr Glöggl, and let me know when you have done so. I must conclude for to-day, and defer the pleasure of writing further till another opportunity. I am, with esteem, yours obediently,

BEETHOVEN.[1]

[Footnote 1: Probst answered the letter as follows:--

"August 18, 1824.

"The many gossiping reports about the differences between you and a publisher here in a similar transaction are the cause, I frankly own, of my wishing first to see your manuscript. The piracy in engraving, so universal in Austria, often prevents the German publisher paying the price for a work which it merits; and even at this moment in Vienna, with regard to your compositions [Schindler mentions three songs with pianoforte accompaniment, six *bagatelles*, and a grand overture], I can see that the birds of prey are on the watch to rob me of them under the shelter of the law."

On one of these letters Beethoven writes in pencil, "Do not listen to gossip; I have no time at this moment to enter on the subject, but I have all the proofs in my own hands; more of this hereafter."]

383.
TO T. HASLINGER.[1]

MY VERY WORTHY FRIEND,--

Have the goodness to send me the Rochlitz article on the Beethoven works, and we will return it to you forthwith by the flying, driving, riding, or migrating post.

Yours,
BEETHOVEN.

[Footnote 1: The *Rochlitz'sche article* is probably the report in the *A.M. Zeitung* of the works performed at the grand concert of May 7.]

384.
TO HERR SCHOTT,--MAYENCE.

1824.

The Overture[1] that you got from my brother was recently performed here, and I received many eulogiums on the occasion.

What is all this compared to the grandest of all masters of harmony above! above! above! Rightfully the *Most High*! While here below all is a mere mockery--*Dwarfs*--and the *Most High*!!

You shall receive the Quartet with the other works. You are open and candid, qualities which I never before found in publishers, and this pleases me. I say so in writing, but who knows whether it may not soon be in person? I wish you would transmit the sum due for the Quartet to P., as at this moment I require a great deal of money, for I derive everything from foreign sources, and sometimes a delay occurs--caused by myself.

[Footnote 1: The Overture to which he alludes is no doubt Op. 124, in C major, *Zur Weihe des Hauses*, published by Schott. It was performed in the great concert of May 23 of this year (1824), which in the estimation of a Beethoven, already absorbed in new great works, might well be termed "recently performed." Schott himself says the letter is written between July 3 and September 17, 1824.]

385.
TO THE ARCHDUKE RUDOLPH.

Baden, August 23, 1824.

YOUR ROYAL HIGHNESS,--

I live--how?--the life of a snail. The unfavorable weather constantly throws me back, and at these baths it is impossible to command one's natural strength. A few days ago, Nägeli, a musical author and poet of considerable repute, wrote to me from Zurich; he is about to publish 200 poems, and among these some are suitable for musical composition. He urged me much to apply to Y.R.H. to request that you would be graciously pleased to subscribe to this collection. The price is very moderate, 20 groschen, or 1 florin 80 kreutzers. Were Y.R.H. to subscribe for six copies, it would immediately be noised abroad, although I am well aware that my illustrious master does not care for anything of the kind; it will suffice for the present if Y.R.H. will condescend to inform me of your will on the subject. The money can be paid when the copies arrive, probably a couple of months hence. I have conveyed Herr Nägeli's request, and now I must ask another favor, on his account, from myself. Everything cannot be measured by line and plummet; but Wieland says: "A little book may be well worth a few *groschen*." Will Y.R.H. therefore honor these poems by permitting your august name to be prefixed to them, as a token of your sympathy for the benefit of this man? the work is not likely to be quite devoid of value. Being convinced of Y.R.H.'s interest in all that is noble and beautiful, I hope I shall not fail in my intercession for Nägeli, and I beg that Y.R.H. will give me a written permission to inform Nägeli that you will be one of his subscribers.

I remain, with all dutiful fidelity and devotion, your R. Highness's obedient servant,

BEETHOVEN.

386.
TO HIS NEPHEW.

Baden, August 29, 1824.

MY DEAR YOUNG SCAMP,--

How active our *mahogany Holz* [wood] is! My plans are decided. We will give the present quartet to Artaria, and the last to Peters. You see I have learned something; I now perceive why I first *explored the path*; it was for your sake, that you might find it smooth. My digestion is terribly out of order, and no physician! I wish to have some ready-made pens, so send some in a letter. Don't write to Peters on Saturday; we had better wait a little, to show him our indifference on the subject.

Since yesterday I have only taken some soup, and a couple of eggs, and drank nothing but water; my tongue is discolored; and without medicine and tonics, whatever my farcical doctor may say, my digestion will never improve.

The third quartet [in C sharp minor, Op. 131] also contains six movements, and will certainly be finished in ten or twelve days at most. Continue to love me, my dear boy; if I ever cause you pain, it is not from a wish to grieve you, but for your eventual benefit. I now conclude. I embrace you cordially. All I wish is that you should be loving, industrious, and upright. Write to me, my dear son. I regret all the trouble I give you, but it will not go on long. Holz seems inclined to become our friend. I expect a letter soon from [illegible].

Your faithful
FATHER.

387.
ROUGH DRAFT OF A LETTER TO PETERS.

1824.

I wrote to you that a quartet ["and a grand one too" is effaced] is ready for you; as soon, therefore, as you let me know that you will accept it for the 360 florins C.M., or 80 ducats, I will at once forward it to you. My works are now paid at a higher rate than ever; besides, you have only yourself to blame in this affair. Your own letters show what you formerly desired to have, and the works I sent you were *what they ought to have been* (the numerous pirated editions prove the truth of this); but the Quartet will convince you that, so far from wishing to take my revenge, I now give you what could not possibly be better, were it intended even for my best friend.

I beg that you will make no delay, so that I may receive your answer by the next post; otherwise I must forthwith return you the 360 florins C.M. I shall, at all events, be rather in a scrape, for there is a person who wishes to have not only this but another newly finished work of mine, though he does not care to take only one. It is solely because you have waited so long (though you are yourself to blame for this) that I separate the Quartet from the following one, now also completed. (Do you think that the latter ought to be also offered here? but, of course, cunningly and warily: *comme marchand coquin!*) You need have no misgivings that I am sending you something merely to fulfil my promise; no, I assure you on my honor as an artist that you may place me on a level with the lowest of men, if you do not find that it is one of my very best works.

388.
TO HANS GEORG NÄGELI,--ZURICH.

Baden, September 9, 1824.

MY MUCH-VALUED FRIEND,--

The Cardinal Archduke is in Vienna, and owing to my health, I am here. I only yesterday received from him a gracious written consent to subscribe to your poems, on account of the services you have rendered to the progress of music. He takes six copies of your work. I will shortly send you the proper address. An anonymous friend is also on the list of subscribers. I mean myself, for as you do me the honor to become my panegyrist, I will on no account allow my name to appear. How gladly would I have subscribed for more copies, but my means are too straitened to do so. The father of an adopted son, (the child of my deceased brother,) I must for his sake think and act for the *future* as well as for the *present*. I recollect that you previously wrote to me about a subscription; but at that time I was in very bad health, and continued an invalid for more than three years, but now I am better. Send also the complete collection of your lectures direct to the Archduke Rudolph, and, if possible, dedicate them to him; you are certain at all events to receive a present, not a very large one probably, but still better than nothing; put some complimentary expressions in the preface, for he understands music, and it is his chief delight and occupation. I do really regret, knowing his talents, that I cannot devote myself to him as much as formerly.

 I have made various applications to procure you subscribers, and shall let you know as soon as I receive the answers. I wish you would also send me your lectures, and likewise Sebastian Bach's five-part Mass, when I will at once remit you the money for both. Pray, do not imagine that I am at all guided by self-interest; I am free from all petty vanity; in godlike Art alone dwells the impulse which gives me strength to sacrifice the best part of my life to the celestial Muse. From childhood my greatest pleasure and felicity consisted in working for others; you may therefore conclude how sincere is my delight in being in any degree of use to you, and in showing you how highly I appreciate all your merits. As one of the votaries of Apollo, I embrace you.

Yours cordially,
BEETHOVEN.

Write to me soon about the Archduke, that I may introduce the subject to his notice; you need take no steps towards seeking permission for the dedication. It will and ought to be a surprise to him.

389.
TO HIS NEPHEW.

Baden, evening, September 14, 1824.

MY DEAR SON,--

Whether it rains heavily to-morrow or not, stifling dust or pouring rain would be equally prejudicial to me. It does grieve me to know that you are so long with this demon; but, pray, strive to keep out of her way. You must give her a letter, written in my name, to the manager of the hospital, in which you must state that she did not come on the 1st, partly because she was unwell, and also from various people having come here to meet me, *Basta cosi!*

I send you 40 florins for the singing-master [corépétiteur]. Get a written receipt from him: how many mistakes are thus avoided! and this should be done by every one who pays money for another. Did not Holz bring Rampel's receipt [the copyist] unasked, and do not others act in the same way? Take the white waistcoat for yourself, and have the other made for me. You can bring the metronome with you; nothing can be done with it. Bring also your linen sheets and two coverlets, and some lead-pencils and patterns; be sure you get the former at the Brandstatt. And now farewell, my dear son; come to my arms as early as you can,--perhaps to-morrow. [The paper is here torn away.]

As ever, your faithful
FATHER.

P.S. All that could be done was to send you by the old woman's *char à banc*, which, however, including everything, costs 8 florins 36 kreutzers.

Do not forget anything, and be careful of your health.

390.
TO HERR NÄGELI.

Vienna, September 16, 1824.

MY ESTEEMED FRIEND,--

I gladly comply with your wish that I should arrange the vocal parts of my last Grand Mass for the organ, or piano, for the use of the different choral societies. This I am willing to do, chiefly because these choral associations, by their private and still more by their church festivals, make an unusually profound impression on the multitude, and my chief object in the composition of this Grand Mass was to awaken, and deeply to impress, religious feelings both on singers and hearers. As, however, a copy of this kind and its repeated revision must cause a considerable outlay, I cannot, I fear, ask less than 50 ducats for it, and leave it to you to make inquiries on the subject, so that I may devote my time exclusively to it.

I am, with high consideration,
Your obedient
BEETHOVEN.

391.
TO SCHOTT,--MAYENCE.

Baden, near Vienna, September 17, 1824.

The Quartet [Op. 127, in E flat major] you shall also certainly receive by the middle of October. Overburdened by work, and suffering from bad health, I really have some claim on the indulgence of others. I am here entirely owing to my health, or rather to the want of it, although I already feel better. Apollo and the Muses do not yet intend me to become the prey of the bony Scytheman, as I have yet much to do for you, and much to bequeath which my spirit dictates, and calls on me to complete, before I depart hence for the Elysian fields; for I feel as if I had written scarcely more than a few notes of music.

I wish your efforts all possible success in the service of art; it is that and science alone which point the way, and lead us to hope for a higher life. I will write again soon. In haste, your obedient

BEETHOVEN.

392.
TO HAUSCHKA.

Baden, September 23, 1824.

MY DEAR AND VALUED FRIEND,--

As soon as I arrive in town, I will write Bernard's Oratorio [see No. 257], and I beg you will also transmit him payment for it. We can discuss when we meet in town what we further require and think necessary, and in the mean-time, I appoint you High and Puissant Intendant of all singing and humming societies, Imperial Violoncello-General, Inspector of the Imperial *Chasse*, as well as Deacon of my gracious master, without house or home, and without a prebendary (like myself). I wish you all these, most faithful servant of my illustrious master, as well as everything else in the world, from which you may select what you like best.[1] That there may be no mistake, I hereby declare that it is our intention to set to music the Bernard Oratorio, the "Sieg des Kreuzes" and speedily to complete the same. Witness this our sign and seal,

LUDWIG VAN BEETHOVEN.

1st P.S. Take care that the venison is not devoured by rats or mice--you understand? Strive for better choice and variety.

Yours, as a Christian and in Apollo,
B.

2d P.S. As for the little flag on the white tower, we hope soon to see it waving again!
[Footnote 1: An allusion to Hauschka's subserviency to all persons in high Court offices.]

393.
TO HERR NÄGELI,--ZURICH.

Vienna, November 17, 1824.

MY MUCH-VALUED FRIEND,--

Deeply absorbed in work, and not sufficiently protected against this late season of the year, I have again been ill; so believe me it was impossible for me to write to you sooner. With regard to your subscription, I have only succeeded in getting one subscriber for two copies, Herr v. Bihler, tutor in the family of His Imperial Highness the Archduke Carl; he tried to get the Archduke also, but failed. I have exerted myself with every one, but, unluckily, people are here actually deluged with things of the same kind. This is all that I can write to you in my hurry. I urged the matter, too, on Haslinger, but in vain; we are really poor here in Austria, and the continued pressure of the war leaves but little for art and science. I will see that the subscriptions are paid, but let me know distinctly where the money is to be sent to. I embrace you in spirit. Always rely on the high esteem of your true friend,

BEETHOVEN.

394.
TO THE ARCHDUKE RUDOLPH.

November 18, 1824.

YOUR ROYAL HIGHNESS,--

On my return from Baden, illness prevented my waiting on Y.R.H. according to my wish, being prohibited going out; thus yesterday was the first time I dared to venture again into the open air. When your gracious letter arrived, I was confined to bed, and under the influence of sudorifics, my illness having been caused by a chill; so it was impossible for me to rise. I feel sure that Y.R.H is well aware that I never would neglect the respect so properly your due. I shall have the pleasure of waiting on you to-morrow forenoon. Moreover, there will be no lack of opportunity here to awaken the interest Y.R.H. takes in music, which cannot fail to prove so beneficial to art,--ever my refuge, thank God!

I remain Y.R.H.'s obedient servant,
BEETHOVEN.

395.
TO SCHOTT,--MAYENCE.

Vienna, November 18, 1824.

I regret being obliged to tell you that some little time must yet elapse before I can send off the works. There was not in reality much to revise in the copies; but as I did not pass the summer here, I am obliged to make up for this now, by giving two lessons a day to H.R.H. the Archduke Rudolph. This exhausts me so much that it almost entirely unfits me for all else. Moreover, I cannot live on my income, and my pen is my sole resource; but *no consideration is shown either for my health or my precious time*. I do hope that this may not long continue, when I will at once complete the slight revision required. Some days ago I received a proposal which concerns you also; its purport being that a foreign music publisher was disposed, &c., &c., to form a connection with you, in order to guard against piracy. I at once declined the offer, having had sufficiently painful experience on these matters. (Perhaps this was only a pretext to spy into my affairs!)

396.
TO CARL HOLZ.

I send you my greetings, and also wish to tell you that I am not going out to-day. I should be glad to see you, perhaps this evening after your office hours.

In haste, your friend,
BEETHOVEN.

I am by no means well.

397.
TO CARL HOLZ.

MY WORTHY HOLZ--BE NO LONGER HOLZ [WOOD]!

The well-beloved government wishes to see me to-day at ten o'clock. I beg you will go in my place; but first call on me, which you can arrange entirely according to your own convenience. I have already written a letter to the *powers that be*, which you can take with you. I much regret being forced to be again so troublesome to you, but my going is out of the question, and the affair must be brought to a close,

Yours,
BEETHOVEN.

398.
TO SCHOTT,--MAYENCE.

Vienna, December 17 [Beethoven's birthday], 1824.

I write to say that a week must yet elapse before the works can be dispatched to you. The Archduke only left this yesterday, and much precious time was I obliged to spend with him. I am beloved and highly esteemed by him, *but*--I cannot live on that, and the call from every quarter to remember "that he who has a lamp ought to pour oil into it" finds no response here.

As the score ought to be correctly engraved, I must look it over repeatedly myself, for I have no clever copyist at present. Pray, do not think ill of me! *Never* was I guilty of anything base!

399.

March, 1825.

MY GOOD FRIENDS,--

Each is herewith appointed to his own post, and formally taken into our service, pledging his honor to do his best to distinguish himself, and each to vie with the other in zeal.

Every individual cooperating in this performance must subscribe his name to this paper.[1]

Schuppanzigh, (*Manu propria.*)
Weiss.
Linke, (M.P.)
Confounded violoncello of the great masters.
Holz, (M.P.)
The *last*, but only as to his signature.

[Footnote 1: In reference to the rehearsals of the first production of the E flat major Quartet, Op. 127, in March, 1825.]

400.
TO SCHINDLER.

The Spring of 1825.

I have waited till half-past one o'clock, but as the *caput confusum* has not come, I know nothing of what is likely to happen. Carl must be off to the University in the Prater; so I am obliged to go, that Carl, who must leave this early, may have his dinner first. I am to be found in the "Wilde Mann" [an inn in the Prater].

To Herr Schindler, *Moravian numskull*.[1]

[Footnote 1: Schindler was a Moravian.]

401.
TO LINKE, VIOLONCELLIST.[1]

DEAR LINKE,--

Having heard Herr v. Bocklet very highly spoken of, I think it would be advisable to ask him kindly to play in the trio at your concert. I do not know him myself, or I would have applied to him on your behalf. Always rely on me when it is in my power to serve you.

Yours truly,
BEETHOVEN.

[Footnote 1: Bocklet, a pianist in Vienna, tells me that he rehearsed the Trio with Holz and Linke in 1825 or 1826 at Beethoven's.]

402.[1]
TO * * *

SIR,--

Through the stupidity of my housekeeper your mother was recently sent away from my house, without my having been informed of her visit. I highly disapprove of such incivility, especially as the lady was not even shown into my apartments. The *rudeness* and *coarseness* of the persons whom I am so unfortunate as to have in my service are well known to every one; I therefore request your forgiveness.

Your obedient servant,
L. V. BEETHOVEN.

[Footnote 1: In the New Vienna *Musik Zeitung* the occasion of this note is thus related:--"In 1825, a well-known artist and *dilettante* in the composition of music published a book of waltzes, each of these being composed by the most popular and celebrated musicians of the day; as no one declined giving a musical contribution to the editor, the profits being intended to enable him to go to Carlsbad for the benefit of the waters there. The work met with unusual support and sympathy. It then occurred to the editor to apply for a contribution to the great Ludwig van Beethoven, with whom he had been acquainted in former days through his father and grandfather. The great musician at once, in the most gracious and amiable manner, promised to comply with the request, and sent him not only a waltz, but (the only one who did so) also a trio, desiring the editor to send in the course of a month for these works, which would by that time be completed. As the editor was in the mean time taken ill, he was not able to call for the work himself, and was thus obliged to give up this interesting visit. He therefore requested his mother to apply for the waltz, &c., and to express his thanks; but the housekeeper, to whom she gave her name, refused to admit her, saying she could not do so, 'for her master was in such a crazy mood.' As at this very moment Beethoven chanced to put his head in at the door, she hurried the lady into a dark room, saying, 'Hide yourself, as it is quite impossible that anyone can speak to him to-day,' getting out of the way herself as fast as she could. A couple of days afterwards Beethoven sent the waltz, &c., to the house of the musical editor in question, with the above letter."]

403.
TO F. RIES.

Vienna, April 9, 1825.

MY DEAR GOOD RIES,--

I write only what is most pressing! So far as I can remember in the score of the Symphony [the 9th] that I sent you, in the first hautboy, 242d bar, there stands [F E D] instead of [F E E]. I have carefully revised all the instrumental parts, but those of the brass instruments only partially, though I believe they are tolerably correct. I would already have sent you my score [for performance at the Aix musical festival], but I have still a concert in prospect, if indeed my health admits of it, and this MS. is the only score I possess. I must now soon go to the country, as this is the only season when I profit by it.

You will shortly receive the second copy of the "Opferlied;" mark it at once as corrected by myself, that it may not be used along with the one you already possess. It is a fine specimen of the wretched copyists I have had since Schlemmer's death. It is scarcely possible to rely on a single note. As you have now got all the parts of the *finale* of the Symphony copied out, I have likewise sent you the score of the choral parts. You can easily score these before the chorus commences, and when the vocal parts begin, it could be contrived, with a little management, to affix the instrumental parts just above the scored vocal parts. It was impossible for me to write all these out at once, and if we had hurried such a copyist, you would have got nothing but mistakes.

I send you an Overture in C, 6/8 time, not yet published; you shall have the engraved parts by the next post. A *Kyrie* and *Gloria*, two of the principal movements (of the solemn Mass in D major), and an Italian vocal duet, are also on their way to you. You will likewise receive a grand march with chorus, well adapted for a musical performance on a great scale, but I think you will find what I have already sent quite sufficient.

Farewell! You are now in the regions of the Rhine [Ries at that time lived at Godesberg, near Bonn], which will ever be so dear to me! I wish you and your wife every good that life can bestow! My kindest and best regards to your father, from your friend,

BEETHOVEN.

404.
TO HERR JENGER,--VIENNA.[1]

1824.

MY ESTEEMED FRIEND,--

It will give me much pleasure to send you some day soon the score of Matthisson's "Opferlied." The whole of it, published and unpublished, is quite at your service. Would that my circumstances permitted me to place at once at your disposal the greater works I have written, before they have been heard. I am, alas! fettered on this point; but it is possible that such an opportunity may hereafter occur, when I shall not fail to take advantage of it.

The enclosed letter is for Hofrath v. Kiesewetter. I beg you will be so good as to deliver it, especially as it concerns yourself quite as much as the Herr Hofrath.

I am, with high esteem, your devoted friend,

BEETHOVEN.

[Footnote 1: This note is addressed to Jenger in Vienna, a chancery official and a musical amateur, connoisseur, factotum, and distinguished pianist. The date is not known. The *Opferlied* he refers to, is undoubtedly the 2d arrangement, Op. 121-b, which according to the Leipzig *A.M. Zeitung* was performed as Beethoven's "most recent poetical and musical work," at the concert in the Royal Redoutensaal, April 4, 1824.]

405.
TO SCHOTT.

I have much pleasure in herewith contributing to the "Cecilia"[1] and its readers some Canons written by me, as a supplement to a humorous and romantic biography of Herr Tobias Haslinger residing here, which is shortly to appear in three parts.

In the *first* part, Tobias appears as the assistant of the celebrated and solid Kapellmeister Fux, holding the ladder for his *Gradus ad Parnassum*. Being, however, mischievously inclined, he contrives, by shaking and moving the ladder, to cause many who had already climbed up a long way, suddenly to fall down, and break their necks.

He now takes leave of this earthly clod and comes to light again in the *second* part in the time of Albrechtsberger. The already existing Fux, *nota cambiata*, is now dealt with in conjunction with Albrechtsberger. The alternating subjects of the Canon are most fully illustrated. The art of creating musical skeletons is carried to the utmost limit, &c.

Tobias begins once more to spin his web as a caterpillar, and comes forth again in the *third* part, making his third appearance in the world. His half-fledged wings bear him quickly to the Paternostergässel, of which he becomes the Kapellmeister. Having emerged from the school of the *nota cambiata*, he retains only the *cambiata* and becomes a member of several learned societies, &c. But here are the Canons.

On a certain person of the name of Schwencke.[2]

On a certain person of the name of Hoffmann.

LUDWIG VAN BEETHOVEN.

[Footnote 1: A periodical published for the musical world, and edited by a society of *savants*, art-critics, and artists; Mayence, B. Schott & Sons. The publishers applied to Beethoven, in the name of the editors, for a contribution to the *Cecilia*.]

[Footnote 2: It appears that Kapellmeister Schwencke in Hamburg, in many complimentary and flowery phrases, had requested Beethoven to send him his autograph. Perhaps Beethoven, to whom the sound of certain names appeared comical, alludes here to this Hamburg Kapellmeister Schwencke.]

406.
TO LUDWIG RELLSTAB.

May 3, 1825.

As I was just starting for the country yesterday, I was obliged to make some preparations myself; so unluckily your visit to me was in vain. Forgive me in consideration of my very delicate health. As perhaps I may not see you again, I wish you every possible prosperity. Think of me when writing your poems.

Your friend,
BEETHOVEN.

Convey my affectionate regards and esteem to Zelter,--that faithful prop of true art.

Though convalescent, I still feel very weak. Kindly accept the following token of remembrance from

Your friend,
BEETHOVEN.

407.
TO * * *

Vienna.

SIR,--

Being on the point of going into the country, and only very recently recovered from an attack of internal inflammation, I can merely write you a few words. In the passage in the "Opferlied," 2d strophe, where it runs thus:--

I wish it to be written thus:--

408.
TO HIS BROTHER JOHANN.

Baden, May 6, 1825.

The bell and bell-pulls, &c., &c., are on no account whatever to be left in my former lodging. No proposal was ever made to these people to take any of my things. Indisposition prevented my sending for it, and the locksmith had not come during my stay to take down the bell; otherwise it might have been at once removed and sent to me in town, as they have no right whatever to retain it. Be this as it may, I am quite determined not to leave the bell there, for I require one here, and therefore intend to use the one in question for my purpose, as a similar one would cost me twice as much as in Vienna, bell-pulls being the most expensive things locksmiths have. If necessary, apply at once to the police. The window in my room is precisely in the same state as when I took possession, but I am willing to pay for it, and also for the one in the kitchen,--2 florins 12 kreutzers for the two. The key I will not pay for, as I found none; on the contrary, the door was fastened or nailed up when I came, and remained in the same condition till I left; there never was a key, so of course neither I myself, nor those who preceded me, could make use of one. Perhaps it is intended to make a collection, in which case I am willing to put my hand in my pocket.

LUDWIG VAN BEETHOVEN.

409.
TO HERR VON SCHLEMMER.[1]

SIR,--

It strikes me as very remarkable that Carl cannot be persuaded to go into good society, where he might amuse himself in a creditable manner. This almost leads me to suspect that he possibly finds recreations, both in the evening and at night, in less respectable company. I entreat you to be on your guard as to this, and on no pretext whatever to allow him to leave the house at night, unless you receive a written request from me to that effect, by Carl. He once paid a visit, with my sanction, to Herr Hofrath Breuning. I strongly recommend this matter to your attention; it is far from being indifferent, either to you or to me; so I would once more urge you to practise the greatest vigilance.

I am, sir,
Your obedient
BEETHOVEN.

[Footnote 1: In 1825, his nephew lived with Schlemmer in the Alleengasse, close to the Karlskirche.]

410.
TO HIS NEPHEW.

Frau Schlemmer is to receive, or has already received, her money by our housekeeper. Some letters must be written to-morrow. Let me know what time would suit you best? Your

UNCLE.

I left my pocket-handkerchief with you.

411.[1]

MY DEAR SON,--

I have this moment got your letter. I still feel very weak and solitary, and only read the horrid letter I enclose! I send you 25 florins to buy the books at once, and you can spend the surplus when you require to do so. Pray bring me back Reisser's note.[2] On Saturday, the 14th of May, I will send a carriage into town to fetch you here; the charge is as yet very reasonable. The old woman is to inquire what hour will suit you best; you can set off at any time before six in the evening, so that you need neglect nothing. Perhaps I may come myself, and then your shirts might be purchased; in which case it would be as well if you were to be at liberty by four o'clock; but if I do not come, which is very possible, drive straight here at five or six o'clock in the evening. You will not thus feel so much fatigued, and you can leave this again on Monday, if nothing is neglected by the delay. You can take the money with you for the Correpetitor. Are you aware that this affair of the Correpetitor, including board and lodging, amounts to 2000 florins a year? I can write no more to-day, I can scarcely guide my pen. Show this letter to Reisser.

Your affectionate
FATHER.

[Footnote 1: I have arranged the following notes to his nephew in their probable succession as to time. Schindler has given some of these in his *Biography*, but quite at random, and disjointed, without any reliable chronological order.]

[Footnote 2: Reisser was Vice-Director of the Polytechnic Institution, where the nephew had been placed for some time. Reisser had also undertaken the office of his co-guardian. Beethoven sometimes writes *Reissig*.]

412.
TO DR. BRAUNHOFER.

Baden, May 13, 1825.

MY ESTEEMED FRIEND,--

Doctor. "How does our patient get on?"

Patient. "Still in a bad way, feeling weak and irritable, and I think that at last we must have recourse to stronger medicines, and yet not too violent; surely I might now drink white wine with water, for that deleterious beer is quite detestable. My catarrhal condition is indicated by the following symptoms. I spit a good deal of blood, though probably only from the windpipe. I have constant bleeding from the nose, which has been often the case this winter. There can be no doubt that my digestion is terribly weakened, and in fact my whole system, and, so far as I know my own constitution, my strength will never be recruited by its natural powers."

Doctor. "I will prescribe for you, and soon, very soon, shall your health be restored."

Patient. "How glad I should be to sit down at my writing-table, with some cheerful companions. Reflect on this proposal." *Finis.*

P.S. I will call on you as soon as I come to town, only tell Carl at what hour I am likely to see you. It would be a good plan to give Carl directions what I am to do. (I took the medicine only once, and have lost it.)

I am, with esteem and gratitude,

Your friend,
BEETHOVEN.

Written on May 11th, 1825, in Baden, Helenenthal, second floor, Anton's-Brücke, near Siechenfeld.

413.
TO HIS NEPHEW.

Baden, May 17.

MY DEAR SON,--

The weather here is abominable, and the cold greater even than yesterday; so much so that I have scarcely the use of my fingers to write; this is the case, however, only in the mountains, and more especially in Baden. I forgot the chocolate to-day, and am sorry to be obliged to trouble you about it, but all will go better soon. I enclose you 2 florins, to which you must add 15 kreutzers; send it if possible with the post in the afternoon; otherwise I shall have none the day after to-morrow; the people of the house will assist you in this. May God bless you! I begin to write again very tolerably; still, in this most dreary, cold stormy weather, it is almost impossible to have any clear conceptions.

Now as ever,
Your good and loving
FATHER.

414.
TO HIS NEPHEW.

Noon, 1 o'clock.

MY DEAR SON,--

I merely wish to let you know that the old woman is not yet returned,--why, I cannot tell. Inquire immediately at Höbel's in the Kothgasse, whether the Höbel who belongs to this place set off from Vienna to Baden? It is really so distressing to me to depend on such people, that if life did not possess higher charms, it would be utterly insupportable in my eyes. You no doubt got my yesterday's letter, and the 2 florins for the chocolate. I shall be obliged to drink coffee to-morrow; perhaps after all it is better for me than chocolate, as the prescriptions of this B. [Braunhofer] have been repeatedly wrong. Indeed he seems to me very ignorant, and a blockhead into the bargain; he must have known about the asparagus. Having dined at the inn to-day, I have a threatening of diarrhoea. I have no more white wine, so I must get it from the inn, and such wine too! for which, however, I pay 3 florins! Two days ago the old woman wrote to me that she wished to end her days in an alms-house; perhaps she will not return to me; so be it in God's name! she will always be a wicked old woman. She ought to make arrangements with the person whom she knows of. She wrote to me in a very different strain from that in which she spoke to you on Sunday, and said "that the people refused to give up the bell-pull." Who knows whether she may not have some interest in the matter? She went into town yesterday at six o'clock, and I begged her to make haste back here this forenoon; if she still comes, I must go to town the day after to-morrow. Leave a written message to say when I am to see you.... Write me a few lines immediately. How much I regret troubling you, but you must see that I cannot do otherwise....

Your attached
FATHER.

How distressing to be in such a state here!
To Herr Carl van Beethoven,
Vienna, Alleengasse 72, Karlskirche, 1ter Étage,
at Herr Schlemmer's.

415.
TO HIS NEPHEW.

MY DEAR SON,--

I sent for the cabinet-maker to-day with the old--witch--to Asinanius'[1] house. Don't forget the paintings, and the things sent in last summer; at all events look for them. I may perhaps come on Saturday; if not, you must come to me on Sunday. May God watch over you, my dear son.

Your attached
FATHER.

I cannot write much. Send me a few words.[2]

[Footnote 1: It was thus Beethoven named his *pseudo*-brother.]

[Footnote 2: Underneath is written in pencil by another hand, "I shall be at the usual place at three o'clock, *s'il vous plait*." The whole appears to be afterwards stroked out.]

416.
TO HIS NEPHEW.

Do send the chocolate at last by the old woman. If Ramler is not already engaged, he may perhaps drive her over. I become daily thinner, and feel far from well; and no physician, no sympathizing friends! If you can possibly come on Sunday, pray do so; but I have no wish to deprive you of any pleasure, were I only sure that you would spend your Sunday properly away from me.

I must strive to wean myself from everything; if I were only secure that my great sacrifices would bring forth worthy fruits!

Your attached
FATHER.

417.
TO HIS NEPHEW.

Wednesday, May 17.

MY DEAR SON,--

The old woman is just come, so you need be under no uneasiness; study assiduously and rise early, as various things may occur to you in the morning, which you could do for me. It cannot be otherwise than becoming in a youth, now in his nineteenth year, to combine his duties towards his benefactor and foster-father with those of his education and progress. I fulfilled my obligations towards my own parents. In haste,

Your attached
FATHER.

The old bell-pull is here. The date of my letter is wrong; it is not May the 17th, but the 18th.

418.
TO HIS NEPHEW.

May 19.

Ask the house agent about a lodging in the Landstrasse, Ungargasse, No. 345, adjoining the Bräuhaus,--four rooms and a kitchen, commanding a view of the adjacent gardens. I hear there are various others too in the Hauptstrasse. Give a gulden to the house agent in the Ungargasse, to promise me the refusal of the lodgings till Saturday, when, if the weather is not too bad, I mean to come on to fetch you. We must decide to-morrow whether it is to be hired from Michaelmas or now. If I do come on Saturday, take care that I find you at home.

Your attached
FATHER.

419.
TO HIS NEPHEW.

Say everything that is kind and amiable from me to my esteemed fellow-guardian, Dr. v. Reissig; I feel still too feeble to write to him myself. I hope he will not object to your coming to me here every Saturday evening. You are well aware that I *never abused* such a permission when you were at Blöchlinger's [see No. 276]. Besides, I feel sure of your intercession *in support of my request*.

Your attached father,
BEETHOVEN.

420.
TO HIS NEPHEW.

Baden, May 23.

I have been assured, though as yet it is only a matter of conjecture, that a clandestine intercourse has been renewed between your mother and yourself. Am I doomed again to experience such detestable ingratitude? No! if the tie is to be severed, so be it! By such ingratitude you will incur the hatred of all impartial persons. The expressions my brother made use of yesterday before Dr. Reissig (as he says); and your own with respect to Schönauer (who is naturally adverse to me, the judgment of the Court being the *exact reverse of what he desired*), were such, that I will not mix myself up with such shameful doings! No! never more!

If you find the *Pactum* oppressive, then, in God's name, I resign you to His holy keeping! I have done my part, and on this score I do not dread appearing before the Highest of all Judges. Do not be afraid to come to me to-morrow; as yet I only *suspect*; God grant that those suspicions *may not prove true*, for to you it would be an incalculable misfortune, with whatever levity my rascally brother, and perhaps your mother also, may treat the matter to the old woman. I shall expect you without fail.

421.
TO HIS NEPHEW.

Baden, May 31, 1825.

MY DEAR SON,--

I intend to come to town on Saturday, and to return here either on Sunday evening, or early on Monday. I beg you will therefore ask Dr. Bach [advocate] at what hour I can see him, and also fetch the key from brother Bäcker's [a brother-in-law of Johann Beethoven's], to see whether in the room inhabited by my unbrotherly brother, the arrangements are such that I can stay a night there; and if there is clean linen, &c., &c. As Thursday is a holiday, and it is unlikely that you will come here (indeed I do not desire that you should), you may easily execute these two commissions for me. You can let me know the result when I arrive on Saturday. I don't send you money, for if you want any, you can borrow a gulden at home. Moderation is necessary for young people, and you do not appear to pay sufficient attention to this, as you had *money without my knowledge, nor do I yet know whence it came*. Fine doings! It is not advisable that you should go to the theatre at *present*, on account of the distraction it causes. The 5 florins procured by Dr. Reissig, I will pay off by instalments, punctually every month. So enough of this! Misled as you have been, it would be no bad thing were you at length to cultivate *simplicity and truth*, for my heart has been so deeply wounded by your deceitful conduct, that it is difficult to forget it. Even were I disposed to submit like an ox to so hard a yoke without murmuring, if you pursue the same course towards others, you will never succeed in gaining the love of any one. As God is my witness, I can think of nothing but you, and my contemptible brother, and the detestable family that I am afflicted with. May God vouchsafe to listen to my prayer, for *never* again can I trust you!

Your Father, alas!
Yet fortunately not your Father.

422.
TO HIS NEPHEW.

Baden, June 9, 1825.

I wish you at least to come here on Sundays. In vain do I ask for an answer. God help you and me!

As ever,
Your attached
FATHER.

I have written to Herr v. Reissig to desire you to come here on Sundays. The *calèche* leaves his house at six o'clock, from the *Kugel, auf der Wieden*. You have only to work and study a little in advance, to lose nothing. I regret being obliged to cause you this annoyance; you are to return the same afternoon at five o'clock, with the *calèche*. Your place is already paid for; you can shave here in the morning, and a shirt and neckcloth will be ready for you, so that you may arrive at the right time.

Farewell. If I reproach you it is not without good cause, and it would be hard to have sacrificed so much, merely to bestow a *commonplace man* on the world. I hope to see you without fail.

If the intrigues are already matured, say so frankly (and naturally), and you will find one who will always be true to the good cause. The lodging A. was again advertised in the paper on Tuesday; could you not have arranged about this? You might at all events have done so through some one else, or by writing, if you were at all indisposed. I should much prefer not moving, if I were not compelled to do so. You know my mode of living here, and it is far worse in this cold stormy weather. My continued solitude only still further enfeebles me, and really my weakness often amounts to a swoon. Oh! do not further grieve me, for the scythe of Death will grant me no long delay!

If I could find a good lodging in the Alleengasse, I would at once engage it.

423.

Tuesday Morning.

MY DEAR SON,--

The two patterns, one placed at the top and the other below, each 21 florins, seem to me the best; the landlord can advise you. For the trousers 88--4-1/2. I enclose 62 florins W.W. 30 kreutzers. Give me an exact account of how you spend this money, for it was hard to earn; still it is not worth while, for the sake of a florin a yard, not to select the best material; so choose, or get some one to choose for you, the best of the two at 21 florins. Order the highest quality for your trousers also; remember you ought never to wear your best clothes at home; no matter who comes, you need never be well dressed in the house.[1] The moment you come home change your good clothes, and be at your ease in those set aside for the purpose. Farewell.

Your attached
FATHER.

P.S. The creature went off yesterday and has not returned; we shall see how this turns out. The old beast was determined to be off, being like a restless wild animal devoid of purpose or reason. May Heaven have pity on me! The new cooking began yesterday.

[Footnote 1: See Weber's narrative in his *Biography*, Vol. II. 510. "The square Cyclopean figure was attired in a shabby coat with torn sleeves."]

424.
TO HIS NEPHEW.

Baden, June 15.

MY DEAR SON,--

I hope you received the 62 florins 30 kreutzers. If you wish to order trousers of the same cloth, do so. You probably chose that at 25 florins, and on such occasions the best quality should not be rejected for the sake of a couple of florins. You may also order two pairs of trousers of the gray cloth. You must let me know the amount of the tailor's bill, &c., &c., which shall be paid by me. "Let not thy left hand know what thy right hand doeth." Such is the sentiment of noble-minded men. You have, alas! only yourself to blame for my being forced to draw your attention to this. Do not forget to call on Riess (??). May Aurora not only awaken you but speed your industry.

Now for my every-day household matters. The maid came indeed, but is not to remain; in the mean time I have spoken pretty plainly to the old woman, *so far* as it is possible to speak to such people.

But let us say no more of all this bedevilment. My brother *Asinanio* has written to me. What I find most trying of all is being alone at dinner, and it is really surprising that I can write to you even tolerably from here. Possibly I may come to town on Saturday, and if so you will perhaps drive out here with me at six o'clock in the evening?

Now farewell, my darling! deserve this name. Retain what money you require; anything you want shall be purchased for you when I come in. I embrace you, and hope you will be my good, studious, noble son.

Now as ever, your attached
FATHER.

I should like to know that you received the money safely. Did the Correpetitor come?

425.
TO HIS NEPHEW.

MY DEAR SON,--

I send you herewith the 90 florins. Get a written receipt from the landlady to prevent all mistakes afterwards; this is the invariable custom with those still under the control of guardians. My wafers are done; cannot you manage to send me a box in some way or other? Acknowledge the receipt of the money at once. God bless you! Do all you possibly can to rid me of that old demon.

Do not involve yourself in any clandestine doings with my brother; above all do nothing clandestine towards me; towards your attached father. Goodnight. Farewell! farewell! The old witch and Satan and I?!

426.
TO HIS NEPHEW.

I rejoice, my dear son, that you take pleasure in this new sphere, and such being the case you must zealously strive to acquire what is necessary for it. I did not recognize your writing; I indeed look only to the *sense* and *meaning*, but you must now attain some outward elegance also. If it is too hard a task for you to come here, give it up; but if you can by any possibility do so, I shall rejoice in my desert home to have a feeling heart near me. If you do come, the housekeeper will settle that you leave Vienna at five o'clock, which leaves you ample time for your studies.

I embrace you cordially.

Your attached
FATHER.

P.S. Don't forget to bring the "Morgenblatt" and Ries's letter.[1]

[Footnote 1: A letter from Ries of this date, in the *Fischhof'sche Handschrift*, is of sufficient interest to be given here at full length:--

Godesberg, June 9, 1825.

Dearest Beethoven,--I returned a few days ago from Aix-la-Chapelle, and feel the greatest pleasure in telling you that your new Symphony [the 9th] was executed with the most extraordinary precision, and received with the greatest applause. It was a hard nut to crack, and the last day I rehearsed the *finale* alone for three hours; but I in particular, and all the others, were fully rewarded by the performance. It is a work beside which no other can stand, and had you written nothing but this you would have gained immortality. Whither will you lead us?

As it will interest you to hear something of the performance, I will now briefly describe it. The orchestra and choruses consisted of 422 persons, and many very distinguished people among them. The first day commenced with a new Symphony of mine, and afterwards Handel's *Alexander's Feast*. The second day began with your new Symphony, followed by the *Davide Penitente* of Mozart, the overture to the *Flaute Magico*, and the *Mount of Olives*. The applause of the public was almost terrific. I had been in Aix-la-Chapelle from the 3d of May on purpose to conduct the rehearsals, and as a mark of the satisfaction and enthusiasm of the public, I was called forward at the close of the performance, when an ode and a laurel crown were presented to me by a lady (a very pretty one too), and at the same moment another poem and a shower of flowers followed from the upper boxes. All was pleasure and contentment, and every one says that this is the finest of the seven Whitsuntide festivals held here.

I cannot sufficiently lament that your other music arrived too late to make use of it. It was indeed utterly impossible to do so. I herewith send you, my dear friend, a check for 40 Louis d'or on Heppenmayer & Co. in Vienna, according to our agreement, and beg you will acknowledge the receipt, that I may settle everything relating to Aix-la-Chapelle.

I am glad that you have not accepted any engagement in England. If you choose to reside there, you must previously take measures to ensure your finding your account in it. From the Theatre alone Rossini got £2500. If the English wish to do anything at all remarkable for you, they must combine, so that it may be well worth your while to go there. You are sure to receive enough of applause, and marks of homage, but you have had plenty of these during your whole life. May all happiness attend you. Dear Beethoven, yours ever,

FERDINAND RIES.]

427.
TO HIS NEPHEW.

Baden, June 28, 1825.

MY DEAR SON,--

As in this heat you may perhaps wish to bathe, I send you two more florins. You must be careful to take a written receipt from those to whom you pay money; for that errors do occur is proved by the blue cloth, and the three florins for the looking-glass. You are a thorough Viennese, and although I do not expect you to become a W.W. (depreciated Vienna currency), still it is no disgrace at your age to give an exact account of all that you receive, as no one is considered to be of age till five and twenty, and even if you had property of your own, you would be obliged to account for it to your guardian at your present years. Let us not refer to the past; it would be easy to do so, but only cause me pain; at last it would come to this, "You are indeed a first-rate guardian," &c. If you had any depth of feeling you would have acted very differently in most things.

Now as to my domestic rabble; yesterday the kitchenmaid was off again and got a fresh place; the cause is difficult to discover from my old witch, who is now once more all smiles, and no longer persists in declaring that she has incurred any *loss* from the weekly bills; what do you think of that?

[The last page of this letter is an illegible fragment.]

428.
TO HIS NEPHEW.

Baden.

MY DEAR GOOD CARL,--

I have just got your letter this evening, and could not help laughing at it. It was not right in the people at Mayence to have acted thus, but since the thing has occurred, it does not signify. Our epoch requires strong minds to scourge those frivolous, contemptible, malicious beings, repulsive as it is to my feelings to cause pain to any man. Besides, I intended a mere jest, and it was far from my intention to let such a thing be printed.[1]

You must ascertain instantly from a magistrate the proper mode of converting the Bank obligations into Rothschild's Austrian Loan, that you may get the authority from a magistrate (not from the *Court* of those *pseudo*-guardians!)

Be good and honest; you have here an instance how people rejoice when such men are properly estimated. Be my own dear precious son, and imitate my virtues, but not my faults; still, though man is frail, do not at least have worse defects than those of

Your sincere and fondly attached
FATHER.

Write to me about the conversation on Sunday--it is of the *Court, courtly*, so you must be on your guard. Holz did not come to-day; whether he is trustworthy I cannot say.

[Footnote 1: There is no doubt that he alludes to the severe castigation of Haslinger in No. 405 and the *canonization* of the two others. See also No. 440, which shows that there was something amiss with Haslinger.]

429.
TO HIS NEPHEW.

To-day is Friday, to-morrow Saturday.

Here comes *Satanas*. To-day her raging fury and madness have somewhat subsided, but if she applies to you, refer her to me the day after to-morrow. During the whole week I was forced to submit and to suffer like a saint. Avaunt! such dregs of the people! What a reproach to our civilization to stand in need of a class like this, and to have those whom we despise so constantly near us. Go with her to-morrow as formerly to the Carolin Thor about the Seltzer water; if the small bottles are as genuine as the larger ones, order some of them, but I think the larger size are more likely to be the *safest*; *ce dépend de votre esprit, votre distinction*, &c. Now farewell, my dear son; take care to get me the genuine, and *not* the artificial Seltzer water, and go yourself to see about it, or I might get Heaven knows what! Farewell again, my good fellow; we are well affected towards you, and shall expect you the day after to-morrow at eight o'clock. Breakfast shall be ready for you, if that early meal does not become as usual a late meal. *Ah! au diable avec ces grands coquins de neveux, allez-vous en, soyez mon fils, mon fils bien aimé. Adieu; je vous baise, votre père sincère comme toujours.*

430.
TO HIS NEPHEW.

The old goose is the bearer of this. She has given you the quills, and you have again told an untruth. Alas! farewell. I await your report about the book. She is going to-day to Katel, so she will have very little time for her stupid blundering. May the Lord one day deliver me from her! *Libera me Domine de illis*, &c.

431.[1]

DEAR SON, DEAR BOY,--

Do not omit the point about "the happiness." I know from my experience of the late Lichnowsky, that those so-called great personages do not like to see an artist, who is at all events their equal, prosperous. *Voilà le même cas, votre Altesse*, sometimes in the context V.A. The address "à son Altesse Monseigneur le Prince," &c., &c. We cannot tell whether he may have that weakness or not. A blank sheet ought to follow with my signature. You might add that he must not regard the newspaper trash, the writers of which, if I chose, would loudly trumpet forth my merits. The Quartet did indeed fail the first time that it was played by Schuppanzigh; for on account of his corpulence he requires more time than formerly to decipher a piece at a glance, and many other circumstances concurred in preventing its success, which were indeed predicted by me; for although Schuppanzigh and two others receive pensions from royal personages [Rasumowsky], their quartet-playing is not what it was when all four were in the habit of constantly playing together. On the other hand, it has been six times performed in the most admirable manner by other artists, and received with the greatest applause; it was played twice over in one evening, and then again after supper. A violinist of the name of Böhm means also to give it at his benefit, and I must now let many others have it.

Mention the Grand Quartet in your letter to Peters at Leipzig; lose no time about this, and desire him to send me an early reply. Mischances of this kind cannot well be avoided, and we must appear rather coy. Seal the enclosed letter to my brother and send it to the post. Desire the tailor in the Kärntnerstrasse to get lining for trousers for me, and to make them long and without straps, one pair to be of kerseymere and the other of cloth. The great-coat can be fetched from Wolf's. The shoemaker's shop is in the "Stadt" in the Spiegelgasse, in front when coming from the Graben. His name is Magnus Senn, at the Stadthaus, No. 1093. Call on Hönigstein [a banker] and be *candid*, that we may really know *how this wretch has acted*; it would be wise to ascertain this before the letter to Galitzin is sent off. It is probable that something else may be found for you this winter, but we can talk over the matter. Before coming here on Saturday call on Zinbrachen in the Naglergasse about the knives, which you can send at once; the old woman made a fine mess of it! When driving home yesterday I met Clement, Holz, Linke, and Rtschaschek [Rzehatschek] in Neudorf; they had all been to call on me while I was in town. They wish to have the Quartet again. Holz drove straight back here from Neudorf and supped with me in the evening, when I gave him the Quartet to take back with him.

The attachment of genuine artists is not to be despised, and cannot be otherwise than gratifying.

Let me hear from you as soon as you have spoken with Hönigstein; write the dedication of the Overture in C [Op. 124] to Galitzin. If the H.'s undertake to forward it, give it to them, but look sharp about it. God be with you, my dear son; I shall expect a letter from you without fail. May God bless you and me. The end must soon come of your attached father. Good-by, you scamp!

N.B. Do not forget in your letter to Galitzin to mention that the Overture is already announced and about to appear, engraved and dedicated to him.

[Footnote 1: He refers to Prince Boris Gallizin and the Quartets he had ordered. The production of the first of them in E flat major had been a failure. See No. 399.]

432.
TO HIS NEPHEW.

MY DEAR SON,--

Send this letter at once to my *pseudo*-brother, and add something yourself. It is impossible to permit this to continue any longer; no soup to-day, no beef, no eggs, and at last *broiled meat* from the inn!

When Holz was with me lately, there was really almost nothing to eat at supper; and such is the woman's bold and insolent behavior, that I have told her to-day I will not suffer her to remain beyond the end of the month. No more to-day. All that is necessary about the magistrate is for me to write a note authorizing you to draw the money, but it would be as well were you to take the opportunity of asking what you are to do about converting the bank shares into a share in Rothschild's Loan. I shall say nothing further, except that I always look on you as my dear son, and one who deserves to be so. *Little* as I require what nourishes the body, as you know, still the present state of things is really too bad, besides being every moment in danger of being poisoned.

Farewell! Be careful, my dear son, of your health in this heat; I trust you will continue well. Shun all that may enervate or diminish your youthful energies. Farewell! A pleasant talk together would be far better than all this writing. Ever your loving and attached father, who fondly presses you to his heart.

433.
TO HIS NEPHEW.

MY DEAR SON,--

The enclosed will show you all. Write this letter to Schlesinger.

To ---- Schlesinger, Berlin,

Emporium of Art and Science.

You can couch some things in better terms. I think we may calculate on 80 ducats. If indispensable, delay the letter to Galitzin, but be sure to dispatch the one to Schlesinger on Saturday. I suppose you received the packet? I beg you will bring me some shaving-soap, and at least one pair of razors; the man who grinds them gets 2 florins. You will know if anything is to be paid. Now pray practise economy, for you certainly receive too much money. All in vain--a Viennese will always be a Viennese! I rejoiced when I could assist my poor parents; what a contrast are you in your conduct towards me! Thriftless boy, farewell!

Your attached
FATHER.

Bring the newspaper with you. You have a great deal to do this time. You no doubt will write before Sunday. Do not flatter that wretch ----. He is a miserable, weak-minded fellow. I embrace you. My health is *no better*.

434.
TO HIS BROTHER JOHANN,--GNEIXENDORF.

Baden, July 13, 1825.

MY WORTHY BROTHER,--

As you have taken such good care of the book, I beg you will take equal care that it be returned to the proprietor here. Another pretty business! As to your wish that I should come to see you, I long ago fully explained myself on that point; so I request that you will never again allude to the subject, for you will find me as immovable as ever. Pray spare me all details, as I am unwilling to repeat what is disagreeable. You are happy, and it is my desire that you should be so; continue thus, for every one is best *in his own sphere*.

I only once made use of your lodgings, but the baking-oven nearly made me ill, so I did not go again; as I have now a lodging of my own, it is not probable that I shall even *once* make use of the room you offer me. When you write, be sure to *seal* your letters, and address them to the care of Carl, in Vienna, as such letters cost a great deal here. I once more urge you to restore the book belonging to the machinist, *an dem Graben*, for such occurrences are really almost incredible, and place me in no small embarrassment. So the book! the book! to be sent to Carl in Vienna with all possible haste and speed. Farewell, most worthy brother! Yours,

LUDWIG.

435.
TO HIS NEPHEW.

Baden, July 15.

MY DEAR SON,--

In your letter to Schlesinger don't forget to ask whether Prince Radziwill is in Berlin. As to the 80 ducats, you can also write that they may be paid in *Conventionsgulden*, at only 4 florins 30 kreutzers to the ducat; but I leave this entirely to yourself, though gold ducats would not be too much from one who has the right of publishing in England and also in France. You must be quite decided too with respect to the four months' bill. A. Mayseder receives 50 ducats for a set of violin variations! Do not fail to call attention to the fact that my bad health and other circumstances constrain me to look more closely after my interests than formerly. Bargaining is odious to me, but it must be so! What are my feelings when I find myself thus alone among these men! Be sure to forward my letter to my brother, that the book may be restored--what a trick! I should have liked, too, to do all I could to benefit my hearing, and here I should have had time to do so. How melancholy to have such a brother! Alas! alas! Farewell! I embrace you from my heart.

Your attached
FATHER.

P.S. Do not be dilatory, and rise early. If you would rather not, pray do not come on Sunday; but at all events write, though not at present, for if you can come we can discuss all matters together.

436.
TO HIS NEPHEW.

Baden, July 18, Monday.

MY DEAR SON,--

You will see from the enclosure all that you wish to know; only observe *moderation*. Fortune crowns my efforts, but do not lay the foundation of misery by mistaken notions; be truthful and exact in the account of your expenses, and give up the theatre for the present. Follow the advice of your guide and father; be counselled by him whose exertions and aspirations have always been directed to your moral welfare, though without neglecting your temporal benefit.

This Herr Thal will call on you, and he will also be at Herr Hönigstein's; you can give him the Overture if you think fit. He is to stay three weeks. You may invite him to dine here. Sunday would be best, as a certain scamp comes on that day at an early hour, in a carriage that I will send for him. Pray show some amiability of manner towards this man; art and science form a link between the noblest spirits, and your future vocation[1] by no means exempts you from this. You might take a *fiacre* and drive to the copyist's if you can spare time. With respect to the transcription of the Quartet, you may tell him that I write very differently now, much more legibly than during my illness; this Quartet must be written out twice, and I can send it at once. I have had the offer of a copyist here, but I don't know what he can do. I should be careful not to be too confidential at first with the *Holz Christi*, or the splinter of the *Holz Christi*.

Write to me forthwith. Perhaps the old goose may go to Vienna the day after to-morrow. Farewell! Attend to my advice.

Your attached
FATHER,
Who cordially embraces you.

You may possibly go to D---- with this Herr Thal; do not, however, show too much anxiety about the money.

[Footnote 1: The nephew had now resolved on a commercial career, and on this account entered the Polytechnic Institution.]

437.
TO HIS NEPHEW.

MY DEAR SON,--

So let it be! Bring G----'s letter with you, for I have scarcely read it myself. My *Signor Fratello* came the day before yesterday with his brother-in-law [see No. 435]--what a contemptible fellow! The old witch, who went almost crazy again yesterday, will bring you the answer about the book from his brother-in-law. If it does not convey a positive certainty on the subject, send this letter at once to the base creature! When Cato exclaimed, with regard to Caesar, "This man and myself!" what can be done in such a case? I don't send the letter, for it will be time enough a couple of days hence. It is too late to-day. I impress my love, as with a seal, on your affectionate attachment to me. If you are likely to miss your work by coming here, then stay where you are.

As ever, your loving and anxious
FATHER.

Three times over:
_____

|: Come soon! :|

438.
TO THE COPYIST.[1]

Read *violino 2do*--the passage in the first *Allegretto* in the 1st violin--thus:--

&c.

So write it in this way; in the first *Allegretto*, mark the signs of expression in all the four parts:

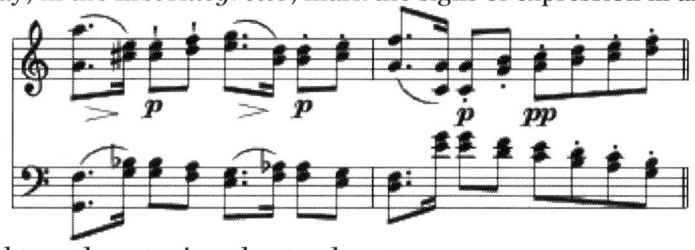

The notes are all right; so do not misunderstand me.

Now, my good friend, as to your mode of writing--*obbligatissimo*; but the signs 𝆏 ══════ ══════ &c., are shamefully neglected, and often, very often, in the wrong place, which is no doubt owing to haste. For Heaven's sake impress on Kempel [a copyist] to copy everything just as it stands; look carefully over my present corrections, and you will find all that you have to say to him. When . is put over a note, ׀ is not to take its place, and *vice versa*. It is not the same thing to write ♩ ♩ ♩ and ♩ ♩ ♩. The ══════ are often purposely placed after the notes. For instance:-- ♫ . The ties to be just as they are now placed. It is not synonymous to write ♫ or thus ♫. Such is our will and pleasure! I have passed no less than the whole forenoon to-day, and yesterday afternoon, in correcting these two pieces, and I am actually quite hoarse from stamping and swearing.

In haste, yours,
BEETHOVEN.

Pray excuse me for to-day, as it is just four o'clock. [The close of this letter has not been deciphered by its possessor, who has traced over the hieroglyphics with a pencil; it reads somewhat to this effect, "to go to Carl at four o'clock. We were much amused," &c.]

[Footnote 1: This letter is evidently written about the same time that the copying of the A minor Quartet (Op. 132) took place, of which the letter treats, and is probably "the enclosure" named in the following note. The corrections, or we ought rather to say revisions, of Beethoven, are all fully and accurately reproduced, at all events in Breitkopf & Härtel's edition.]

439.
TO HIS NEPHEW.

Tuesday, August 2.

MY DEAR SON,--

Send the enclosed to-morrow morning (Wednesday) to the post; as it refers to corrections, *haste is absolutely necessary*. We must have done with this evil old creature! I have scarcely enough to eat, and am forced also to endure the sauciness and insolence of this most malicious old witch--and with such wages too! I think I must ask my *pseudo*-brother to come, and would be glad to engage again the woman from Winter's, in the Kothgasse, who at least knew how to cook.

Write me a few lines to-morrow, and direct here. I send you another florin. Do not neglect your bathing; continue well, and guard against *illness*. Spend your money *on good objects alone*. Be my dear son! What a frightful discord would it be, were you to prove *false* to me, as many persons maintain that you already are! May God bless you!

Your attached
FATHER.

N.B. Send off the letter to-morrow (Wednesday). I have heard nothing as yet of the knives, and my made pens also begin to fail.

440.
TO HIS NEPHEW.

Baden, August

MY DEAR SON,--

I am in mortal anxiety about the Quartet--namely, the third, fourth, fifth, and sixth parts, that Holz took away, while the first bars of the third movement have been left here; the number of these sheets is 13. *I hear nothing of Holz.* I wrote to him yesterday, and he is not usually remiss in writing. What a sad business it will be if he has lost it! He drinks hard, *entre nous*. Tranquillize me on this point as quickly as possible. You can find out Linke's lodgings from Haslinger; he was here to-day and very friendly, and brought some of the sheets and other things, and begged hard for the new quartets. Never interfere in this kind of business; it can only lead to what is unpleasant. For Heaven's sake pacify me about the Quartet--a serious loss. The sketch is only written on small fragments of paper, and I could not manage to write out the whole exactly from these.

Your attached
FATHER.

I must remind you that next Sunday and Monday are holidays, so that you may arrange accordingly. On this occasion you could perhaps, when I come in, return with me here on Saturday evening, which would give you the whole of Sunday morning to yourself.

441.
TO ZMESKALL.

1825.

MY GOOD FRIEND,--

I had scarcely got home when I bethought me of the stuff I may have written yesterday. Give the enclosed to Kuhlau; you know all the rest. Write to me as soon as possible, or come here, next Thursday being a holiday, but write beforehand. Ask if the cook understands anything about game, that she may take the command of my game preserves for me. As to Carl, it would be better for him to tell me about it at the *Atrapper* at *Rosen*. All this *prestissimo*! As for my friendship, think of me always as *Cantum firmum*. Farewell!

Ever your friend,
BEETHOVEN.

442.
TO HERR FRIEDRICH KUHLAU.

Baden, September 3, 1825.

I must admit that the champagne went a little to my head yesterday, and I learned once more from experience, that such things rather prostrate than promote my energies; for, though able to respond fluently at the moment, still I can no longer recall what I wrote yesterday.

Sometimes bear in mind your attached

BEETHOVEN.

443.
TO HIS NEPHEW.

September 6, 1825.

MY DEAR SON,--

I see perfectly well how troublesome it would be for you all to come here; we must therefore make an appointment to meet every Friday at Schlesinger's, when I will come to town; for, in case any thing goes amiss, I must be present. This is the best plan, and settles the affair. He was here yesterday, and said that he would pay for the Quintet as soon as you sent it to him.

It will be enough if they play the new one only, but you can judge what is best. If they prefer Thursday, I can be present then. Only see that they come to an arrangement as quickly as possible, so that the money may be transmitted to Peters in Leipzig, to whom, however, you must on no account allude. Schlesinger scarcely expects to be still in Vienna on Sunday; haste is therefore necessary. The ducats must be in gold; mention, as a precedent, that others do this.

Be sure to write to me by the old woman to-day. All I want is a rehearsal, to see whether corrections are required. Make no delays, and take care that the old woman sets off in good time. The best plan would be to fix where I am to come to in town every Friday for rehearsals. If Schlesinger has brought you the Quartet (the first), pray stand on no ceremony, for it is clear he means to pay.

Your letter has this moment come. So Holz is not to be here till Thursday, and who can tell whether even this is certain? Your letter changes everything, as Friday is now decided on. Holz can inform me whether we meet here or in Vienna. Our main point now is with Schlesinger, for we must delay no longer. If he is only waiting for the rehearsal, he certainly shall not have it. He said yesterday that he would not publish the quartets here; I told him it was a matter of entire indifference to me. May God bless you and keep you!

Your attached
FATHER.

444.
TO HIS NEPHEW.

September.

MY DEAR SON,--

Do not forget to give Tobias [Haslinger] the receipt together with the money. The gentleman ought to have come a little sooner; but as the affair stands, you must do as he advises. I do not wish now that you should come to me on the 19th of September. It is better to finish your studies. God has never yet forsaken me, and no doubt some one will be found to close my eyes. The whole thing seems to me to have been some artful collusion, in which my brother (*pseudo*) has played a part. I also know that you have no pleasure now in coming to me--which is only natural, for my atmosphere is too pure for you. Last Sunday you again borrowed 1 florin 15 kreutzers from the housekeeper, from a mean old kitchen wench,--this was already forbidden,--and it is the same in all things. I could have gone on wearing the out-of-doors coat for two years--to be sure I have the shabby custom of putting on an old coat at home--but Herr Carl! What a disgrace it would be! and why should he do so? Herr Ludwig van Beethoven's money-bags are expressly for this purpose.

You had better not come next Sunday, for true harmony and concord can never exist with conduct such as yours. Why such hypocrisy? Avoid it, and you will then become a better man, and not require to be deceitful nor untruthful, which will eventually benefit your moral character. Such is the impression you have made on my mind--for what avail even the most gentle reproofs? They merely serve to embitter you. But do not be uneasy; I shall continue to *care for you* as much as ever. *What feelings* were aroused in me when I again found a florin and 15 kreutzers charged in the bill!

Do not send any more such flimsy notes, for the housekeeper can see through them in the light. I have just received this letter from Leipzig, but I don't mean to send the Quartet yet; we can talk of this on Sunday. Three years ago I only asked 40 ducats for a quartet; we must therefore refer to the exact words you have written.

Farewell! He who, though he did not give you life, has certainly provided for it, and above all striven to perfect your mental culture, and been more than a father to you, earnestly implores you to pursue steadily the only true path to all that is good and right. Farewell!

Bring back the letter with you on Sunday.

Your attached and kind
FATHER.

445.
TO HERR VON SCHLESINGER.

Vienna, September 26, 1825.

Si non per Por-tus, per mu-ros, per mu-ros, per mu-ros.

My worthy friend, I wish you the loveliest bride! And I take this opportunity of asking you to present my compliments to Herr Marx, in Berlin, and beg him not to be too hard on me, and sometimes to allow me to slip out at the backdoor.

Yours,
BEETHOVEN.

446.
TO HIS NEPHEW.

Baden, October 4.

MY DEAR SON,--

Like the sage Odysseus, I know the best course to take; if you come on Saturday, you need not fear the cold, for a portion of the old window-shutters is still here, with which we can protect ourselves. I hope also to get rid of my cold and catarrh here; at the same time this place is a great risk in my rheumatic condition, for wind, or rather hurricanes, still prevail here. As to Biedermann, you must inquire whether Schlesinger gave him a commission; for if this be not the case, we ought to write at once to Peters. You could scarcely write to me to-day, but I hope to hear from you to-morrow, and to see you positively on Saturday. I wish you never may have cause to feel ashamed of your want of love for me; if I alone suffer, what matters it? I wish and hope that all the pretexts you made here to go into Vienna may prove true.

Rest assured that you may at all times expect every possible kindness from me, but can I hope for the same from you? When you see me irritable, ascribe it solely to my great anxiety on your account, for you are exposed to many dangers. I hope at all events to get a letter from you to-morrow; do not cause me uneasiness, but think of my sufferings. I ought not, properly, to have any such apprehensions, but what sorrow have I not already experienced?!

As ever, your attached
FATHER.

Remember that I am all alone here, and subject to sudden illness. [On the outside:] *N'oubliez pas de demander des quittances, et donnez-moi aussi vite que possible des nouvelles.*

447.
TO HIS NEPHEW.

MY DEAR SON,--

Say no more! only come to my arms; not one harsh word shall you hear! For God's sake do not bring misery on your own head. You shall be received as lovingly as ever. We can discuss in a friendly manner what is to be done and settled as to the future. I pledge my word of honor you shall meet with no reproaches from me, which, indeed, could no longer avail. You need expect only the most affectionate care and assistance from me. Only come! Come to the faithful heart of--

Your father,
BEETHOVEN.
Volti sub.

Set off the moment you receive this letter. *Si vous ne viendrez pas, vous me tuerez sûrement. Lisez la lettre et restez à la maison chez vous. Venez embrasser votre père, vous vraiment adonné. Soyez assuré que tout cela restera entre nous.* For God's sake come home to-day, for we cannot tell what risks you run,--hasten,--hasten to me!

448.
TO HIS NEPHEW.

October 5.

DEAR AND MUCH-BELOVED SON,--

I have just received your letter. I was a prey to anguish, and resolved to hurry into Vienna myself this very day. God be praised! this is not necessary; follow my advice, and love and peace of mind, as well as worldly happiness, will attend us, and you can then combine an inward and spiritual existence with your outer life. But it is well that the *former* should be esteemed superior to the *latter*. *Il fait trop froid.* So I am to see you on Saturday? Write to say whether you come early or in the evening, that I may hasten to meet you. I embrace and kiss you a thousand times over, *not my lost, but my new-born son.*

I wrote to Schlemmer; do not take it amiss, but my heart is still too full [a piece is here torn away]. Live! and my care of the son *I have found again* will show only love on the part of your father. [On the cover:] *Ayez la bonté de m'envoyer* a lucifer-match bottle and matches from Rospini, *ou en portez avec vous, puisque de celle de Kärnthnerthor on ne veut pas faire usage.*

449.
TO HIS NEPHEW.

Immediate. Baden, October 14.

I write in the greatest haste to say, that even if it rains, I shall certainly come in to-morrow forenoon; be sure, therefore, that I find you at home.

I rejoice at the thoughts of seeing you again, and if you detect any heavy clouds lowering, do not attribute them to deliberate anger, for they will be wholly chased away by your promise to strive more earnestly after the true and pure happiness, based on active exertion. Something hovered before me in my last letter, which though perhaps *not quite justly* yet called forth a dark mood; this, after all that has passed, was indeed very possible; still who would not rejoice when the transgressor returns to the right path?--and this I hope I shall live to see. I was especially pained by your coming so late on Sunday, and hurrying away again so early. I mean to come in to-morrow with the joiner and to send off these old hags; they are too bad for anything. Until the other housekeeper arrives, I can make use of the joiner. More of this when we meet, and I know you will think I am right. Expect me then to-morrow without fail, whether it rains or not.

Your loving
FATHER,
Who fondly embraces you.

450.
TO THE ABBÉ MAXIMILIAN STADLER.

February 6, 1826.

REVEREND AND HONORED SIR,--

You have really done well in rendering justice to the *manes* of Mozart by your inimitable pamphlet, which so searchingly enters into the matter [the Requiem], and you have earned the gratitude of the lay and the profane, as well as of all who are musical, or have any pretensions to be so. To bring a thing of this kind forward as H.W.[1] has done, a man must either be a great personage, or a nonentity. Be it remembered also that it is said this same person has written a book on composition, and yet has ascribed to Mozart such passages as the following:--

and has added such things as,--

as samples of his own composition! H.W.'s astonishing knowledge of harmony and melody recall the old composers of the Empire,--Sterkel, [illegible,] Kalkbrenner (the father), André, &c.

Requiescant in pace! I especially thank you, my dear friend, for the pleasure you have conferred on me by your pamphlet. I have always accounted myself one of Mozart's greatest admirers, and shall continue to be so to my last breath. I beg, venerable sir, for your blessing, and I am, with sincere esteem and veneration, yours,

BEETHOVEN.

[Footnote 1: Gottfried Weber, the well-known theorist, who was one of those engaged in the dispute as to the genuineness of Mozart's Requiem.]

451.
TO GOTTFRIED WEBER.

April 3, 1826.

Holz tells me that it is your intention to publish a larger size of the engraving representing Handel's monument, in St. Peter's Church in London. This affords me extreme pleasure, independent of the fact that I was the person who suggested this. Accept my thanks beforehand.

I am your obedient
BEETHOVEN.

452.
TO HERR PROBST, MUSIC PUBLISHER,--LEIPZIG.

Vienna, June 3, 1826.

SIR,--

I always consider myself in some degree bound to make you the offer of my compositions when it is possible to do so. I am at this moment more at liberty than usual. I was obliged to give my minor works to those who took the greater ones also, as without the former they refused to accept the latter. So far as I remember, however, you wished to have nothing to do with the greater works. In this view, I offer you an entirely new Quartet for two violins, viola and violoncello; you must not, however, be surprised at my demanding the sum of 80 gold ducats for it. I assure you, upon my honor, that the same sum has been remitted to me for several quartets. I must request you, in any event, to write to me on this point as soon as possible. Should you accept my offer, I beg you will send the money to some bank here, where I can receive it on delivery of the work. If the reverse be the case, I shall equally expect an immediate reply, as other publishers have already made me offers. I have also the following trifles ready, with which I can supply you. A Serenade-congratulatory-Minuet, and an *Entr'acte*, both for a full orchestra,--the two for 20 gold ducats. In the hope of a speedy answer,

I am, sir, your obedient
BEETHOVEN.

453.
TO STEPHAN V. BREUNING.[1]

MY DEAR AND MUCH-LOVED STEPHAN,--

May our temporary estrangement be forever effaced by the portrait I now send. I know that I have rent your heart. The emotion which you cannot fail now to see in mine has sufficiently punished me for it. There was no malice towards you in my heart, for then I should be no longer worthy of your friendship. It was *passion* both on *your* part and on *mine*; but mistrust was rife within me, for people had come between us, unworthy both of *you* and of *me*.

My portrait[2] was long ago intended for you; you knew that it was destined for some one--and to whom could I give it with such warmth of heart as to you, my faithful, good, and noble Stephan?

Forgive me for having grieved you; but I did not myself suffer less when I no longer saw you near me. I then first keenly felt how dear you were, and ever will be to my heart. Surely you will once more fly to my arms as you formerly did.

[Footnote 1: Schindler places this letter in the summer of 1826, when his nephew attempted self-destruction in Baden, which reduced Beethoven to the most miserable state of mind, and brought afresh to his recollection those dear friends of his youth, whom he seemed almost to have forgotten in the society of Holz and his colleagues. Schindler states that the more immediate cause of this estrangement was Breuning having tried to dissuade him from adopting his nephew. Dr. v. Breuning in Vienna is of opinion that the reunion of the two old friends had already occurred in 1825, or even perhaps at an earlier period. I am not at present capable of finally deciding on this discrepancy, but I believe the latter assertion to be correct.]

[Footnote 2: Schindler says, "It was Stieler's lithograph, which the *maestro* had previously sent to Dr. Wegeler." See No. 459.]

454.
TO STEPHAN VON BREUNING.

MY BELOVED FRIEND,--

You are harassed by work, and so am I--besides, I am still far from well. I would have invited you to dinner ere this, but I have been obliged to entertain people whose most highly prized author is *the cook*, and not finding his interesting productions at home, they hunt after them in the kitchens and cellars of others [Holz for instance]. Such society would not be very eligible for you, but all this will soon be altered. In the mean time do not buy Czerny's "School for the Pianoforte;"[1] for in a day or two I expect to get some information about another. Along with the "Journal des Modes" that I promised to your wife, I also send something for your children. I can always regularly transmit you the journal--you have only to express your wish on any point, for me to comply with it at once.

I am, with love and esteem, your friend,
BEETHOVEN.

I hope we shall soon meet.

[Footnote 1: Czerny, *The Vienna Pianoforte Teacher; or, theoretical and practical mode of learning how to play the piano skilfully and beautifully in a short time by a new and easy method*. Vienna: Haslinger. See No. 455.]

455.
TO STEPHAN V. BREUNING

MY DEAR GOOD FRIEND,--

I can at length realize my boast, and send you Clement's long-promised "Pianoforte School" for Gerhard [Breuning's eldest son]. If he makes the use of it that I advise, the results cannot fail to be good. I shall see you very shortly now, and cordially embrace you.

Your
BEETHOVEN.

456. [1]
TO CARL HOLZ.

TESTIMONIAL FOR C. HOLZ.

Vienna, August 30, 1826.

I am happy to give my friend Carl Holz the testimonial he wishes, namely, that I consider him well fitted to write my Biography hereafter, if indeed I may presume to think that this will be desired. I place the most implicit confidence in his faithfully transmitting to posterity what I have imparted to him for this purpose.

LUDWIG VAN BEETHOVEN.

[Footnote 1: Carl Holz ceded his rights to Dr. Gassner, who however died in 1851 without having completed any biography of Beethoven. In the *maestro's* bequest, which Gassner's widow was so kind as to show me, there was nothing new (at least to me) except two letters included in this collection and a couple of anecdotes. Schindler also states that Beethoven subsequently repented of the authority he had given Holz and declared he did so too hastily.]

457.
TO CARL HOLZ.

Both the gentlemen were here, but they have been admonished on every side to observe the most strict secrecy with regard to the Order. Haslinger declares that in this respect you are a son of the deceased Papageno. *Prenez garde!*

I told Carl to-day it was definitively settled that he could not quit the hospital except with you or me. I dine at home to-morrow, so I shall be very glad if you can come. As you have no official work to-morrow you might arrive later, but it is very necessary that you should come. *Portez-vous bien, Monsieur terrible amoureux.*[1]

Your *indeclinable* friend,
BEETHOVEN.

[Footnote 1: This letter contains all kinds of dashes and flourishes, which prove that the *maestro* was in his happiest mood when he wrote it. His nephew was at that time in the hospital, probably owing to his attempt at suicide.]

458.
TO THE KING OF PRUSSIA.

YOUR MAJESTY,--

One of the greatest pieces of good fortune of my life is your Majesty having graciously permitted me respectfully to dedicate my present work [the 9th Symphony] to you.

Your Majesty is not only the father of your subjects, but also a patron of art and science; and how much more precious is your gracious permission to me, from being myself so fortunate as to be numbered among your subjects, being a citizen of Bonn.

I beg your Majesty will vouchsafe to accept this work as a slender token of the profound admiration with which I regard your virtues.

I am, your Majesty's obedient humble servant,

LUDWIG VAN BEETHOVEN.

459.
TO WEGELER.

Vienna, October 7, 1826.

MY OLD AND BELOVED FRIEND,--

I really cannot express the pleasure your letter and that of your Lorchen caused me. An answer speedy as an arrow's flight ought indeed to have responded, but I am always rather indolent about writing, because I think that the better class of men know me sufficiently without this. I often compose the answer in my head, but when I wish to write it down I generally throw aside the pen, from not being able to write as I feel. I recall all the kindness you have ever shown me; for example, your causing my room to be whitewashed, which was an agreeable surprise to me. It was just the same with all the Breuning family. Our separation was in the usual course of things; each striving to pursue and to attain his object; while at the same time the everlasting and immutable principles of good still held us closely united. I cannot unfortunately write so much to you to-day as I could wish, being confined to bed,[1] so I limit my reply to some points in your letter.

You write that in some book I am declared to be the natural son of the late King of Prussia; this was mentioned to me long ago, but I have made it a rule never either to write anything about myself, or to answer anything written by others about me. I therefore gladly devolve on you the duty of making known to the world the respectability of my parents, and especially that of my mother.

You write to me about your son. There is no possible doubt that when he comes here he will find a friend and a father in me, and whenever it may be in my power to serve or to assist him, I will gladly do so.

I still have the *silhouette* of your Lorchen, by which you will see how dear to me to this hour are all those who were kind and loving to me in the days of my youth. As to my diploma, I may briefly state that I am an Honorary Member of the Royal Academy of Science in Sweden [see No. 338] and in Amsterdam, and that I have been presented with the Honorary Citizenship of Vienna. A Dr. Spiecker lately took with him to Berlin my last Grand Symphony with Choruses; it is dedicated to the King, and I wrote the dedication with my own hand. I had previously applied at the Embassy for permission to dedicate the work to the King, which has now been accorded.[2] By desire of Dr. Spiecker I gave him the manuscript I had myself corrected, and with my own amendments, to present to the King, as it is to be deposited in the Royal Library. I received a hint at the time about the second class of the Order of the Red Eagle; I do not know what the result may be, for I have never sought such distinctions, though in these days for many reasons they would not be unwelcome to me. Besides, my maxim has always been,--*Nulla dies sine linea*; and if I allow my Muse to slumber, it is only that she may awake with fresh vigor. I hope yet to usher some great works into the world, and then to close my earthly career like an old child somewhere among good people.[3] You will soon receive some music through the Brothers Schott, in Mayence. The portrait which I now send you is indeed an artistic masterpiece, but not the last that has been taken of me. I must tell you further, what I know you will rejoice to hear, with regard to marks of distinction. The late King of France sent me a medal with the inscription, *Donné par le Roi à M. Beethoven*, accompanied by a very polite letter from *le premier gentilhomme du Roi, le Duc de Châtres*.

My beloved friend, excuse my writing more to-day, for the remembrance of the past has deeply affected me, and not without many tears have I written this letter. The oftener you write the more pleasure will you confer on me. There can be no question on either side as to our friendship, so farewell. I beg you will embrace your dear children and your Lorchen in my name, and think of me when you do so. May God be with you all.

As ever, your attached friend, with sincere esteem,

BEETHOVEN.

[Footnote 1: On which account this letter is dictated, and only signed by Beethoven, who was at that time at his brother's house in the country--Gneixendorf, near Krems, on the Danube.]

[Footnote 2: In consequence of his application to the King of Prussia to subscribe to his Mass, of which he had sent the MS., Beethoven received the following intimation:--

To the Composer Ludwig van Beethoven.

Berlin, Nov. 25, 1826.

"It gave me great pleasure to receive your new work, knowing the acknowledged value of your compositions. I thank you for having sent it to me, and present you with a ring of brilliants, as a token of my sincere appreciation.

"FRIEDRICH WILHELM."

Schindler adds that the stones in the ring were false, and casts a suspicion of fraud on the Chancery Director of that day, W----.]

[Footnote 3: It was during those weeks that he wrote the second *Finale* to the B. flat major Quartet, Op. 130, little anticipating that this was to be his "Swan song."]

460.
TO TOBIAS HASLINGER.[1]

No time is left to-day for further words and vocalization. I beg you will at once deliver the enclosed letter. Pray forgive my causing you this trouble; but, as you are the owner of an artistic post-office, it is scarcely possible not to take advantage of this.

You will perceive that I am now at Gneixendorf. The name sounds like the breaking of an axletree. The air is healthy. The *memento mori* must be applied to all else. Most marvellous and best of all Tobiases, we salute you in the name of the arts and poets!

I remain yours,
BEETHOVEN.

[Footnote 1: The music alone and the words "I remain" at the close, are in Beethoven's writing. The rest is probably written by his nephew, with whom he had been obliged to take refuge in the house of his odious brother near Krems, because the police had intimated to the young delinquent that he must leave Vienna. See No. 435 on the subject of Beethoven's repugnance to live in his brother's family circle, whose ignoble wife treated the gray-haired and suffering *maestro* as badly as possible.]

461.
TO TOBIAS HASLINGER.

GNEIXENDORF, October 13, 1826.

BEST OF ALL TOBIASES,--
[Here follow eight bars of music.]

We are writing to you from the castle of our *Signor Fratello*. I must again intrude on you by the polite request to post the two enclosed letters without delay.

I will repay you for the time I kept the "School for the Pianoforte" and all the other expenses as soon as I return to Vienna. I am staying here longer, owing to the weather being so fine, and also not having gone to the country at all during the summer. A quartet[1] for Schlesinger is already finished; only I don't know which is the safest way to send it to you, that you may give it to Tendler and Manstein and receive the money in return. Schlesinger will probably not make the remittance in *gold*, but if you can contrive that I should get it, you would very much oblige me, as all my publishers pay me in gold. Besides, my worthy *Tobiasserl*, we stand in need of money, and it is by no means the same thing whether we have money or not. If you get a sight of Holz make sure of him, and nail him at once. The passion of love has so violently assailed him that he has almost taken fire, and some one jestingly wrote that Holz was a son of the deceased Papageno.

Most astounding, most admirable, and most *unique* of all Tobiases, farewell! If not inconvenient, pray write me a few lines here. Is Dr. Spiecker still in Vienna? I am, with highest consideration and fidelity,

Yours,
BEETHOVEN.

[Footnote 1: Probably the one in F, Op. 135.]

462.
TO CARL HOLZ.

Dec. 1826.

YOUR OFFICIAL MAJESTY,--

I wrote to you on my arrival here a few days ago, but the letter was mislaid; I then became so unwell that I thought it best to stay in bed. I shall therefore be very glad if you will pay me a visit. You will find it less inconvenient, because every one has left Döbling to go to town. I only add, in conclusion,[1]

As ever, your friend,
BEETHOVEN.

[Footnote 1: Here Beethoven's own writing begins. The slight indisposition that he mentions, in the course of a few days became a serious illness, the result of which was dropsy, and from this the *maestro* was doomed never to recover. Indeed from that time he never again left his bed.]

463.
TO DR. BACH.[1]

Vienna, Wednesday, Jan. 3, 1827.

MY RESPECTED FRIEND,--

I hereby declare, at my decease, my beloved nephew, Carl van Beethoven, sole heir of all my property, and of seven bank shares in particular, as well as any ready money I may be possessed of. If the law prescribes any modifications in this matter, pray endeavor to regulate these as much as possible to his advantage.

I appoint you his curator, and beg that, together with Hofrath Breuning, his guardian, you will supply the place of a father to him.

God bless you! A thousand thanks for all the love and friendship you have shown towards me.

LUDWIG VAN BEETHOVEN.

[Footnote 1: The signature alone is in Beethoven's writing.]

464.
TO WEGELER.

Vienna, February 17, 1827.

MY OLD AND WORTHY FRIEND,--

I received your second letter safely through Breuning. I am still too feeble to answer it, but you may be assured that its contents were most welcome and agreeable to me.[1] My convalescence, if indeed I may call it such, makes very slow progress, and there is reason to suspect that a fourth operation will be necessary, although the medical men have not as yet decided on this. I arm myself with patience, and reflect that all evil leads to some good. I am quite surprised to find from your last letter that you had not received mine. From this one you will see that I wrote to you on the 10th of December last. It is the same with the portrait, as you will perceive from the date, when you get it. "Frau Steffen spake the word:" Michael Steffen insisted on sending them by some private hand; so they have been lying here until this very day, and really it was a hard matter to get them back even now. You will receive the portrait by the post, through the Messrs. Schott, who have also sent you the music.

How much is there that I would fain say to you to-day; but I am too weak,[2] so I can only embrace you and your Lorchen in spirit. With true friendship and attachment to you and yours,

Your old and faithful friend,
BEETHOVEN.

[Footnote 1: Wegeler had reminded him of Blumenauer, who, after being operated on for dropsy, lived for many years in perfect health. He at the same time suggested to him the plan of going with him in the ensuing summer to one of the Bohemian baths, proposing to travel by a circuitous route to the Upper Rhine, and from thence to Coblenz.]

[Footnote 2: Beethoven's last letter to Wegeler. The signature alone is his.]

465.
TO SIR GEORGE SMART,--LONDON.

Feb. 22, 1827.

I remember that some years ago the Philharmonic Society proposed to give a concert for my benefit. This prompts me to request you, dear sir, to say to the Philharmonic Society that if they be now disposed to renew their offer it would be most welcome to me. Unhappily, since the beginning of December I have been confined to bed by dropsy,--a most wearing malady, the result of which cannot yet be ascertained. As you are already well aware, I live entirely by the produce of my brains, and for a long time to come all idea of writing is out of the question. My salary is in itself so small, that I can scarcely contrive to defray my half-year's rent out of it. I therefore entreat you kindly to use all your influence for the furtherance of this project,--your generous sentiments towards me convincing me that you will not be offended by my application. I intend also to write to Herr Moscheles on this subject, being persuaded that he will gladly unite with you in promoting my object. I am so weak that I can no longer write, so I only dictate this. I hope, dear sir, that you will soon cheer me by an answer, to say whether I may look forward to the fulfilment of my request.

In the mean time, pray receive the assurance of the high esteem with which I always remain, &c., &c.

466.
TO HERR MOSCHELES.

Vienna, Feb. 22, 1827.

DEAR MOSCHELES,--

I feel sure that you will not take amiss my troubling you as well as Sir G. Smart (to whom I enclose a letter) with a request. The matter is briefly this. Some years since, the London Philharmonic Society made me the handsome offer to give a concert in my behalf. At that time I was not, God be praised! so situated as to render it necessary for me to take advantage of this generous proposal. Things are, however, very different with me now, as for fully three months past I have been entirely prostrated by that tedious malady, dropsy. Schindler encloses a letter with further details. You have long known my circumstances, and are aware how, and by what, I live: a length of time must elapse before I can attempt to write again, so that, unhappily, I might be reduced to actual want. You have not only an extensive acquaintance in London, but also the greatest influence with the Philharmonic; may I beg you, therefore, to exercise it, so far as you can, in prevailing on the Society to resume their former intention, and to carry it soon into effect.

The letter I enclose to Sir Smart is to the same effect, as well as one I already sent to Herr Stumpff.[1] I beg you will yourself give the enclosed letter to Sir Smart, and unite with him and all my friends in London in furthering my object. Your sincere friend,

BEETHOVEN.

[Footnote 1: Stumpff, a Thuringian maker of harps, came to Vienna in 1824, recommended to our *maestro* by Andreas Streicher in a letter of Sept. 24, in these words:--"The bearer of this is Herr Stumpff, an excellent German, who has lived for thirty-four years in London. The sole reason of his going to Baden is to see you, my revered Beethoven, the man of whom Germany is so proud. Pray receive him in a kind and friendly manner, as beseems the saint to whose shrine the pious pilgrim has made so long a journey." In 1826 he presented Beethoven with the English edition of Handel's works in 40 folio volumes, which the *maestro* constantly studied during his last illness. Gerhard v. Breuning, when a youth of fourteen, either held up the separate volumes for him, or propped them against the wall.]

467.
TO SCHINDLER.

The end of February, 1827.

When we meet we can discuss the mischance that has befallen you. I can send you some person without the smallest inconvenience. Do accept my offer; it is, at least, something. Have you had no letters from Moscheles or Cramer? There will be a fresh occasion for writing on Wednesday, and once more urging my project. If you are still indisposed at that time, one of my people can take the letter, and get a receipt from the post-office.

Vale et fave. I need not assure you of my sympathy with your misfortune. Pray allow me to supply board for you in the mean time. I offer this from my heart. May Heaven preserve you! Your sincere friend,

BEETHOVEN.

468.
TO BARON VON PASQUALATI.[1]

March 6, 1827.

MY MUCH-ESTEEMED OLD FRIEND,--

My warmest thanks for the kind present you have sent me for the benefit of my health; as soon as I have found what wine is most suitable for me I will let you know, but not abuse your kindness. I like the *compote* much, and shall again apply to you for some. Even this costs me an effort. *Sapienti pauca.*

Your grateful friend,
BEETHOVEN.

[Footnote 1: Traced in feeble and trembling characters. Some other hand has written on it, "March 6, 1827."]

469.
TO BARON VON PASQUALATI.

MY ESTEEMED FRIEND,--

I beg you will send me some more of the cherry *compote*, but without lemons, and quite simple. I should also like a light pudding, almost liquid, my worthy cook not being very experienced in invalid diet. I am allowed to drink *champagne*, and I wish you would send me for to-day a champagne glass with it. Now, as to wine, Malfatti wished me to drink moselle, but declared that no genuine moselle could be got here; so he gave me several bottles of *Krumbholzkirchner*,[1] deeming this best for my health, as no really good moselle is to be had. Pray forgive my troubling you, and ascribe it chiefly to my helpless condition.

I am, with much esteem, your friend,
BEETHOVEN.

[Footnote 1: Gumpoldskirchner--a celebrated and generous Austrian wine.]

470.
TO SIR GEORGE SMART,--LONDON.

March 6, 1827.

DEAR SIR,--

I make no doubt that you have already received through Herr Moscheles my letter of February 22, but as I found your address by chance among my papers, I do not hesitate to write direct to yourself, to urge my request once more on you in the strongest terms.

I do not, alas! even up to the present hour, see any prospect of the termination of my terrible malady; on the contrary, my sufferings, and consequently my cares, have only increased. I underwent a fourth operation on the 27th of February, and possibly fate may compel me to submit to this a fifth time, and perhaps oftener. If this goes on, my illness will certainly continue one half the summer, and in that case, what is to become of me? How am I to subsist until I can succeed in arousing my decayed powers, and once more earn my living by my pen? But I do not wish to plague you by fresh complaints; so I only refer you to my letter of the 22d February, and entreat you to use all your influence with the Philharmonic Society to carry now into execution their former proposal of a concert for my benefit.

471.
TO BARON VON PASQUALATI.

MY WORTHY FRIEND,--

I am still confined to my room; be so good, therefore, as to tell me, or rather, I should say, write to me, the name of the person who values this house, and where he is to be found. If you have any Muterhall [?] medicine I beg you will think of your poor Austrian musician and citizen of the guild.

BEETHOVEN.

472.[1]
TO BARON VON PASQUALATI.

March 14, 1827.

MY ESTEEMED FRIEND,--

Many thanks for the dish you sent me yesterday, which will suffice for to-day also. I am allowed to have game; and the doctor said that fieldfares were very wholesome for me. I only tell you this for information, as I do not want them to-day. Forgive this stupid note, but I am exhausted from a sleepless night. I embrace you, and am, with much esteem, your attached friend.

[Footnote 1: In a tremulous hand,--"March 14, 1827."]

473.
TO HERR MOSCHELES.

Vienna, March 14, 1827.

MY DEAR MOSCHELES,--

I recently heard, through Herr Lewisey,[1] that in a letter to him of the 10th February, you had made inquiries as to the state of my health, about which such various rumors have been circulated. Although I cannot possibly doubt that you have by this time received my letter of February 22d, which explains all you wish to know, still I cannot resist thanking you for your sympathy with my sad condition, and again imploring you to attend to the request contained in my first letter. I feel already certain that, in conjunction with Sir Smart and other friends, you are sure to succeed in obtaining a favorable result for me from the Philharmonic Society. I wrote again to Sir Smart also on the subject.

I was operated on for the fourth time on the 27th of February, and now symptoms evidently exist which show that I must expect a fifth operation. What is to be done? What is to become of me if this lasts much longer? Mine has indeed been a hard doom; but I resign myself to the decrees of fate, and only constantly pray to God that His holy will may ordain that while thus condemned to suffer death in life, I may be shielded from want. The Almighty will give me strength to endure my lot, however severe and terrible, with resignation to His will.

So once more, dear Moscheles, I commend my cause to you, and shall anxiously await your answer, with highest esteem. Hummel is here, and has several times come to see me.

Your friend,
BEETHOVEN.

[Footnote 1: Schindler mentions, on Beethoven's authority, that this gentleman translated Beethoven's letters to Smart into English, which his nephew had previously done.]

474.[1]
TO SCHINDLER.--

March 17, 1827.

WONDERFUL! WONDERFUL! WONDERFUL!--

Both the learned gentlemen are defeated, and I shall be saved solely by Malfatti's skill! You must come to me for a few minutes without fail this forenoon.

Yours,
BEETHOVEN.

[Footnote 1: Schindler dates this note March 17, 1827, and says that these are the last lines Beethoven ever wrote. They certainly were the last that he wrote to Schindler. On the back of the note, in another writing (probably Schindler's), the receipt is given in pencil for the bath with hay steeped in it, ordered by Malfatti, which the poor invalid thought had saved his life. The "learned gentlemen" are Dr. Wawruch and the surgeon Seibert, who had made the punctures.]

475.
TO MOSCHELES.

Vienna, March 18, 1827.

No words can express my feelings on reading your letter of the 1st of March. The noble liberality of the Philharmonic Society, which almost anticipated my request, has touched me to my inmost soul.[1] I beg you, therefore, dear Moscheles, to be my organ in conveying to the Society my heartfelt thanks for their generous sympathy and aid.

[Say[2] to these worthy men, that if God restores me to health, I shall endeavor to prove the reality of my gratitude by my actions. I therefore leave it to the Society to choose what I am to write for them--a symphony (the 10th) lies fully sketched in my desk, and likewise a new overture and some other things. With regard to the concert the Philharmonic had resolved to give in my behalf, I would entreat them not to abandon their intention. In short, I will strive to fulfil every wish of the Society, and never shall I have begun any work with so much zeal as on this occasion. May Heaven only soon grant me the restoration of my health, and then I will show the noble-hearted English how highly I value their sympathy with my sad fate.] I was compelled at once to draw for the whole sum of 1000 gulden, being on the eve of borrowing money.

Your generous conduct can never be forgotten by me, and I hope shortly to convey my thanks to Sir Smart in particular, and to Herr Stumpff. I beg you will deliver the metronomed 9th Symphony to the Society. I enclose the proper markings.

Your friend, with high esteem,
BEETHOVEN.

[Footnote 1: A hundred pounds had been sent at once.]
[Footnote 2: In the original the words placed within brackets are dictated by Beethoven himself, and were indeed the last he ever dictated--but they are crossed out.]

476.
CODICIL.[1]

Vienna, March 23, 1827.

I appoint my nephew Carl my sole heir. The capital of my bequest, however, to devolve on his natural or testamentary heirs.

LUDWIG VAN BEETHOVEN.[2]

[Footnote 1: See No. 463. Schindler relates:--"This testament contained no restrictions or precautionary measures with regard to his heir-at-law, who, after the legal forms connected with the inheritance were terminated, was entitled to take immediate possession of the whole. The guardian and curator, however, knowing the unexampled levity of the heir, had a valid pretext for raising objections to these testamentary depositions. They therefore suggested to the *maestro*, to alter his intentions in so far as to place his property in trust; his nephew to draw the revenue, and at his death the capital to pass to his direct heirs. Beethoven, however, considered such restraints as too severe on the nephew whom he still so dearly loved in his heart [since December of the previous year the young man had been a cadet in a royal regiment at Iglau, in Moravia], so he remonstrated against this advice; indeed he reproached Hofrath Breuning as the person who had suggested such harsh measures. A note, still extant, written by Breuning to Beethoven, shows the state of matters, in which he still maintains, though in moderate language, the absolute necessity of the above precautions. This mode of argument seemed to make an impression on the *maestro*, who at last promised to yield his own wishes. By his desire, Breuning laid the codicil of three lines before him, and Beethoven at once proceeded to copy it, which was no easy matter for him. When it was finished he exclaimed, 'There! now I write no more!' He was not a little surprised to see on the paper the words 'heirs of his body' changed into 'natural heirs.' Breuning represented to him the disputes to which this destination might give rise. Beethoven replied that the one term was as good as the other, and that it should remain just as it was. *This was his last contradiction.*"]

[Footnote 2: Next day, at noon, he lost consciousness, and a frightful death-struggle began, which continued till the evening of March 26, 1827, when, during a violent spring storm of thunder and lightning, the sublime *maestro* paid his last tribute to that humanity for which he had made so many sacrifices in this world, to enter into life everlasting, which, from his life and actions, few could look forward to more hopefully.]

INDEX.

Academies, concerts given by Beethoven, so called. The grand concerts of the year 1824.

Address and appeal to London artists, from Beethoven.

Adlersburg, Dr. von, Court advocate and barrister at Vienna, "a most inconsiderate character," for some time Beethoven's lawyer.

Aesthetical observations on particular subjects.

Albrechtsberger, the popular theorist and composer, Kapellmeister at St. Stephen's in Vienna, for some time, about the year 1795, Beethoven's instructor in musical composition.

Amenda of Courland, afterwards rector in Talsen.

"A.M.Z." *See* Leipzig "Allgemeine Musikalische Zeitung."

André, composer and music publisher in Offenbach on the Maine.

Archduke Carl.

Arnim, Frau von. *See* Brentano, Bettina.

Artaria, print and music publisher in Vienna.

Attorney, power of.

Augarten, the well-known park near Vienna, in which morning concerts were frequently given.

Augsburg.

Austria, Beethoven's sentiments respecting that country, his second father-land.

Bach, Dr. Johann Baptist, Court advocate and barrister, from the year 1816 Beethoven's lawyer at Vienna.

Bach, Johann Sebastian.

Baden, near Vienna, a favorite watering-place, to which Beethoven often resorted.

Bauer, chief secretary to the Austrian Embassy in London.

Baumeister, private secretary to the Archduke Rudolph.

Beethoven's brother Carl, born at Bonn in 1774, instructed in music by Beethoven; afterwards came to Vienna, where he occupied the appointment of cashier in the Government Revenue (died Nov. 15, 1815).

His brother Johann, born in 1776, an apothecary, first in Linz, afterwards in Vienna, and at a later period proprietor of Gneixendorf, an estate near Krems, on the Danube; named by Beethoven, "Braineater," "Pseudo-brother," "Asinanios," &c.

His brother Ludwig Maria.

His father, Johann, son of Ludwig van Beethoven, Kapellmeister to the Elector of Cologne, Court tenor singer at the Electoral Chapel at Bonn, a man possessing no considerable mental endowments, but an excellent musician, and Beethoven's first instructor in music. Unhappily, he was so addicted to habits of intemperance, that he greatly impoverished his family, the care of which, owing to the father's recklessness, devolved entirely upon his son Ludwig (died Dec. 1792).

His grandfather, Ludwig van Beethoven, Kapellmeister to the Elector of Cologne (died 1774).

His mother, Maria Magdalena Kewerich, the wife, first of Leym of Ehrenbreitstein, cook to the Elector of Treves, and afterwards of Johann van Beethoven, in Bonn, Court tenor singer to the Elector of Cologne. She gave birth to her illustrious son Ludwig on Dec. 17, 1770, and died July 17, 1787.

His nephew, Carl, son of his brother Carl, Beethoven's ward from the year 1815. Entered the Blöchlinger Institute, at Vienna, June 22, 1819.
Letters to him from Beethoven.

His sister-in-law, Johanna, wife of his brother Carl and mother of his nephew, named by Beethoven "The Queen of the Night."

Beethoven's *Works. In General.*

I. *For pianoforte only.*
Sonatas of the year 1783.

Op. 22.
Op. 31.
Op. 90.
Op. 106.
Op. 109.
Op. 111.
Variations.
Bagatelles.
"Allegri di Bravoura."
    II. *For pianoforte with obbligato instruments.*
For pianoforte and violin:--Sonatas.
Sonatas with violoncello.
Twelve Variations in F on the Theme from "Figaro," "Se vuol ballare."
Rondo.
Variations with violoncello and violin.
for hautboys and horn.
Trios.
Concertos.
Fantasia with chorus.
    III. *Quartets.*
    IV. *Instrumental pieces.*
Septet.
Quintets.
Violin Romance.
    V. *Orchestral music.*
Symphonies.
The Ninth.
Minuet and Interlude.
Music for the ballet of "Prometheus."
"Egmont."
"King Stephen."
"The Ruins of Athens."
"Wellington's Victory at Vittoria."
March to "Tarpeia."
Gratulation Minuet.
Marches.
Overtures.
    VI. *Vocal music.*
"Adelaide."
"Ah! Perfido."
"Heart, my Heart," and "Knowest Thou the Land?"
"To Hope."
Aria for bass voice with chorus.
Terzet on Count Lichnowsky.
Canon for Spohr.
"The Glorious Moment."
On Mdlle. Milder-Hauptmann.
Scotch songs.
Canon for Schlesinger;
for the Archduke Rudolph;
on Tobias Haslinger.
Various songs;
two grand songs with chorus from Goethe and Matthisson.
Choruses.

"Empitremate."
Elegy.
"Meeresstille und glückliche Fahrt."
Opferlied.
Canons;
for Rellstab;
for Braunhofer;
for Kuhlau;
for Schlesinger.
Terzet.

    VII. *Operas*.

Grillparzer's "Melusina."
"Fidelio" in Dresden.

    VIII. *Church music and Oratorios*.

"Missa solennis."

    Benedict, Julius, in London, a composer, the pupil of C.M. von Weber.

    Berlin.

    Bernard, Carl, an author, editor of the "Wiener Zeitschrift."

    Bihler, J.N., a special admirer of Beethoven, one of the subscribers to, and the bearer of, the address presented to Beethoven in the year 1824, in which the master was requested again to present himself and his works to the Viennese public.

    Birchall, music publisher in London.

    "Birne, zur goldnen," an eating-house in the Landstrasse, Vienna.

    Blöchlinger, proprietor of an educational institution at Vienna.

    Bocklet, Carl Maria, of Prague, pianist in Vienna.

    Böhm, Joseph, a distinguished concerto violinist, professor at the Vienna Conservatory, and the teacher of Joachim.

    Bolderini.

    Bonn, residence of the Elector of Cologne, and Beethoven's birthplace, which he left in the year 1792, never again to visit.

    Braunhofer, Dr., for some time Beethoven's surgeon at Vienna.

    Breitkopf & Härtel, the well-known book and music publishers in Leipzig.

    Brentano, Bettina, became Frau von Arnim in 1811.

    Brentano, Clemens, the poet.

    Brentano, F.A., merchant at Frankfort, an admirer of Beethoven's music. *See also* Tonie.

    Breuning, Christoph von.

    Breuning, Dr. Gerhard von, Court physician at Vienna, son of Stephan von Breuning.

    Breuning, Eleonore von, daughter of Councillor von Breuning, in Bonn, the friend and pupil of Beethoven; in 1802 became the wife of Dr. Wegeler, afterwards consulting physician at Coblenz.

    Breuning, Frau von, widow of Councillor von Breuning, into whose house Beethoven was received as one of the family, and where he received his first musical impressions.

    Breuning, Lenz (Lorenz), youngest son of the "Frau Hofrath."

    Breuning, Stephan von, of Bonn; came to Vienna in the spring of 1800, where he became councillor, and died in 1827.

    Browne, Count, of Vienna, an admirer of Beethoven's music.

    Brühl, the, a village and favorite pleasure resort near Vienna.

    Brunswick, Count Franz von, of Pesth, one of Beethoven's greatest admirers and friends in Vienna.

    Bonaparte, Ludwig, King of Holland.

    "Cäcilia, a Journal for the Musical World," &c.

    Carl, Archduke. *See* Archduke Carl.

    Carlsbad.

    Cassel.

    Castlereagh, the well-known English minister.

Cherubini. Visited Vienna in 1805.

Clement, Franz, born 1784, died 1842, orchestral director at the "Theater an der Wien."

Clementi.

Collin, the famous Austrian poet.

Cornega, a singer in Vienna commended to Beethoven by Schindler.

Court Theatre, Beethoven's letter to the directors of the.

Cramer, John, the celebrated London pianist, also a music publisher.

Czerny, Carl, in Vienna, the well known writer of pianoforte studies.

Czerny, Joseph, in Vienna.

Deafness of Beethoven.

De la Motte-Fouqué, the poet of "Undine," which he had arranged as an Opera libretto for T.A. Hoffmann.

Del Rio, Giannatasio, proprietor of an academy at Vienna, under whose care Beethoven placed his nephew Carl from the year 1816 to 1818.

Diabelli, Anton, composer and music publisher in Vienna.

Döbling, Ober- and Unter-Döbling, near Vienna, Beethoven's occasional summer residence.

Dresden.

Drossdick, Baroness Thérèse, to whom Beethoven was greatly attached.

Duport, director of the Kärnthnerthor Theatre in the year 1823.

Eisenstadt, in Hungary, the residence of Prince Esterhazy, where Beethoven remained on a visit in the years 1794 and 1808.

English language, Beethoven's correspondence in the.

Erdödy Countess, in Vienna, one of Beethoven's best friends.

Ertmann, Baroness Dorothea (*née* Graumann), a friend of Beethoven, and one of the most accomplished pianists in Vienna; she especially excelled in the performance of Beethoven's compositions.

Esterhazy, Prince Paul, son of the protector of Haydn, and himself, at a later period, an ardent admirer of that master.

France.

Frank, Dr.

Frank, Frau, in Vienna.

"Frau Schnaps," Beethoven's housekeeper during the latter years of his life; called also "The Fast-sailing Frigate" and "The Old Goose."

French language, Beethoven's correspondence in the.

Fries, Count, in Vienna, an admirer of Beethoven's works.

Fux, the well-known old theorist and composer, in Vienna, author of the "Gradus ad Parnassum."

Gallizin, Prince Nikolaus Boris, at St. Petersburg, a zealous friend of art, from whom Beethoven received an order for his last quartet.

Gebauer, Franz Xaver, founder of the "Concerts Spirituels" at Vienna.

Gerardi, Mdlle.

Girowetz, Court musical director at the "Burgtheater."

Giuliani, a celebrated guitar player at Vienna.

Gläser, Beethoven's copyist from the year 1823.

Gleichenstein, Baron, of Rothweil, near Freiburg in Breisgau, a friend of Beethoven at Vienna. He left Vienna about the year 1815, and only revisited that city once afterwards, in 1824.

Gneixendorf, the estate of Beethoven's brother Johann, near Krems, on the Danube, which Beethoven visited, accompanied by his nephew, in the autumn of 1826.

Goethe.

Gratz, in Styria.

Grillparzer.

Guicciardi, Countess Giulietta, Beethoven's "immortal beloved."

Hammer-Purgstall, the distinguished Orientalist in Vienna.

Handel.

Haslinger, Tobias, music publisher at Vienna.

Hauschka, Vincenz, Government auditor, a friend of Beethoven.

Heiligenstadt, near Vienna, a favorite summer residence of Beethoven, where, among other works, the "Pastoral Symphony" was written by him.

Hetzendorf, a favorite suburban residence near Vienna.

Hoffmann, Th. Amadeus.

Hofmeister, Kapellmeister and music publisher, first in Vienna, and afterwards in company with Kühnel in Leipzig (now Peters's Bureau de Musique). *See also* Peters.

Holz, Carl, Government official at Vienna, an accomplished violinist, born in 1798; became a member of the Schuppanzigh Quartets in 1824, and afterwards director of the Concerts Spirituels in that capital; a Viennese of somewhat dissolute habits, by whom even the grave master himself was at times unfavorably influenced.

Homer, especially the Odyssey, a favorite study of Beethoven.

Hönigstein, a banker in Vienna.

Hummel, Johann Nepomuk, the celebrated composer and pianist, a pupil of Mozart, and for some time Beethoven's rival in love matters, having married the sister of the singer Röckel, to whom Beethoven also was much attached (*see also* Schindler's "Biography," i. 189).

Hungary, Beethoven there.

Imperial Court at Vienna.

Imperial High Court of Appeal, letter from Beethoven to the.

Jenger, Chancery officer in the Imperial War Office at Vienna, a passionate lover of music.

Kalkbrenner.

Kandeler, testimonial from Beethoven in favor of.

Kanne, F.A., at Vienna, highly appreciated in his day as a poet, composer, and critic, an intimate friend of Beethoven, and occasionally his guest (*see also* Schindler's "Biography," i. 228).

Kauka, Dr., Beethoven's advocate in Prague.

Kiesewetter, Councillor von, in Vienna, the popular writer on the science of music, one of the subscribers to the great address presented to Beethoven in February, 1824.

Kinsky, Prince Ferdinand, of Bohemia, one of Beethoven's most devoted patrons in Vienna.

Kinsky, Princess.

Kirnberger, of Berlin, the well-known theorist.

Koch, Barbara, of Bonn, daughter of the landlord of the "Zehrgaden," the friend of Eleonore von Breuning, an amiable and intelligent lady, at whose house the leading persons of the town were accustomed to assemble; she afterwards became governess to the children of Count Belderbusch, whom she married in 1802.

Könneritz, Von, principal director of the Court band and Opera in Dresden.

Kraft, Anton, a celebrated violoncello-player in Vienna.

Kuhlau, Friedrich, the distinguished flute-player, a great admirer of Beethoven's music.

Kühnel, in Leipzig. *See* Hofmeister.

Laibach, the Philharmonic Society of.

Landrecht, Beethoven's address to the honorable members of the.

Leidesdorf, M.J., composer and music publisher in Vienna, a subscriber to the great address presented to Beethoven in 1824.

Leipzig "Allgemeine Zeitung," established in 1798; its remarks at first unfavorable towards Beethoven.

Lichnowsky, Count Moritz, brother of Prince Carl Lichnowsky, and, like him, the friend and patron of Beethoven. Schindler, in his "Biography," i. 241, n., relates as follows:-- "The acute perception of the Count led him, on a nearer acquaintance with the work, to surmise that it had been written with some special intentions. On being questioned on this matter, the author replied that he had intended to set the Count's love-story to music, and that if he needed titles for it, he might write over the first piece, 'Fight between Head and Heart,' and over the second, 'Conversation with the Loved One.' After the death of his first wife, the Count had fallen deeply in love with a distinguished opera singer, but his friends protested against such an alliance. After a contest of many years' duration, however, he at last succeeded, in 1816, in removing all hindrances to their union."

Lichnowsky, Prince Carl, a friend and pupil of Mozart, and afterwards a most zealous patron of Beethoven in Vienna (died April 15, 1814).

Liechtenstein, Princess, in Vienna, Beethoven's patroness.

Linke, born 1783, a distinguished violoncello player, member of the Rasumowsky Quartets.

Lobkowitz, Prince, one of Beethoven's most zealous patrons in Vienna.

London, England, and the English.

Luther.

Maelzel, mechanician to the Imperial Court of Vienna, the well-known inventor of the metronome.

Malchus, a youthful friend of Beethoven in Bonn, in later years Minister of Finance of the kingdom of Westphalia, and afterwards of that of Wirtemberg (died at Stuttgart in 1840).

Malfatti, Dr., a celebrated surgeon in Vienna; Beethoven under his treatment in 1814.

Marconi, contralto singer in Vienna.

Marx, A.B., music director and professor at the University of Berlin; edited, when in his twentieth year, the "Berliner Musikzeitung," a journal whose publication, unfortunately, lasted but a few years only. Next to T.A. Hofmann, he was the first who fully and thoroughly appreciated Beethoven's music in all its depth and grandeur, and who manfully and intelligently defended the lofty genius of the master against the base attacks to which it was at times exposed; he has remained until the present day the most efficient representative of the progress of musical art.

Matthisson, the poet.

Maximilian Franz, youngest brother of the Emperor Joseph II., Elector of Cologne from the year 1785, and one of the noblest and most zealous patrons of the young Beethoven, on whom, in 1785, he conferred the appointment of Court organist, and in 1787, with a view to the further cultivation of his talents, sent him to Vienna, assisting him in every way until the year 1794, at which period his country fell entirely under the dominion of France (died in 1801).

Maximilian, Friedrich, Elector of Cologne until the year 1784; the first noble patron of Beethoven, whom he placed under the instruction of the Court organist Von der Eeden, and afterwards, on the death of that musician, under Neefe; as an acknowledgment for which kindness, and in proof of the success which had attended his studies, the young composer, then only eleven years of age, dedicated his first sonatas to his benefactor.

Mayseder, the celebrated violinist (died at Vienna in 1863).

Meyer, Friedrich Sebastian, a singer (born 1773, died 1835), the husband of Mozart's eldest sister-in-law, who frequently, even in Beethoven's presence, made some boastful remark in praise of his deceased relative; such as "My brother-in-law would not have written that!."

Metronome, an instrument for measuring tune in music, invented about the year 1815 by Maelzel, of Vienna, and often employed and spoken of by Beethoven.

Milder-Hauptmann, Mdlle., the celebrated singer, first in Vienna and afterwards in Berlin.

Mödling, a village near Vienna, and Beethoven's favorite summer residence.

Mollo, music publisher in Vienna, afterwards the firm of Steiner & Co., and at a later period that of Haslinger.

Mölk, the celebrated abbey on the Danube.

Mölker Bastei, the, at Vienna, on several occasions Beethoven's residence in the house of Baron von Pasqualati (*see also* Schindler's "Biography," i. 187).

Moscheles.

Mosel, Hofrath Ignaz von, in Vienna, a well-known music writer, and the founder of the Conservatory of Music in that capital.

Mozart.

Munich.

Mythological subjects, reference made to, by Beethoven, who, as it is well known, possessed a considerable acquaintance with ancient history.

Nägeli, Hans Georg, the distinguished founder of men's vocal unions in Switzerland, also a popular composer of vocal music, a music publisher, and, at a later period, educational inspector in Zurich.

Napoleon, when General Bonaparte, so greatly admired by Beethoven, that on the occasion of that General's appearance, the master was incited to compose the "Eroica," which he dedicated to him ("Napoleon Buonaparte--Luigi van Beethoven"). On hearing, however, of the coronation of his hero as Emperor, he angrily cast aside the intended presentation copy of his work, and refused to send it to him.

Neate, Charles, a London artist, and a great admirer of Beethoven, with whom he became acquainted in Vienna in the year 1816.

Nussböck, town sequestrator at Vienna, for some time the guardian of Beethoven's nephew.

Nussdorf, a favorite summer residence on the Danube, near Vienna.

Oliva, a philologist and friend of Beethoven. According to Schindler ("Biography," i. 228), he repaired to St. Petersburg in 1817, in which city he settled as professor of German literature; Schindler is, however, mistaken in the date which he has given.

Oppersdorf, Count Franz von, Beethoven's friend and patron.

Pachler-Koschak, Marie, of Gratz, to whom Beethoven was warmly attached.

Papageno.

Paris.

Parry, Captain, wrote on the music of the Esquimaux.

Pasqualati, Baron von, merchant in Vienna, an ardent admirer of Beethoven, and his constant benefactor. In 1813 Beethoven again occupied apartments appropriated to his use by the Baron at his residence on the Mölker Bastei, and remained there until 1816.

Penzing, a village near Vienna, a favorite summer residence.

Peters, C.F., "Bureau de Musique" in Leipzig (*see also* Hofmeister).

Peters, councillor of Prince Lobkowitz at Vienna, a friend of Beethoven.

Philharmonic Society in London. In Laibach.

Pianoforte, Beethoven's remarks concerning the.

Pilat, editor of the "Austrian Observer."

Plutarch.

Portraits of Beethoven.

Potter, Cipriani, pianist in London.

Prague.

Prince Regent, the, afterwards George IV. of England.

Probst, music publisher in Leipzig.

Prussia.

Punto (*alias* Stich) a celebrated horn player, to whom Beethoven was mainly indebted for his knowledge of that instrument (died 1804).

"Queen of the Night." *See* Beethoven's sister-in-law.

Radziwill, Prince, at Berlin, a devoted patron of music and the composer of music to "Faust."

Rampel, Beethoven's copyist about the year 1824.

Rasumowsky, Count, afterwards Prince, Russian ambassador at Vienna, an ardent lover of music.

Recke, Elise von der, the well-known poetess.

Reisser, vice-director of the Polytechnic Institution at Vienna, co-guardian of Beethoven's nephew in the year 1825.

Religious and moral sentiments on particular subjects.

Rellstab, Ludwig, a writer and poet, for many years editor of the "Vossische Zeitung," in Berlin.

Ries, Ferdinand, son of the preceding, a pupil of Beethoven and a distinguished composer. Quitted Vienna in 1805, and, with the exception of a short residence there, on his return from Russia in the autumn of 1808, never again returned to that capital (Schindler, i. 227).

Ries, Franz, Court musician to the Elector of Cologne, a helpful friend to Beethoven (born 1755).

Rochlitz, Friedrich, the well-known writer on the science of music, and for nearly twenty-five years editor of the Leipzig "Allgemeine Musikzeitung," a man who, notwithstanding his entire lack of historical acumen and his limited acquaintance with the technicalities of music, did very much towards liberating the art from its mechanical condition, and promoting its intellectual appreciation by the public. He was in Vienna in the year 1822, where he became personally acquainted with Beethoven, but never fully appreciated the genius of the master,--a circumstance which Beethoven himself most deeply felt, even after the retirement of Rochlitz from the editorship of that journal, and which formed the subject of many ironical remarks on the part of Beethoven respecting these representatives of the so-called Old-German national composers.

Röckel, singer of the part of Florestan in Vienna in 1806, still living at Bath, in England.

Rode, the celebrated violinist; came to Vienna in the winter of 1812-13, where he became acquainted with Beethoven.

Rudolph, Archduke, youngest brother of the Emperor Franz, born 1788, died 1831, a passionate lover of music, and himself a composer; he became Beethoven's pupil in 1808, and in 1819 Cardinal-Archbishop of Olmütz.

Russia.

Rzehatschek, in Vienna.

Salieri, Kapellmeister at Vienna, a contemporary and rival of Haydn and Mozart, for some time Beethoven's instructor in the dramatic style.

Salomon, J.P., of Bonn, the celebrated violinist, until the year 1782 director of the concerts of Prince Heinrich of Prussia; he afterwards came to London, where he became chiefly instrumental in the introduction of German music into that capital; as is well known, it was owing to him also that J. Haydn was induced to visit England.

Sarastro.

Sartorius, royal censor at Vienna (*see also* Schindler's "Biography," ii. 69).

Saxony. *See also* Dresden.

Schade, Dr., advocate at Augsburg, a helpful friend of the young Beethoven.

Schenk, the well-known composer of the "Village Barber," for some time Beethoven's instructor in Vienna (died 1836).

Schiller.

Schindler, Anton, of Moravia, Beethoven's sincere friend and biographer (born 1790, died 1864); he became acquainted with Beethoven towards the end of March, 1814.

Schlemmer, for many years Beethoven's copyist until 1823.

Schlemmer, a gentleman living in the Alleengasse, auf der Wieden, in whose house Beethoven placed his nephew Carl (not to be confounded with the copyist of the same name).

Schlesinger, Moritz, music publisher in Berlin and Paris.

Schmidt, Dr., army surgeon in Vienna.

Schoberlechner, Franz, pianist.

Scholz, music director in Warmbrunn.

Schönauer, Dr., Court advocate and barrister at Vienna, appointed by Beethoven's brother Carl testamentary trustee to his nephew--an intriguing lawsuit-pettifogger.

Schott, music publisher in Mayence.

Schröder, Wilhelmine, the great singer.

Schuppanzigh, Ignaz, born 1776, died 1830, the celebrated violinist, whose extraordinary corpulence was a frequent subject of Beethoven's witticisms; he was, however, the first who fully appreciated Beethoven's music for stringed instruments, which he performed in a masterly manner. Resided in Russia from 1816 to 1823.

Schweiger, Joseph Freiherr von, chamberlain to the Archduke Rudolph.

Schweizer, Ed. Friedrich von, chamberlain to the Archduke Anton, an admirer of Beethoven's music and subscriber to the address of February 1824.

Sebald, Auguste, the singer.

Seibert, Dr., surgeon in Vienna, Beethoven's operator.

Seyfried, Ignaz Ritter von, the well-known composer, publisher of the spurious edition of "Studies by Ludwig van Beethoven," Kapellmeister in Vienna.

Shakespeare, deeply read and greatly admired by Beethoven.

Siboni, a distinguished tenorist in Vienna.

Sight, Beethoven's weakness of.

Simrock, Court musician (horn player) to the Elector of Cologne, and music publisher in Bonn, a friend of Beethoven's early days.

His son, the present proprietor of the business in Bonn, at Vienna in the summer of 1816.

Sketch by Beethoven.
Smart, Sir George, music publisher in London, a great admirer of Beethoven's music.
Smetana, Dr., surgeon at Vienna; gained considerable popularity by his treatment of deafness.
"Society of Friends to Music in the Austrian States" at Vienna.
Sonntag, Henriette, the celebrated singer.
Spiecker. Dr., of Berlin.
Spohr.
Stadler, Abbé Maximilian (born 1748, died 1833), a composer, and the friend of Mozart; an opponent of the Beethoven school of music (*see* Schindler's "Biography," i. 80; ii. 109).
Standenheim, a celebrated physician in Vienna.
Stein, pianoforte manufacturer at Vienna, brother of Frau Nanette Streicher.
Steiner, S.A., music publisher in Vienna, succeeded by T. Haslinger.
Sterkel, Franz Xaver, a pleasing pianist and composer, whom Beethoven visited at Aschaffenburg in 1791, and greatly astonished by his pianoforte playing.
Stoll, a young poet at Vienna.
Streicher, Andreas, the well-known friend of Schiller's early days. He married, when in his nineteenth year, Nanette Stein, only daughter of the celebrated pianoforte manufacturer at Augsburg, whom he took with him to Vienna, where he first became teacher of the pianoforte, and afterwards, by the assistance of his wife, who had made herself acquainted with her father's art, founder of the celebrated Streicher pianoforte manufactory. Schindler, in his "Biography," i. 187, speaks of the interest taken by Frau Streicher in Beethoven's domestic matters.
Stumpff, harp manufacturer in London, an admirer of Beethoven's works.
Swedish Academy of Music.
Theatres:
Josephstadt;
Kärnthnerthor;
"An der Wien."
Tiedge, the poet of "Urania," and also of the song "An die Hoffnung," so much admired by Beethoven, and several times set to music by him.
Tonie, Antonie, of Birkenstock, daughter of a family in Vienna from which Beethoven received great kindness from the first period of his residence in that capital, and in which, in the year 1810, Bettina lived, who afterwards became the wife of B.A. Brentano, a merchant in Frankfort, to whom Beethoven was greatly indebted.
Töplitz, in Bohemia.
Trautmannsdorf, Prince, High Chamberlain.
Travels and travelling projects of Beethoven. *See also* London.
Treitschke, stage poet at Vienna.
Unger, the celebrated singer.
University, the, of Vienna.
Ursulines, convent of the, at Gratz, in Styria, music supplied by Beethoven in aid of.
Varenna, Kammerprocurator at Gratz.
Varnhagen von Ense.
Vering, Dr., army surgeon at Vienna.
Vienna, Beethoven's settled residence from the year 1792, of which, however, he never spoke favorably.
Wawruch, Dr., clinical professor, Beethoven's last surgeon.
Weber, Carl Maria von.
Weber, Gottfried, theorist and composer.
Wegeler, Dr., of Bonn, an early friend of Beethoven.
Weigl, Joseph, composer of the "Swiss Family," Kapellmeister at Vienna.
Weinmüller, singer at the Kärnthnerthor Theatre.
Weiss, tenor player at Vienna.
Westphalia, Beethoven offered the appointment of Kapellmeister to the King of, in 1808.
Wieden, a suburb of Vienna, on several occasions Beethoven's residence.

Wieland.
Wills, Beethoven's.
Wolf, Dr., advocate in Prague.
Zelter, the song composer and friend of Goethe, director of the Academy of Vocal Music at Berlin.
Zmeskall von Domanowecz, Court secretary at Vienna, one of Beethoven's earliest friends in the Imperial city, a good violoncello player and also a composer.
Zulehner, music publisher at Mayence.
Zurich.

THE END

Printed in Poland
by Amazon Fulfillment
Poland Sp. z o.o., Wrocław
08 May 2022

37a5aa05-02dd-4a54-8376-cf48dfbd1946R01